CONCISE DICTIONARY OF BIOLOGY

A Perfect Reference for Aspirants of IAS, IIT-JEE, AIEEE, CBSE-PMT, and Students of All Age Groups

I0129578

Editorial Board

V&S PUBLISHERS

Published by:

V&S PUBLISHERS

F-2/16, Ansari road, Daryaganj, New Delhi-110002
☎ 23240026, 23240027 •Fax: 011-23240028
Email: info@vspublishers.com

Branch : Hyderabad
5-1-707/1, Brij Bhawan (Beside Central Bank of India Lane)
Bank Street, Koti, Hyderabad - 500 095
☎ 040-24737290
E-mail: vspublishershyd@gmail.com

Follow us on:

All books available at **www.vspublishers.com**

© **Copyright:** **V&S PUBLISHERS**
ISBN 978-93-815886-3-5
Edition: 2012

Printed at: Param Offsetters, Okhla, New Delhi

Contents

Publisher's Note

Innumerable books are available in the market on science and its allied branches, like, physics, chemistry, and biology et al, both as textbook and reference manual. Written for different age-groups and class, quite a number of these books come replete with jargon-filled terms; and just fail to connect with readers' inclination and curiosity level. On top of that, new words keep finding their way into the books every other day. Every new addition contributes to difficulty in comprehending the matter.

An average reader is interested only in knowing what a specific word means without getting lost with heavy sounding inputs.

Following an open-ended discussion with a cross-section of students and other stakeholders we realised that many books on science (physics, chemistry and biology) take readers' understanding of scientific terms for granted and make short passing references while alluding to the term in the text. Presentations of this nature in no way assist readers in understanding the subject properly.

You need to suffer no longer.

V&S Publishers has come out with four dictionaries of terms; in science, physics, chemistry and biology. These have been compiled to help readers grasp the meaning of popular scientific terms. For easy reference terms have been arranged alphabetically. Terms that have come into the reckoning even in the early 2012 have been incorporated and suitably explained in such a way that an average secondary and senior secondary student can grasp them easily. High resolution images, illustrations and examples, where appropriate, have been added for reader's convenience. For all readers, who have not made a special study of any science subject, explanations of terms will be found to be easily comprehensible.

An attempt has been made to include important scientific charts, tables, constants, conversion tables as appendices to make this dictionary more useful. A glossary of Nobel Prize winners and their contributions is an added attraction.

We would be happy to have your views and comments about the book.

Introduction

What is Biology?

Biology is one of the three essential studies of science. Anyone interested in science has to study biology, chemistry, and physics. Chemistry looks at the different kinds of substances and molecules that exist, and physics looks at the way the world and the universe work. Biology is the fascinating study of life and is incredibly important for the advancement of modern society.

The study of biology helps us understand ourselves and other life forms. For many of us the most interesting part of biology may be the study of ourselves; how our body works; how it reacts to diseases; how we resemble or differ from other people such as our sisters, brothers and parents. We also learn how we and other living things came on this Earth, as part of the origin of life and the process of evolution of organisms. The study of man is not complete unless we also make a comparative study of other animals. For example, by studying the working of muscles in a frog, or the digestive, respiratory and nervous system of a mammal such as the rabbit, we can understand how such systems work in our own bodies.

By studying plants we have found that certain plants have medicinal value from which it is possible to manufacture drugs (e.g. penicillin and streptomycin) which have proved effective in the treatment of certain diseases. An ever-increasing human population requires more and more food. Food production can be increased by a careful study of plants and soil. Above all, biology helps us to understand ourselves and the world we live.

Why is the study of Biology Important?

Biology is important for a number of reasons, but in particular because it is used in nearly every field. If we do not understand biology, nobody would be able to understand how bodies work seamlessly, and of course, how other lives on the earth (e.g. plants) function.

If it were not for biology, we would not be able to understand the environment in which we live. Biology involves and contains many secrets of nature. Biology is incredibly complex and vast, and possesses the ability to explain many 'unknowns' found within nature everyday by individuals and scientists. It allows us to build upon the technology that allows people to be cured from illnesses or diseases and allows for society to obtain better overall well-being and health.

Without biology there would be no doctors; there would be no hospitals and there would be no real way to help people with the problems that they experience with their body. It is because of the progression of biological studies that the world's population is healthier than ever before. It is incredibly important for biology to continue being studied for this reason. That's why it has been promoted so highly in educational establishments.

How is Biology Classified?

Botany – Botany involves the study of plant life, the structure, growth, diseases, chemical and physical properties, metabolism and evolution of the fungi, algae and plant species. Botany implies the importance of study of plant life on earth because they generate food, fibers, medicines, fuel and oxygen.

Zoology – Zoology is the study of animals and animal life, including classification, physiology, development, and behaviour. Major studies on human health and wellness, besides research in medicine, is studied under zoology.

Though Zoology and Botany are considered to be principle branches of biology, there are at least 50 other branches. Some important ones among them are mentioned below:

Agriculture – The study of producing crops from the land, with an emphasis on practical applications.

Biochemistry – The study of the chemical reactions required for life to exist and function, usually a focus on the cellular level

Biophysics – The study of biological processes through physics, by applying the theories and methods traditionally used in the physical sciences.

Biotechnology – A new and sometimes controversial branch of biology that studies the manipulation of living matter, including genetic modification.

Bioengineering – The study of biology through the means of engineering with an emphasis on applied knowledge and especially related to biotechnology.

Bioinformatics – It is the study, collection, and storage of genomic data with the help of information technology (IT).

Ecology – The study of the ecosystem as a complete unit, with an emphasis on how species and groups of species interact with other living beings and non-living elements.

Environmental Biology – The study of the natural world, as a whole or in a particular area especially as affected by human activity.

Genetics – It is the study of genes – the hereditary aspects of all living organisms. The study of inheritance of traits from the parent is the subject matter of genetics.

Marine Biology – The study of ocean ecosystems, plants, animals, and other living beings.

Medicine – The study of the human body in health and disease, with allopathic medicine focusing on alleviating or curing the body from states of disease

Microbiology – The study of microscopic organisms (microorganisms) and their interactions with other living things.

Molecular Biology – The study of biology and biological functions at the molecular level, some cross over with biochemistry.

Pathology – The study of diseases, and the causes, processes, nature, and development of disease.

Pharmacology – The study and practical application of preparation, use, and effects of drugs and synthetic medicines.

Physiology – The study of the functioning of living organisms and the organs and parts of living organisms.

Great Biologists of All-time

Aristotle (384 – 322 B.C.) – Greek philosopher and scientist. He is sometimes called the father of biology. He was able to describe plant and animal specimens received from all parts of the far-flung Alexandrian Empire. Out of 400 treatises that Aristotle wrote only 30 survive. Of these, most important in connection with biology are his Enquiry into Animals, Motion of Animals, Gait of Animals, Parts of Animals and Generation of Animals. When read from the standpoint of modern knowledge of the subject, these books are obviously riddled with error, myth, and rumour, but they nevertheless served as the starting point of all subsequent biological thought and are the ultimate source of natural history as a field of study.

Charles Robert Darwin (1809 –1882) – An English naturalist. He established that all species of life have descended over time from common ancestors, and proposed the scientific theory that this branching pattern of evolution resulted from a process that he called natural selection. Darwin published his theory with compelling evidence for evolution in his 1859 book *On the Origin of Species*, overcoming scientific rejection of earlier concepts of transmutation of species.

Walther Flemming (1843 –1905) – A German biologist and a founder of cytogenetics. Flemming investigated the process of cell division and the distribution of chromosomes to the daughter nuclei, a process he called mitosis. His discovery of mitosis and chromosomes is considered one of the 100 most important scientific discoveries of all times.

Oswald Avery (1877 – 1955) – An American physician and medical researcher. He was one of the first molecular biologists and a pioneer in immunochemistry, but he is best known for his discovery in 1944, with his co-workers Colin MacLeod and Maclyn McCarty, that DNA is the material of which genes and chromosomes are made.

Gregor Mendel (1822– 1884) – An Austrian scientist, who gained fame as the founder of the new science of genetics. Mendel demonstrated that the inheritance of certain traits in pea plants follows particular patterns. This theory is now referred to as the laws of Mendelian inheritance. Although the significance of Mendel's work was not recognised until the turn of the 20th century, the independent rediscovery of these laws formed the foundation of the modern science of genetics.

Louis Pasteur (1822 –1895) – French chemist and microbiologist. He is remembered for his remarkable breakthroughs in the causes and preventions of diseases. He created the first vaccines for rabies and anthrax. He is best known for inventing a method to stop milk from causing sickness, a process that came to be called pasteurisation. He is regarded as one of the founders of microbiology. Pasteur also made many discoveries in the field of chemistry, most notably the molecular basis for the asymmetry of certain crystals

Linus Carl Pauling (1901 – 1994) – American chemist, biochemist, peace activist. He was one of the most influential chemists in history and among the first scientists to work in the fields of quantum chemistry and molecular biology. He is one of only two people awarded Nobel Prizes in different fields (the chemistry and peace prizes). Besides being the greatest architect of chemistry, Pauling was a founder of molecular biology and a pioneer in quantum mechanics. Pauling combined chemistry and physics to solve various puzzles related to the nature of chemical bonding which now are fundamental to modern theories of molecular structure. Pauling determined crystal structure by X-ray crystallography and the structure of gas molecules by electron diffraction.

Francis Crick and James Watson – The discovery of the structure of deoxyribose nucleic acid (DNA) by Francis Crick and James Watson in 1953 was one of the most far-reaching discoveries of the 20th century, the stuff of which genes are made. Biotechnology and genetic engineering, sciences that have developed so dramatically, owe their origins to this understanding of the structure of DNA and the ability to manipulate it. Disease resistant crops, specially designed drugs, scientific testing procedures, even treatments for hereditary illnesses have now become possible through these technologies. One of the most ambitious projects of the twentieth century has been to map the entire human genome – to determine the genetic code of DNA in man.

The Future of Biology

It's very difficult to predict where science and technology are going, even over a short time-span, for the obvious reason that the greatest advances are often the least expected. And science follows them. And within science, this is going to be a century of biology. We are entering an age of synthesis. So many discoveries have been made in biology in the cell, at the molecular level, and on up to the development of organisms. Increasingly now, these discoveries are beginning to throw light upon ecosystems and the processes of evolution beyond what we already had.

The world is on the edge, really, of mastering disease, particularly genetic disease. There would be genetic engineering in time that will allow the correcting of molecular structure to eliminate genetic disease that is crippled such a large percentage of the human population today. It'll be able to treat many diseases. Biology will also be crucial for feeding a world of seven billion people today, and possibly 10 billion by mid-century. And we need all the biology and all the advances we can find in agriculture, especially. We're going to switch worldwide to dry land agriculture. There is not enough water in many countries to feed all those people and to restore soil to arable condition. So this means that we have to have genetically modified organisms. Some people may not like the idea. But that's one of those necessities brought about by the human condition.

That's for future generations to decide. But it's up to this generation, and the ones immediately to come, to decide where not to go, and what mistakes not to make to forfeit the future.

A

Abc soil
Soil that has a surface layer, subsoil, and a lower layer of loose rock material is called this. The layers are said to be it's A, B, and C horizons.

Abdomen
Region of the body furthest from the mouth. In insects, the third body region behind the head and thorax.

Abelia
(Genus of plants) Plants from Mexico, Himalaya and Eastern Asia from Caprifoliaceae Family. There are about 30 species, all of them showing tubular flowers.

Aberrant
This describes a plant or species that is different in some way from the group in which it is placed.

Abiogenesis
Early theory that held that some organisms originated from nonliving material.

Ablastous
Means without germ or bud.

Abnormal hemoglobin
Hemoglobin molecule with a different shape due to an altered amino acid sequence (ultimately caused by an altered DNA base sequence), such as in the inherited disease sickle-cell anemia.

Abruptly pinnate
This describes a pinnate leaf that ends without an odd leaflet or tendril. It ends in a matched pair of leaflets.

Abscisic acid
A plant hormone that promotes dormancy in perennial plants and causes rapid closure of leaf stomata when a leaf begins to wilt.

Absolute filtration
Total retention of target particles of a given size, generally under a well-defined test or operational protocol.

Absolute rating
A filter value that expresses the smallest particle that will be completely retained under a standard test method (with attendant experimental uncertainty) consistent with the filter's application.

Absolute time
One of the two types of geologic time (relative time being the other), with a definite age date established mostly by the decay of radioactive elements, although ages may also be obtained by counting tree rings, decay of a specific type of atom, or annual sedimentary layers (such as varves in lakes or layers in a glacier). The term is in some disfavor because it suggests an exactness that may not be possible to obtain.

Absorption

The process by which the products of digestion are transferred into the body's internal environment, enabling them to reach the cells.

Absorptive feeders

Animals such as tapeworms that ingest food through the body wall.

Abyssal plain

The ocean floor offshore from the continental margin, usually very flat with a slight slope.

ACAP (Agreement on the Conservation of Albatrosses and Petrels)

The Agreement on the Conservation of Albatrosses and Petrels (ACAP) binds signing countries to putting forth immediate efforts to reduce albatross deaths due to fishing lines.

Accidental

Pertaining to species that do not occur in a region under normal circumstances.

Acclimation

Reversible physiological or morphological changes an organism experiences in response to changing environmental conditions; such physiological changes enable the organism to tolerate the new environmental conditions.

Accrete

To add terranes (small land masses or pieces of crust) to another, usually larger, land mass.

Acetyl coa

An intermediate compound formed during the breakdown of glucose by adding a two-carbon fragment to a carrier molecule (Coenzyme A or CoA).

Acetylcholine

A chemical released at neuromuscular junctions that binds to receptors on the surface of the plasma membrane of muscle cells, causing an electrical impulse to be transmitted. The impulse ultimately leads to muscle contraction.

Achene

Type of indehescent dry fruit. Achenes are fruits with a solitary seed , not attached to the carpel . Sometimes achenes appear joined together in what it is known as poly-achenes.

Acicular

Type of leaf needle-shaped. Several times longer than wide; ending sharply at the apex.

Acid

A substance that increases the number of hydrogen ions in a solution.

Acid rain

The precipitation of sulphuric acid and other acids as rain. The acids form when sulphur dioxide and nitrogen oxides released during the combustion of fossil fuels combine with water and oxygen in the atmosphere.

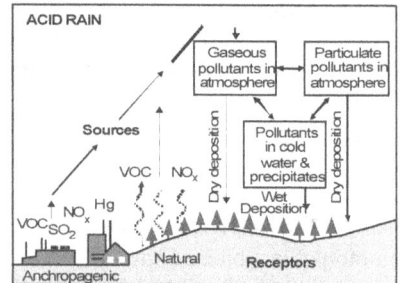

Acoelomates

Animals that do not have a coelom or body cavity; e.g., sponges & flatworms.

Acquired immunodeficiency syndrome (AIDS)

A collection of disorders that develop as a result of infection by the human immunodeficiency virus (HIV), which attacks helper T cells, crippling the immune system and greatly reducing the body's ability to fight infection; results in premature death brought about by various diseases that overwhelm the compromised immune system.

Actin

The protein from which microfilaments are composed; forms the contractile filaments of sarcomeres in muscle cells.

Action potential

A reversal of the electrical potential in the plasma membrane of a neuron that occurs when a nerve cell is stimulated; caused by rapid changes in membrane permeability to sodium and potassium.

Active site

The region of an enzyme to which a substrate binds and at which a chemical reaction occurs.

Active transport

Transport of molecules against a concentration gradient (from regions of low concentration to regions of high concentration) with the aid of proteins in the cell membrane and energy from ATP.

Activity space

The range or spectrum of environmental conditions and characteristics suitable for the normal activity of an organism.

Adaptation

Tendency of an organism to suit its environment; one of the major points of Charles Darwin's theory of evolution by natural selection: organisms adapt to their environment. Those organisms best adapted will have a greater chance of surviving and passing their genes on to the next generation.

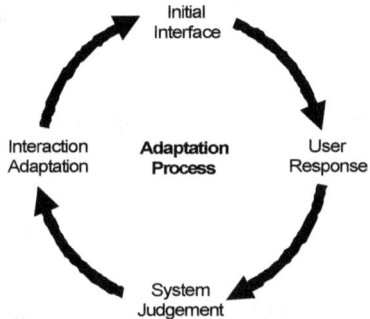

Adaptive function

A mathematical expression that takes into account the fitnesses of a phenotype in each of several different environments to produce a measurement of the general fitness of the phenotype in a varied environment.

Adaptive radiation

The development of a variety of species from a single ancestral form; occurs when a new habitat becomes available to a population. Evolutionary pattern of divergence of a great many taxa from a common ancestral species as a result of novel adaptations or a recent mass extinction. Examples: mammals during the Cenozoic Era after the extinction of dinosaurs at the close of the Mesozoic Era flowering plants during the Cretaceous Period diversified because of their reproductive advantages over gymnosperm and non-seed plants that dominated the floras of the world at that time.

Additive

Something that is added to a fertilizer to improve its chemical or physical condition.

Adelphous

Means having stamens united into sets; used mostly in combination, as in monoadelphous.

Adenine

One of the four nitrogen-containing bases occurring in nucleotides, the building blocks of the organic macromolecule group known as nucleic acids (DNA and RNA). Adenine is also the base in the energy carrying molecule ATP (adenosine triphosphate) which is the energy coin of the cell.

Adenosine diphosphate

Lower energy form of ATP, having two (instead of the three in ATP) phosphhate groups attached to the adenine base and ribose sugar.

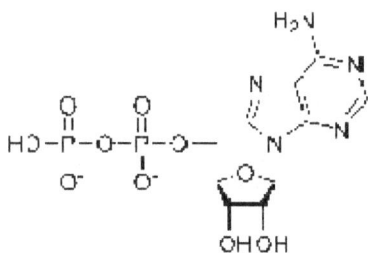

Adenosine triphosphate

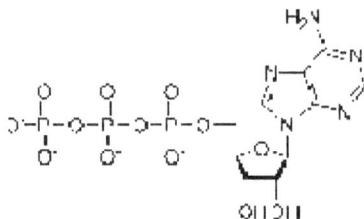

A common form in which energy is stored in living systems; consists of a nucleotide (with ribose sugar) with three phosphate groups. The energy coin of the cell.

Adhesion

The ability of molecules of one substance to adhere to a different substance.

Adnate

In botany, grown together or attached.

Adnation

Fusion of unlike parts such as the labellum (of an Orchid) with the column.

Adnexed

In botany, annexed or touching, but not attached.

Adobe soil

Dense, clay-like soil, also called gumbo, that is also high-alkaline.

Adosculation

In botany, the fertilization of plants by the falling of the pollen on the pistils.

Adpressed

Lying close and flat.

Adrenocorticotropic hormone (ACTH)

A hormone produced by the anterior pituitary that stimulates the adrenal cortex to release several hormones including cortisol.

Adsorb

To accumulate on the soil's surface.

Adsorption

The binding of molecules to a surface as a result of a chemical or physio-electric interaction between the membrane surface and the molecule.

Adsortion
Condensation on the soil's surface.

Adult
The mature stage of an organism, usually recognized by the organism's attaining the ability to reproduce.

Adventitious
Type of root. Adventitious roots grow from a stem and are used by some plants to spread along the surface of the soil., like in the ivy or strawberry.

Adventitious
In botany, appearing in an abnormal or unusual position or place; occurring as a straggler or away from its natural position, such as roots on aerial stems.

Adventitious buds
The buds appearing in an unusual place; for example, buds on leaves.

Adventitious roots
Roots that develop from the stem following the death of the primary root. Branches from the adventitious roots form a fibrous root system in which all roots are about the same size; occur in monocots.

Adventive
A plant that has been introduced, but isn't naturalized yet.

Aerial behaviour
A type of behaviour exhibited by dolphins and whales in which the animal comes out above the surface of the water (for example, leaps, jumps, or bow rides). Such actions are thought to be forms of communicative or playful behaviour.

Aerobic
Pertaining to the presence of free oxygen. Aerobic organisms require oxygen for their life processes.

Affluent
Influent, or fluid entering a filter or filter system; opposite of effluent.

After-shaft
A double feather that grows from the shaft of a body feather. An after-shaft is important in maintaining warmth and is known to occur in grouse, quail, and relatives.

Agar
polysaccharides used to gel liquids for bacteria media and human foods including ice cream. Does not melt at room temperature like gelatin. Only a few marine bacteria can digest agar. Agar is obtained from seaweeds (algae) by heating, acid, and freezing.

Age class
The set of individuals in a population that are all of a particular age or fall within a specfied age group.

Age structure
The relative proportion of individuals in each age group in a population.

Aggregates
Fairly random associations of animals with little or no internal organization; form in response to a single stimulus and disperse when the stimulus is removed; one of the three broad classes of social organization.

Aglanoema
Genus of plants. Plants from tropical South Asia of the Arum Family - Areaceae - there are about 20 species. Some of them used in gardening. Anagloema simplex is used to aromatize cigars.

Agonistic
Pertaining to behaviour that opposes other that of other individuals and causes conflicts.

Aigrette

Breeding feathers characteristic of herons and egrets that are used in courtship displays. Aigrette feathers are long and loose.

Air diffusion rate

The rate at which air diffuses through the wetted pores of a membrane at a given differential pressure. Measuring the air diffusion rate is a method used to check the integrity of a membrane filter.

Air flow

The amount of air that flows through a filter related to contamination, differential pressure, filter area, and filter porosity. In membrane separations, generally expressed as l / minute / cm^2 at a given pressure.

Air sac

A structure unique to the respiratory system of birds. Air sacs are thin-walled structures and through which air flows as the bird breathes.

Airfoil

A structure that creates lift as a result of the differential airflow over that occurs over its top and bottom surfaces. An example of an airfoil in the animal world is a bird's wing.

Albinism

Genetic condition caused by the body's inability to manufacture pigments; an autosomal recessive trait.

Aldosterone

A hormone secreted by the adrenal glands that controls the reabsorption of sodium in the renal tubule of the nephron.

Alga

Single celled green plants usually growing in water; often in long chain, visible to naked eye.

Alginate

Component of the cell walls of many rhodophytes and kelps. Alginates have an affinity for water, and so help to slow dessication when the algae are exposed to the air; they are commercially important in the production of paper, toothpaste, beer, and frozen foods.

Alkaline

Term pertaining to a highly basic, as opposed to acidic, subtance. For example, hydroxide or carbonate of sodium or potassium.

Allele

One of multiple alternate gene forms that are possible at a chromosomal location.

Alleles

Alternate forms of a gene.

Allergens

Antigens that provoke an allergic reaction.

Allergy

An immune reaction of the body which causes discomfort and possible harm.

Alligator

A crocodilian that occurs in subtropical regions and can be distinguished from a crocodile in that it has a broader snout.

Allochthonous

Refers to something formed elswhere than its present location..

Allopatric

Pertaining to organisms that have different ranges due to geographical separation.

Alluvial fan

A fan-shaped deposit of sand, mud, etc. formed by a stream where its velocity has slowed, such as at the mouth of a ravine or at the foot of a mountain.

Alpha decay
Type of radioactive decay in which a radioisotope emits a large but slow-moving particle consisting of two protons and two neutrons.

Alpha diversity
A measurement of the variety of organisms that inhabit a defined region or habitat.

Alpha helix
A short, spiral-shaped section within a protein structure.

Alternate
Type of leaf springing one per node at different levels of the stem.

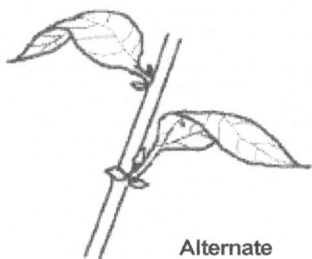

Alternate

Alternation of generations
A life cycle in which a multicellular diploid stage is followed by a haploid stage and so on; found in land plants and many algae and fungi.

Altitudinal gradient
As altitude increases, a gradient of cooler, drier conditions occurs.

Altricial
Refers to animals with young that are unable to move on their own after hatching or birth, and require extensive parental care. Songbirds, dogs, and humans are examples of species with altricial young.

Altruism
A type of behaviour in which an individual acts to further the welfare of other individuals.

Alula
A set of feathers on the leading edge of a bird's wing located close to the base of the primary feathers that, when raised and lowered, affect the airflow over the wing by increasing or decreasing lift during flight.

Alveoli
Tiny, thin-walled, inflatable sacs in the lungs where oxygen and carbon dioxide are exchanged.

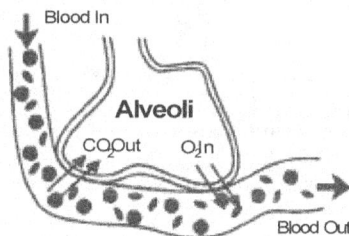

Alveolus
A term used to identify a small cavity, sac, or depression in the body. For example, the tiny cavities within the lungs or the depression in which a tooth sits.

Amber
Fossilization where the organism is entrapped in resin and preserved whole.

Ambient surrounding
Ambient temperature would be the room temperature.

Ambulacra
Row of tube feet of an echinoderm.

Amensalism
A symbiotic relationship in which members of one population inhibit

the growth of another population without being affected.

Amino acid

The subunits (monomers) from which proteins (polymers) are assembled. Each amino acid consists of an amino functional group, and a carboxyl acid group, and differs from other amino acids by the composition of an R group.

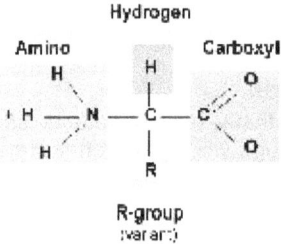

Hydrogen
Amino   Carboxyl

R-group
(variant)

Amino acid sequence

Also known as the primary structure of a protein/polypeptide; the sequence of amino acids in a protein/polypeptide controlled by the sequence of DNA bases.

Ammonite

n. One of a group of extinct, shelled, marine cephalopods related to squids; cephalopods are within the larger group Mollusca, which includes clams and snails. Ammonite shells were generally coiled, though some non-coiled forms did exist. The group went extinct 65 million years ago at the end of the Cretaceous Period.

Amniocentesis

A method of prenatal testing in which amniotic fluid is withdrawn from the uterus through a needle. The fluid and the fetal cells it contains are analyzed to detect biochemical or chromosomal disorders.

Amnion

A delicate membrane that encloses an embryo of higher vertebrates (occurs in reptiles, birds, and mammals).

Amniote

Any of a group of land-dwelling vertebrates that have an amnion during embryonic development, including reptiles, birds, and mammals. Most extant mammals give live birth, the egg being retained inside the body during gestation.

Amniote egg

An egg with compartmentalized sacs (a liquid-filled sac in which the embryo develops, a food sac, and a waste sac) that allowed vertebrates to reproduce on land.

Amniotic egg

An egg that can be laid on land due to the presence of a fluid-filled amniotic sac (amnion) that cushions and protects the developing embryo. amniote - n. Any of a group of land-dwelling vertebrates that have an amnion during embryonic development, including reptiles, birds, and mammals. Most extant mammals give live birth, the egg being retained inside the body during gestation.

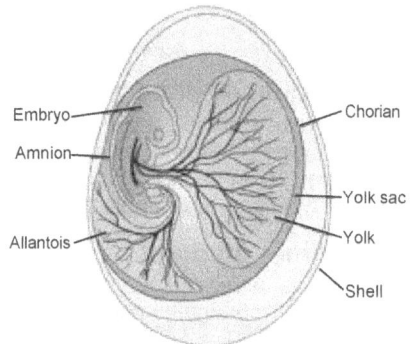

Embryo, Amnion, Allantois, Chorian, Yolk sac, Yolk, Shell

Amoebocytes

Amoeboid cells in sponges that occur in the matrix between the epidermal and collar cells. They transport nutrients.

Amoeboid
Having no definite shape to the cell, able to change shape.

Amphibians
Class of terrestrial vertebrates which lay their eggs (and also mate) in water but live on land as adults following a juvenile stage where they live in water and breathe through gills. Amphibians were the first group of land vertebrates; today they are mostly restricted to moist habitats.

Amphiesma
The outer covering of a dinoflagellate, consisting of several membrane layers.

Amphisbaenian
A wormlike (long and slender) reptile that has a short tail, and scales arranged in rings and is well-adapted to burrowing.

Amplexus
A mating position used by frogs and toads, in which the male holds the female with its front legs and fertilization usually takes place outside of the female's body and thus often requires a moist or aquatic environment.

Anabolic reactions
Reactions in cells in which new chemical bonds are formed and new molecules are made; generally require energy, involve reduction, and lead to an increase in atomic order.

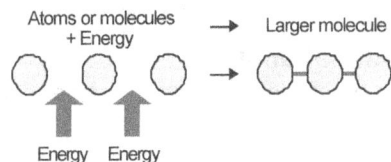

Atoms or molecules + Energy → Larger molecule

Energy   Energy

Anacardiaceae
The Cashew family - Anacardiaceae - comprises about 600 species of plants which live in temperate and subtropical countries. They are mainly trees and bushes, which contain in their stems big quantities of latex and tanines, very frequently used in resin and tanning industries. We also have very well known edible plants, such as mangoes (Mangifera indica) or pistachios.

Anaerobic
Pertaining to the absence of free oxygen. Anaerobic organisms do not require oxygen for their life processes, in fact oxygen is toxic to many of them. Most anaerobic organisms are bacteria or archaeans.

Anagensis
Evolutionary change along an unbranching lineage; change without speciation.

Analogous structures
Body parts that serve the same function in different organisms, but differ in structure and embryological development; e. g., the wings of insects and birds.

Anaphase
Phase of mitosis in which the chromosomes begin to separate.

Anaphylaxis
A severe allergic reaction in which histamine is released into the circulatory system; occurs upon

subsequent exposure to a particular antigen; also called anaphylactic shock.

Anapsid
A vertebrate distinguished by a skull with no openings in the side behind the eyes, e.g. turtles.

Anastomosis
A branching and interconnecting network of tubes such as blood vessels, nerves, or leaf veins that branch and reconnect to form a plexus.

Ancestor
Any organism, population, or species from which some other organism, population, or species is descended by reproduction.

Andesite
Igneous volcanic rock, less mafic than basalt, but more mafic than dacite; rough volcanic equivalent of diorite.

Androecium
It is the male reproductive part of the flower. We can find in it the stamens which were leaves that suffered a transformation to carry the pollen.

Anemophily
Seed plants which are pollinated by wind are said to be anemophilous.

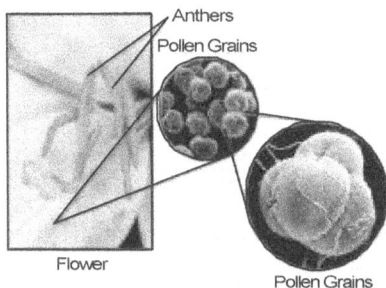

Anthers
Pollen Grains

Flower

Pollen Grains

Aneuploidy
Variation in chromosome number involving one or a small number of chromosomes; commonly involves the gain or loss of a single chromosome.

Angina
Chest pain, especially during physical exertion or emotional stress, that is caused by gradual blockage of the coronary arteries.

Angiogenesis
Blood vessel formation, which usually accompanies the growth of malignant tissue.

Angiosperms
Flowering plants. First appearing at least 110 million years ago from an unknown gymnosperm ancestor, flowering planbts have risen to dominance in most of the world's floras. The male gametophyte is 2-3 cells contained within a pollen grain; the female gametophyte is usually eight cells contained within an ovule which is retaind on the sporophyte phase of the plant's life cycle.

Parts of Flower

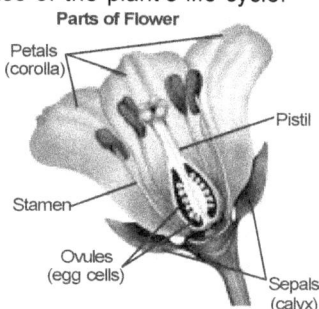

Petals (corolla)

Pistil

Stamen

Ovules (egg cells)

Sepals (calyx)

Anglet angulate
Type of stem forming an angle, not round.

Angstrom
A unit of length used for measuring atomic dimensions. One angstrom equals 10^{-10} metres.

Animalia

Animal Kingdom. Multicellular eukaryotic group characterized by heterotrophic nutritional mode, usually organ and tissue development, and motility sometime during the organism's life history.

Annelida

The taxonomic group (phylum) of animals that includes segmented worms.

Annual

Type of plant according to the stem. Plants with a year life-time generally belong to this group.

Antagonistic muscles

A pair of muscles that work to produce opposite effects&emdash;one contracts as the other relaxes: for example, the bicep and tricep muscles on opposite sides of your upper arm.

Antelope

The term antelope refers to approximately 90 species of even-toed ungulates that belong to the family Bovidae. Most antelope are native to Africa, though some species are native to Asia. The term antelope does not correspond to a single taxonomic group.

Antenna

A sensory aparatus (also referred to as a 'feeler') that is located on the head of an arthropod.

Anther

The top of a stamen's filament; divided into pollen sacs in which the pollen grains form.

Antheridium

The organ on a gametophyte plant which produces the sperm cells.

Anthophyte

A flowering plant, or any of its closest relatives, such as the Bennettitales, Gnetales, or Pentoxylales.

Antibiotic resistance

Tendency of certain bacteria to develop a resistance to commonly over-used antibiotics.

Antibiotic-resistant bacteria

A strain of bacteria with slight alterations (mutations) in some of their molecules that enable the bacteria to survive drugs designed to kill them.

Antibiotics

Substances produced by some microorganisms, plants, and vertebrates that kill or inhibit the growth of bacteria.

Antibodies

several sizes of structurally similar protein molecules which are able to bind to specific proteins or other substances; forming a main line of defense in animals against foreign items.

Antibody

A protein produced by certain white blood cells in response to a foreign substance (antigen). Each antibody can bind only to a specific antigen.

Antibody-mediated immunity

Immune reaction that protects primarily against invading viruses and bacteria through antibodies produced by plasma cells; also known as humoral immunity.

Anticline

A fold of rock layers that is convex upwards. Antonym of syncline.

Anticodon
A sequence of three nucleotides on the transfer RNA molecule that recognizes and pairs with a specific codon on a messenger RNA molecule; helps control the sequence of amino acids in a growing polypeptide chain.

Antidiuretic hormone (ADH)
A hormone produced by the hypothalamus and released by the pituitary gland that increases the permeability of the renal tubule of the nephron and thereby increases water reabsorption; also known as vasopressin.

Antigen
Any foreign or "non-self" substance that, when introduced into the body, causes the immune system to create an antibody.

Antigenic determinant
The site on an antigen to which an antibody binds, forming an antigen-antibody complex.

Antinutrients
Chemicals produced by plants as a defense mechanism; inhibit the action of digestive enzymes in insects that attack and attempt to eat the plants.

Antler
A bony structure that grows on the head of a deer. Contrasted with horns, antlers are often branched (whereas horns do not branch).

Anus
End of the digestive tract, or gut, through which waste products of digestion are excreted, as distinct from the mouth.

Aorta
The artery that carries blood from the left ventricle for distribution throughout the tissues of the body. The largest diameter and thickest walled artery in the body.

Aperture
Small opening, for example the opening in the test of a foram.

Apical meristem
A meristem (embryonic tissue) at the tip of a shoot or root that is responsible for increasing the plant's length.

Apnea
A disorder in which breathing stops for periods longer than 10 seconds during sleep; can be caused by failure of the automatic respiratory centre to respond to elevated blood levels of carbon dioxide.

Apocrine glands
Sweat glands that are located primarily in the armpits and groin area; larger than the more widely distributed eccrine glands.

Apomorph
A new trait or structural feature that arises in an evolving lineage that is dissimilar from the ancestral line.

Apoptosis
A normal cellular process involving a genetically programmed series of events leading to the death of a cell.

Aposematic
Characteristics (such bright colouration) that act as warnings to other animals (especially predators) and signal that an animal has defences (for example, a poisonous frog that is brightly coloured).

Appendicular skeleton
The bones of the appendages (wings, legs, and arms or fins) and of the pelvic and pectoral girdles that join

the appendages to the rest of the skeleton; one of the two components of the skeleton of vertebrates.

Appendix
Blind sac at the end of the large intestine that usually ruptures during final exams; a vestigial organ in humans.

Aptenia
Genus of plants. Plants from South Africa of the Aizoazeae family containing 2 species of succulents plants, with flowers very similar to those of daisies.

Arboreal
Pertaining to animals that are adapted to life in the tree tops, tree-dwelling.

Archaea
Proposed, but not widely accepted, sixth taxonomic kingdom that would include the archaebacteria.

Archaebacteria
Ancient (over 3.5 billion years old) group of prokaryotes; some biologists want to place this group into a separate Kingdom, the Archaea. Most currently place it within the Kingdom Monera.

Archaeocyathids
An extinct group of animals that were part of Cambrian-aged reef environments, but which were extinct by the close of the Cambrian Period.

Archean
The Archean Eon (3800 to 2500 MYA) was the time period in which the first life forms appeared on our planet. At that time, Earth was very different from what it is today. The atmosphere was composed of toxic gases such as methane and ammonia.

Archean/proterozoic era
The period of time beginning 4.6 billion years ago with the formation of the Earth and ending 570 million years ago.

Archegonium
The organ on a gametophyte plant which produces the egg cell, and nurtures the young sporophyte.

Archipelago
A group of islands; an expanse of water with scattered islands.

Aridity
The condition of receiving sparse rainfall; associated with cooler climates because cool air can hold less water vapor than warm air. Many deserts occur in relatively warm climates, however, because of local or global influences that block rainfall.

Arrector pili
A muscle running from a hair follicle to the dermis. Contraction of the muscle causes the hair to rise perpendicular to the skin surface, forming "goose pimples."

Arteries
Thick-walled vessels that carry blood away from the heart. Singular = artery.

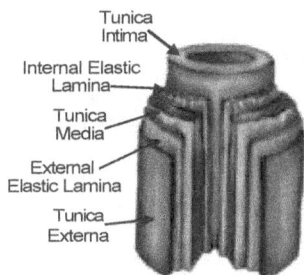

Arterioles
The smallest arteries; usually branch into a capillary bed.

Arthropod

A taxonomic group of animals that includes spiders, crabs, insects, and centipedes and whose bodies possess pairs of jointed limbs and in most cases an exoskeleton or hard exterior covering.

Artificial selection

A type of selection in which individuals are chosen (by a breeder) to mate and produce offspring with particular characteristics desired by the breeder.

Ascomycetes

Division of fungi that contains the yeasts and morels; ascomycetes produce an ascus (or sac) in which ascospores are produced.

Ascus

Structure produced by sac fungi in which sexual ascospores develop.

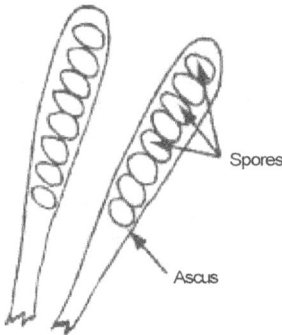

Asexual reproduction

A type of reproduction involving only one parent that usually produces genetically identical offspring. Asexual reproduction occurs without meiosis or syngamy, and may happen though budding, by the division of a single cell, or the breakup of an entire organism into two or more parts.

Aspect diversity

A measure of the variety of the physical appearances of species that live in the same habitat and are hunted by predators that use visual hunting skills to identify and capture prey.

Asphalt

A dark bituminous substance found in natural beds. Residue from petroleum distillation.

Assortment

A way in which meiosis produces new combinations of genetic information. Paternal and maternal chromosomes line up randomly during synapsis, so each daughter cell is likely to receive an assortment of maternal and paternal chromosomes rather than a complete set from either.

Aster

Short fibres produced by cells during mitosis and meiosis. These radiate from the centriole (if it is present).

Asteroid impacts

Hypothesis that links certain mass extinction events with the impact of a comet or asteroid, most notably the mass extinction 65 million years that caused the disappearance of dinosaurs and many other reptilian groups. Asteroid impacts early in earth history also contributed to the formation of the atmosphere and oceans.

Asthma

A respiratory disorder caused by allergies that constrict the bronchioles by inducing spasms in the muscles surrounding the lungs, by causing the bronchioles to swell, or by clogging the bronchioles with mucus.

Asymmetric membrane

A membrane that is made such that the pore size increases through the membrane matrix.

Asymmetrical
In animals, a term referring to organisms that lack a general body plan or axis of symmetry that divides the body into mirror-image halves.

Atmosphere
The envelope of gases that surrounds the Earth; consists largely of nitrogen (78%) and oxygen (21%).

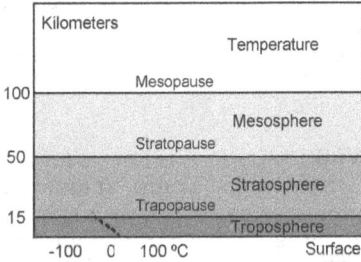

Kilometers

Temperature

Mesopause

100

Mesosphere

Stratopause

50

Stratosphere

Trapopause

15

Troposphere

-100 0 100 °C   Surface

Atmospheric pressure
Pressure at any point in an atmosphere attributable solely to the weight of the atmospheric gases at that point. Expressed as 1 barg, approximately 75 cm of mercury (14.7 lbs/in^2) at sea level.

Atom
The smallest indivisible particle of matter that can have an independent existence.

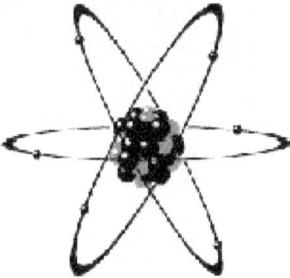

Atomic number
The number of protons in the nucleus of an atom.

Atomic weight
The sum of the weights of an atom's protons and neutrons, the atomic weight differs between isotopes of the same element.

Atrioventricular (AV) node
Tissue in the right ventricle of the heart that receives the impulse from the atria and transmits it through the ventricles by way of the bundles of His and the Purkinje fibres.

Atrioventricular (AV) valve
The valve between each auricle and ventricle of the heart.

Auricle
The chamber of the heart that receives blood from the body returned to the heart by the veins. Also referred to as atrium.

Auriculars
A group of feathers that covers the side of a bird's head where the bird's ear openings are located.

Autochthonous
Refers to something formed in its present location.

Autoclave, autoclavability
An autoclave is a device that uses saturated steam at a specified pressure over time to kill microorganisms and thus achieve sanitization or sterilization. Because many materials change properties when exposed to moisture, heat, and pressure, products destined for this process must be specially engineered for autoclavability. A sterilizing grade air filter is required to maintain sterility during air inrush after autoclaving.

Autonomic nervous system
The part of the vertebrate nervous

system that is made up of the motor neurons that innervate the animal's internal organs and that are in most cases not voluntarily controlled by the animal.

Autonomic system

The portion of the peripheral nervous system that stimulates smooth muscle, cardiac muscle, and glands; consists of the parasympathetic and sympathetic systems.

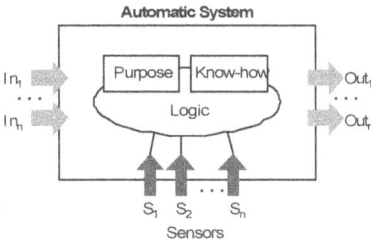

Autosomes

The chromosomes other than the sex chromosomes. Each member of an autosome pair (in diploid organisms) is of similar length and in the genes it carries.

Autotroph

Any organism that is able to manufacture its own food. Most plants are autotrophs, as are many protists and bacteria. Contrast with consumer. Autotrophs may be photoautotrophic, using light energy to manufacture food, or chemoautotrophic, using chemical energy.

Autotrophic

Refers to organisms that synthesize their nutrients and obtain their energy from inorganic raw materials.

Autotrophs

Organisms that synthesize their own nutrients; include some bacteria that are able to synthesize organic molecules from simpler inorganic compounds.

Auxins

A group of hormones involved in controlling plant growth and other functions; once thought responsible for phototropism by causing the cells on the shaded side of a plant to elongate, thereby causing the plant to bend toward the light.

Avalonia

A separate plate in the Early Paleozoic consisting of much of Northern Europe, Newfoundland, Nova Scotia, and some coastal parts of New England.

Aves

A taxonomic group (class) of vertebrates, also known commonly as 'birds', whose distinguishing characteristics include feathers, endothermy, and the production of amiotic eggs.

Axial skeleton

The skull, vertebral column, and rib cage; one of the two components of the skeleton in vertebrates.

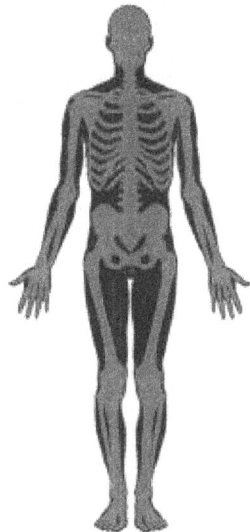

Axial Skeleton

Axil
The angle formed between a leaf stalk and the stem to which it is attached. In flowering plants, buds develop in the axils of leaves.

Axillary buds
The axillary bud is an embryonic shoot which lies at the junction of the stem and petiole of a plant. Axillary buds can be used to differentiate if the plant is single-leafed or multi-leafed.

Axons
An axon is a long, slender projection of a nerve cell, or neuron, that conducts electrical impulses away from the neuron's cell body or soma.

AZT (azido-deoxythymidine)
Zidovudine (INN) or azidothymidine (AZT) (also called ZDV) is a nucleoside analog reverse-transcriptase inhibitor (NRTI), a type of antiretroviral drug used for the treatment of HIV/AIDS. It is an analog of thymidine.

B

B cells

Type of lymphocyte responsible for antibody-mediated immunity; mature in the bone marrow and circulate in the circulatory and lymph systems where they transform into antibody-producing plasma cells when exposed to antigens.

B memory cells

Long-lived B cells that are produced after an initial exposure to an antigen and play an important role in secondary immunity. They remain in the body and facilitate a more rapid responce if the antigen is encountered again.

Back flushing, backwash

Reversing the permeate flow to mechanically clean the membrane.

Back flushing, backwash

Reversing the permeate flow to mechanically clean the membrane.

Bacteria

Single celled organisms non-green (except the blue-green bacteria {algae}) which have cell wall compositions different than other living organisms.

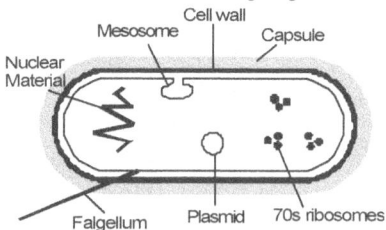

Bacteriophage

Virus which infects and destroys a bacterial host. Some phages, however, will incorporate their DNA into that of their host, and remain dormant for an extended period. For this reason, they have become essential tools of genetic engineers.

Bacterium (pl. Bacteria)

A primitive, one-celled microorganism without a nucleus. Bacteria live almost everywhere in the environment. Some bacteria may infect humans, plants, or animals. They may be harmless or they may cause disease.

Balanced polymorphisim

The maintenance of more than one allele in a population due to the superiority (in selection terms) of the heterozygote over both homozygotes.

Baleen

A fibrous structure in the mouths of some whales (baleen whales or Mysticetes) that enables the whale to filter food from the water for ingestion.

Baltica

A separate continental plate of the Early Paleozoic composed of the United Kingdom, Scandinavia, European Russia and Central Europe; named for the Baltic Sea.

Banded iron formation

Rock consisting of alternating light and dark layers of iron-rich chert (the dark layers have more iron minerals) formed from 3.8 to 1.7 billion years ago.

Banding
The practice of attaching metal or plastic bands around the legs of birds (or other animals) to mark individuals for identification on recapture.

Barachois
A lagoon separated from the ocean by a sandbar, which was deposited in a delta after the last glaciation. The term is used in Atlantic Canada, where the landform is common.

Barbel
A long tubercle (projection) that serves as a sensory appendage and is attached to an animal's lips or mouthparts.

Barbicels
Small hook-like structures on barbules that link adjoining barbules to form the rigid, interlocked structure of the feather vane.

Barbs
The structures that branch from the main shaft of a feather and form the feather's vanes.

Barbules
Small structures that grow from the barbs of a bird's feather. Barbules overlap and interlock to give a feather rigidity.

Bark
The outer layer of the stems of woody plants; composed of an outer layer of dead cells (cork) and an inner layer of phloem.

Barr body
Inactivated X-chromosome in mammalian females. Although inactivated, the Barr body is replicated prior to cell division and thus is passed on to all descendant cells of the embryonic cell that had one of its X-chromosomes inactivated.

Barren
Characterized by sparse vegetation due to limitations in the physical environment (such as a harsh climate or the chemical properties of the soil).

Barrier island
A long, narrow island that runs parallel to the mainland and is separated from it by a lagoon.

Barriers to gene flow
Factors, such as geographic, mechanical, and behavioural isolating mechanisms that restrict gene flow between populations, leading to populations with differing allele frequencies.

Basal
Relating to, located at, or forming the base.

Basal body
A structure at the base of a cilium or flagellum; consists of nine triplet microtubules arranged in a circle with no central microtubule.

Basal group
The earliest diverging group within a clade; for instance, to hypothesize that sponges are basal animals is to suggest that the lineage(s) leading to sponges diverged from the lineage that gave rise to all other animals.

Basalt
Highly mafic igneous volcanic rock, typically fine-grained and dark in colour; rough volcanic equivalent of gabbro.

Base

A chemical component (the fundamental information unit) of DNA or RNA. There are four bases in DNA: adenine (A), thymine (T), cytosine (C), and guanine (G). RNA also contains four bases, but instead of thymine, RNA contains uracil (U).

Base pair

two bases, each containing the element nitrogen, held together by relatively weak chemical bonds. Two base pairs make up DNA molecules: adenine and thymine, and guanine and cytosine.

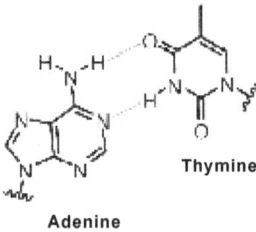

Thymine

Adenine

Basement rock

The oldest rocks in a given area; a complex of metamorphic and igneous rocks that underlies the sedimentary deposits. Usually Precambrian or Paleozoic in age.

Basic plumage

If a bird species only molts once a year, their basic plummge is the set of feathers they have throughout the year. If a bird species experiences two molts per year, the basic plumage is (in most cases) the plumage grown after a complete molt and is present during the bird's non breeding season.

Basidia

Specialized club-shaped structures on the underside of club fungi (Basidiomycetes) within which spores form (sing.: basidium).

Basidiomycetes

The club fungi, a major group of fungi that all produce a structure (basidium) on which basidiospores are produced. Includes mushrooms and toadstools.

Basidiospores

The spores formed on the basidia of club fungi (Basidiomycetes).

Basin

Any large depression in which sediments are deposited.

Basin and range province

One of the most extensive systems of fault-bounded mountains separated by sediment-filled valleys, extending across Idaho, Oregon, Nevada, Utah, Arizona, New Mexico, California, and northern Mexico.

Basin and range topography

The surface features typical of the Basin and Range Province.

Batesian mimicry

The resemblance between a mimic species (which is not harmful or unpaletable if ingested) and a model species (which is harmful or unpaletable if ingested).

Beak

Narrow, protruding jaws that usually do not contain teeth. Present in various groups of vertebrates including some cetaceans.

Bedrock

The general term referring to the rock underlying other unconsolidated material, i.e. soil.

Bell-flower

The bellflower family - campanulaceae. It includes about 2000 species, spread all around the world. They are mainly annual herbs.

America during the Last Glacial Maximum, about 21,000 years ago; it served as a migration route for people, animals, and plants. Also known as Beringia.

Berry
Type of fruits. Berries are fruits with very soft epicarp and with the mesocarp and endocarp very fleshy . For instance, tomatoes and grapes.

Beta decay
Type of radioactive decay in which a radioisotope emits a small, negatively-charged and fast-moving particle from its nucleus. The beta particle is similar in size, charge, and speed to an electron and is formed when a neutron in the radioisotope's nucleus converts to a proton.

Beta diversity
A measure of the variety of organisms in a region. Beta diversity is influenced by the turnover of species among habitats.

Beta rating, beta ratio
A standard method of rating a filter's ability to remove particles.

Beta sheet
A pleated section within a protein structure.

Bicarbonate ions
A weak base present in saliva that helps to neutralize acids in food.

Big bang theory
A model for the evolution of the universe that holds that all matter and energy in the universe were concentrated in one point, which suddenly exploded. Subsequently, matter condensed to form atoms, elements, and eventually galaxies and stars.

Beneficial
Useful, offering benefits. Beneficial insects produce honey or eat harmful insects.

Benguela upwelling
The Benguela Upwelling is a 9000-square kilometre patch of sea off the coast of Namibia where the northbound Benguela Current periodically churns up nutrients from deeper waters.

Benign
Not cancerous; does not invade nearby tissue or spread to other parts of the body.

Benthic
Organisms that live on the bottom of the ocean are called benthic organisms. They are not free-floating like pelagic organisms are.

Benthic zone
One of the two basic subdivisions of the marine biome; includes the sea floor and bottom-dwelling organisms.

Bering land bridge
The vast tundra plain that was exposed between Asia and North

Bilabiate

Type of flower. Flower presenting irregular corollas with two very distinctive lips, the upper one made by joining two petals and the lower one by joining three.

Bilateral symmetry

A type of symmetry in which an organism's body possesses two equal halves that are symmetrical when compared on either side of a midline. Most animals exhibit bilateral symmetry.

Biliary system

The bile-producing system consisting of the liver, gallbladder, and associated ducts.

Bill

A bird's jaws which consist of bone and a hornlike outer layer of keratin.

Binary fission

The method by which bacteria reproduce. The circular DNA molecule is replicated; then the cell splits into two identical cells, each containing an exact copy of the original cell's DNA.

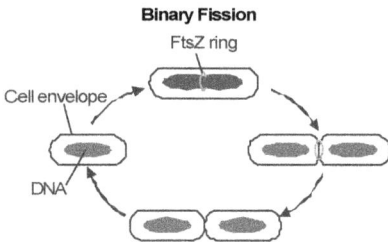

Binary Fission

FtsZ ring

Cell envelope

DNA

Binding

The process by which some components in a feed solution adhere to the membrane. Binding can be desirable in some instances, but often, as in the case of protein binding during sterile filtration, can result in a loss of valuable product.

Binding sites

Areas on the ribosome within which tRNA-amino acid complexes fit during protein synthesis.

Bindweed

The Bindweed family - convulvulaceae - comprises about 1500 species of plants scattered worldwide. Some are shrubs; other trees. Many of them are climbing plants. There are also some parasites. Some species, such as Ipomoea batatas (sweet potato) is cultivated in many places around the world because of its tubercles; other ones, like the Mexican Exogonium purga (jalap) or the Indian Operculina turpethum contain medicinal and purgative properties in their tuberous roots. Some members of this family are used in gardening , like in the case of the Ipomoema genus, and more precisely the species Ipomoea acuminata, which , after being cultivated for many years , can be found in the wild as a naturalized species.

Binocular vision

A type of vision in which an animals two eyes face forward providing overlapping fields of view that enable the animal to judge depth.

Binoculars

Binoculars, also referred to as field glasses, are optical magnification instruments that consist of two telescopes mounted together so that you can view objects that are at a distance.

Binomial nomenclature

A method of identifying and naming organisms using two names. The first name is the genus name, and the second is the species name. Names are usually Latin or Greek in origin. Binomial system of nomenclature

A system of taxonomy developed by Linnaeus in the early eighteenth century. Each species of plant and animal receives a two-term name; the first term is the genus, and the second is the species.

Biochemical
Organic compounds made by living organisms: proteins, vitamins, fats, etc.

Biochemical cycle
The flow of an element through the living tissue and physical environment of an ecosystem; e. g., the carbon, hydrogen, oxygen, nitrogen, sulphur, and phosphorus cycles.

Biochemical reactions
Specific chemical processes that occur in living things.

Biochemistry
That division of chemistry which studies the compounds made by living things.

Biodiversity
A measure of the variety of organisms in a habitat or ecosystem. Can be measured by the number of species or genetic variation in an area or ecosystem.

Biogeography
The study of the geographic distribution of organisms throughout the landscape. Examines the how geographical variation in the physical environment manifests variation in the biotic components that inhabit the area.

Biological/biotic factors
Living factors such as decomposers, scavengers and predators.

Bioluminescence
The production of light by a chemical reaction within an organism. The

process occurs in many bacteria and protists, as well as certain animals and fungi.

Bioluminescent
Refers to organisms that emit light under certain conditions.

Biomass
The weight of living material (expressed as a dry weight) in some unit such as an organism, population, or community. Biomass is often cited as weight per unit area (biomass density).

Biome
A bunch of vegetal communities. Vegetal communities sharing similar fisiognomy, induce by a similar climate.

Biosafety tests
A class of tests that determine whether a filter's materials of construction can induce systemic toxicity, skin irritation, sensitization reaction, or other biological responses. These tests are often completed by labs in vivo or in vitro. For example, United States Pharmacopoeia XXVII Class VI Plastics Test involves both the implantation and extraction of drug product contact surfaces to demonstrate that these materials are not toxic to various mammalian cells.

Biosphere
All ecosystems on Earth as well as the Earth's crust, waters, and atmosphere on and in which organisms exist; also, the sum of all living matter on Earth.

Biostratigraphy
The study of rock layers (e.g., distribution, environment of deposition, age) based on their fossils.

Biostratinomy
The study of what happens between the death of an organism and burial.

Biota
The living components (fauna and flora) of an ecosystem or habitat.

Biotechnology
A set of biological techniques developed through basic research and now applied to research and product development.

Bioturbation
The disturbance of sediment by organisms, e.g. burrows, trails, or complete mixing.

Bipedal
Describes an animal that walks on two legs.

Bipinnate
Describing a pinnate leaf in which the leaflets themselves are further subdivided in a pinnate fashion.

Biramous
Arthropod appendages that are biramous have two branches, an outer branch and an inner branch. These branches may have separate functions; in crustaceans, for instance, the inner branch of a leg is used for walking, while the outer branch may be paddle-shaped or feathery and often functions as a gill.

Bird
A bird is an animal that belongs to the Class Aves. Birds are a diverse group of vertebrates that evolved from reptiles during the Mesazoic Era about 150 million years ago.

Birth rate
The average number of offspring produced per individual per unit of time. Birth rate is often expressed as a function of age.

Bisporangiate
When a flower or cone produces both megaspores and microspores, it is said to be bisporangiate. Most flowers are bisporangiate.

Bladder
A hollow, distensible organ with muscular walls that stores urine and expels it through the urethra.

Blade
Any broad and flattened region of a plant or alga, which allows for increased photosynthetic surface area.

Blanketing
The use of nitrogen or other inert gas to hold a tank such that product is not exposed to atmospheric air. Hydrophobic filter cartridges are typically used for blanketing.

Blastocoel
The fluid-filled cavity at the centre of a blastula.

Blastocyst
The developmental stage of the fertilized ovum by the time it is ready to implant; formed from the morula and consists of an inner cell mass, an internal cavity, and an outer layer of cells (the trophoblast).

Blastula
A ball of cells surrounding a fluid-filled cavity (the blastocoel) that is produced by the repeated cleavage of a zygote.

Blending
Term applied to 19th century belief that parental traits "blended" in their offspring; disproven by Mendel's work.

Blinded

When a filter is "blinded," it means that particles have filled the pores, and the flow through the filter from the feed side to the permeate side is reduced or stopped.

Blood

Fluid which circulates throughout the body of an animal, distributing nutrients, and often oxygen as well.

Blood group or type

One of the classes into which blood can be separated on the basis of the presence or absence of certain antigens; notably, the ABO types and the Rh blood group.

Blow down

The act of draining a system or of introducing constituents into a reactor through the use of gas at a positive pressure. Care must be exercised to prevent pressures above the maximum operating pressure.

Blowhole

A hole on top of a cetacean's head through which air is inhaled and exhaled. The blowhole is found on top of the head so as to prevent water from flowing into the lungs.

Blueschist

Metamorphic rock formed under great pressures, but not so great temperatures.

Body fossil

The actual remains (however permineralized, compressed or otherwise post-mortem altered) of an organism; includes bones, shells, and teeth.

Bolus

A mass of chewed food mixed with salivary secretions that is propelled into the espohagus during the swallowing phase of digestion.

Bony fish

A term applied collectively to all groups of fish with bony (as opposed to cartilaginous) skeletons.

Book lung

A set of soft overlapping flaps, covered up by a plate on the abdomen, through which oxygen is taken up and carbon dioxide given off. Characteristic of many terrestrial arachnids such as scorpions and spiders.

Borage

The Borage family - boraginaceae. It comprises about 2000 species scattered all around the world. They are mainly herbs and shrubs.

Bottlenecks

Drastic short-term reductions in population size caused by natural disasters, disease, or predators; can lead to random changes in the population's gene pool.

Boundary layer

A layer of slow-moving water or air that lies just above the surface of an object.

Bow riding

The behaviour of cetaceans (commonly dolphins) in which they swim or 'ride' the crests of ocean waves.

Brachiopods

A phylum of hinge-shelled animals that have left an excellent fossil record; brachiopods live on or in the ocean floor.

Brachydactly

Human genetic disorder that causes production of an extra digit; an autosomal dominant trait. Sometimes referred to as polydactly.

Bract
Part of the flower. Pieces under the flower with foliacious structure, different to the calyx .

Braided river
A river characterized by a network of channels that split and entwine, rather than a single channel for water and sediment. Braided rivers are common in upland areas closer to mountain fronts where the slope, and consequently water velocity, lessens and the river begins to deposit sediment. Braiding is the result of the channel becoming clogged with sediment.

Brain
Collection of nerve cells usually located at the anterior end of an animal, when present at all. The nerves coordinate information gathered by sense organs, locomotion, and most internal body activities.

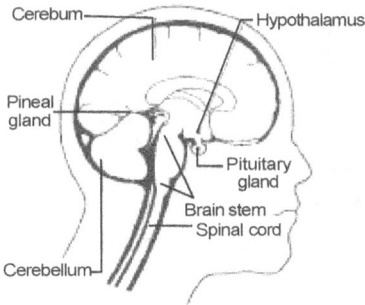

Brain stem
The portion of the brain that is continuous with the spinal cord and consists of the medulla oblongata and pons of the hindbrain and the midbrain.

Branched
They do not have a primary root. They resemble to the branches of a tree.

Breccia
A rock composed of angular fragments of older rocks; distinguished from a conglomerate in that the component rocks are not rounded and worn.

Breeding system
The type of breeding behaviours characteristic of a population (polygyny, outcrossing, or selective mating) and the ways in which members of the population adapt to these breeding behaviours.

Brilles
Transparent layers that cover the eyes of all snakes and some lizards. Brilles cannot be moved (in contrast to lids).

Bristles
Long, stiff feathers that are often found near a bird's mouth or eyes. The function of bristles is not well-understood and it is thought they may serve to funnel food into a bird's mouth or provide protection to the bird's eyes.

Broken stick model
A model that describes the relative abundance of species by random segmentization of a line representing the resources of the environment.

Bronchi
Tubes that carry air from the trachea to the lungs (sing.: bronchus).

Bronchioles
Small tubes in the lungs that are formed by the branching of the bronchi; terminate in the alveoli.

Bronchitis
A respiratory disorder characterized by excess mucus production and swelling of the bronchioles; caused by long-term exposure to irritants

such as cigarette smoke and air pollutants.

Brood parasite

A bird that lays its eggs in the nest of another bird (either another species or another individual of the same species) so that the young will be raised by the host parents.

Brood parasitism

A method of reproduction seen in birds that involves the laying of eggs in the nests of other birds. The eggs are left under the parantal care of the host parents.

Brood patch

An area that develops on the lower abdomen of birds in which the feathers drop off and the skin thickens and becomes densely populated with blood vessels. It is used in incubation to keep eggs and young warm.

Brood reduction

A reproductive strategy in which a female bird produces more eggs than she would normally be capable of raising.

Brooding

A behaviour in birds in which the parents continue to warm nestlings or young that are unable to maintain their own body temperatures.

Brown algae

Multicellular protistans placed in the Division Phaeophyta, includes kelp.

Brush border

The collection of microvilli forming a border on the intestinal side of the epithelial cells of the small intestine.

Bryophyte

Plants in which the gametophyte generation is the larger, persistent phase; they generally lack conducting tissues. Bryophytes include the Hepaticophyta (liverworts), Anthocerotophyta (hornworts), and Bryophyta (mosses).

Bubble point

The minimum pressure required to overcome the capillary forces and surface tension of a liquid in a fully-wetted membrane filter. The bubble point value is determined by observing when bubbles first begin to emerge on the permeate side or downstream side of a fully-wetted membrane filter when pressurized with a gas on the feed (upstream) side of the membrane filter.

Bubble point test

The test procedure for determining the bubble point of the largest pores in a microfiltration membrane.

Bud

Part of the stem that are responsible for plant growth, either new stems , flowers or buds .

Bud sports

Buds that produce fruit that is different from the rest of the fruit on the tree; vegetatively propagated by grafting cuttings onto another plant.

Budding

1. Asexual production of new organisms; usually found in yeast;
2. The process by which HIV and similar viruses leave the cell (other than by lysing).

Buffer exchange

Filtration process used for the exchange of smaller ionic solutes, whereby the feed solution is washed, usually repeatedly, and one buffer is removed and replaced with an alternative buffer.

Buffers

Chemicals that maintain pH values within narrow limits by absorbing or releasing hydrogen ions.

Bulb

Bulbs are in fact buds adapted to leave under the ground, that store food provisions. Onions are bulbs.

Bulbourethral glands

Glands that secrete a mucus-like substance that is added to sperm and provides lubrication during intercourse.

Bursae

Small sacs lined with synovial membrane and filled with synovial fluid; act as cushions to reduce friction between tendons and bones.

Bush

Type of plant according to the stem. Bushes are ligneous plants shorter than one metre tall

Buttercup

Buttercup family - ranunculaceae. it comprises about 2000 species of plants mainly spread in temperate countries. Most of them are herbs and lianas having big flowers, so they are very valuable in gardening. They are also very well known because many of them are poisonous plants.

C

Caiman
A relative of the alligator that is found in Central and South America.

Calamus
The hollow, proximal portion of the feather shaft that attaches the feather to the skin.

Calcereous
Describes structures that contain calcium such as shells, exoskeletons, and bones and function to support or protect an animal.

Calcite
A common crystalline form of natural calcium carbonate, CaCO3, that is the basic constituent of limestone, marble, and chalk. Also called calcspar.

Calcitonin
A hormone produced by the thyroid that plays a role in regulating calcium levels.

Calcium carbonate
A white compound, $CaCO_3$, that occurs naturally as marble, chalk, limestone, and calcite. It is used by many marine invertebrates, such as corals and echinoderms, and by protists, such as coccolithophorids, to construct their exoskeletons. Calcium carbonate, in the form of calcite, is also incorporated into the eggshells of amniotes, except for turtles whose eggs are composed of aragonite ($CaCO_3$ + magnesium).

Caldera
A large circular volcanic depression, often originating due to collapse.

Caliche
A sedimentary deposit commonly made of calcium carbonate and formed from the leaching of minerals from the top layers of soil. Caliche deposits characterize arid and semi-arid environments.

Call matching
A vocalization in birds characterized by the male and female of a pair duplicating the other's flight call. Call matching is often a behaviour exhibited by members of the finch family.

Calvin cycle
Calvin-Benson Cycle or Carbon Fixation. Series of biochemical, enzyme-mediated reactions during which atmospheric carbon dioxide is reduced and incorporated into organic molecules, eventually some of this forms sugars. The enzymes in the Calvin cycle are functionally equivalent to many enzymes used in other metabolic pathways such as gluconeogenesis and the pentose phosphate pathway, but they are to be found in the chloroplast stroma instead of the cell cytoplasm, separating the reactions.

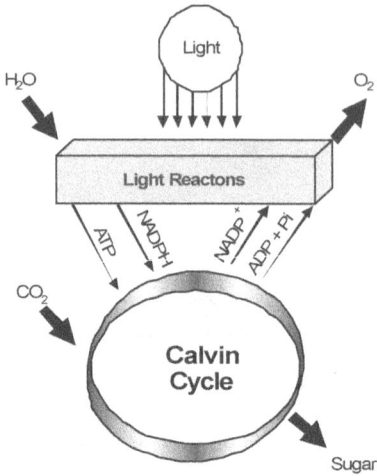

Diagram labels: Light, H_2O, O_2, Light Reactons, ATP, NADPH, NADP$^+$, ADP + Pi, CO_2, Calvin Cycle, Sugar

Calyx

It is the green section of the flower. It is more consistent than the corolla . It is formed by green leaf- like pieces called sepals. They are meant to protect the flower bud.

Cambium

A lateral meristem in plants. Types of cambiums include vascular, cork, and intercalary.

Cambrian

Geologic period that begins the Paleozoic Era 570 million years ago. Marked in its beginning by a proliferation of animals with hard, preservable parts, such as brachiopods, trilobites, and archaeocyathids.

Cambrian explosion

The Cambrian Explosion (570 to 530 million years ago) refers to an unprecedented and unsurpassed period of evolutionary innovation in the history of our planet.

Cambrian period

The Cambrian Period (543 to 505 million years ago) is the first time period of the Paleozoic Era. It is preceded by the Precambrian.

Camouflage

Colouration or patterns that help an animal to appear to blend with its surroundings. Camouflage is common among invertebrates.

Campanulate

Type of flower. these flowers are narrower than tubular , in the shape of a bell.

Campodactyly

A dominant trait in which a muscle is improperly attached to bones in the little finger, causing the finger to be permanently bent.

Canadian shield

A broad area of Precambrian rock that covers most of Canada, from the Great Lakes to the Arctic Ocean and from Labrador to Northwest Territories. It forms the centre of the original North American craton (Laurentia) around which the rest of the continent was added.

Cancer

Diseases in which abnormal cells divide without control. Cancer cells can invade nearby tissue and can spread through the bloodstream and lymphatic system.

Candidate species

A species of plant or animal for which FWS or NOAA Fisheries has sufficient information about its biological vulnerability and threats to warrant a proposal to list as endangered or threatened.

Canine tooth

A sharp tooth positioned near the front of the jaws present in mammals (and most prominent in carnivores)

that has a single point that is shaped for peircing and holding onto food.

Canopy
Layer of vegetation elevated above the ground, usually of tree braches and epiphytes. In tropical forests, the canopy may be more than 100 feet above the ground.

Capillaries
Small, thin-walled blood vessels that allow oxygen to diffuse from the blood into the cells and carbon dioxide to diffuse from the cells into the blood.

Capillary
A tube with a very thin lumen, by analogy with the smallest vessels in the human circulatory and lymphatic system. In filtration, descriptive of the pores in a membrane.

Capillary bed
A branching network of capillaries supplied by arterioles and drained by venules.

Capsid
The protcin "shell" of a free virus particle.

Capsule
Type of deshincent dry food. Capsules are fruits derived from compound ovaries. They have many openings, like in the case of the oppium poppy.

Carapace
A hard shell or shield-like structure on the dorsal side of an animal's body. Also refers more specifically to the upper side of a turtle or tortoise shell.

Carbohydrates
Organic molecules composed of carbon, hydrogen, and oxygen that serve as energy sources and structural materials for cells of all organisms.

Carbonate
A mineral composed mainly of calcium (Ca) and carbonate (CO_3) ions, may also include magnesium (Mg), iron (Fe) and others. n. Rock or sediments derived from debris of organic materials composed mainly of calcium and carbonate (e.g., shells, corals, etc.) or from the inorganic precipitation of calcium (and other ions) and carbonate from solution (seawater). For example, limestone or dolomite.

carbonate platform
A broad (hundreds of metres), flat, shallow submarine expanse of carbonate rock, more common in the early-middle Paleozoic.

carbonate bank
A narrow (tens of metres), fairly flat, shallow, submarine plateau of carbonate rock, more common from the middle-late Paleozoic to the present, e.g., the Bahama Banks.

Carboniferous period
The Carboniferous Period (360 to 286 million years ago), also known as the Age of Amphibians, is the fifth of six periods during the Paleozoic Era.

Cardiac cycle
One heartbeat; consists of atrial contraction and relaxation, ventricular contraction and relaxation, and a short pause.

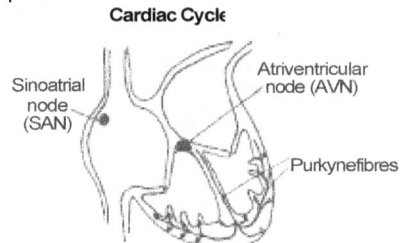
Cardiac Cyck

Cardiac muscle
The type of muscle that is found in the walls of the heart. Cardiac muscle is striated but branched, unlike the straight-shaped striated skeletal muscle cells.

Cardiovascular system
The human circulatory system consisting of the heart and the vessels that transport blood to and from the heart.

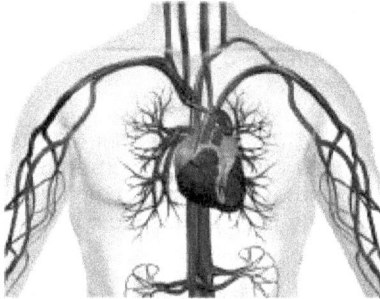

Carnasial tooth
A sharp, premolar tooth present in carnivores that is adapted for efficient tearing and slicing through the meat of their prey.

Carnivore
An animal that consumes primarily the flesh of other animals. More specifically used in reference to members of the Order Carnivora.

Carotenoids
Carotenoids are a class of organic pigments that absorb blue light and as a result are responsible for red, orange, and yellow hues.

Carpals
The bones that make up the wrist joint.

Carpel
It is the female reproductive part of the flower. Similar to a base-expanded bottle, stands upright in the middle of the flower. Its green colour denotes it derives from a transformed leaf.

Carrageenan
Chemical extracted from red algae that is added to commercial ice creams as an emulsifying agent.

Carrying capacity
The maximum population size that can be regularly sustained by an environment; the point where the population size levels off in the logistic growth model.

Cartridge or cartridge filter
A filtration or separations device having a membrane encapsulated within a housing. The housing normally has feed and permeate ports and, in the case of cross flow filters, a retentate port. All of these ports may be used to control the flow parameters of fluid into and out of the housing and through the membrane.

Caruncle
A bright-coloured area of skin (featherless) on the face or neck of a bird (most prominent in turkeys and relatives).

Caryopsis
Type of indehescent dry fruit. Caryopsys are fruits with the seed stuck to the pericarp .

Casparian strip
In plants, an impermeable waxy layer between the cells of the endodermis that stops water and solutes from entering the xylem, except by passing through the cytoplasm of adjacent cells.

Casque
A raised structure located on the head of a lizard (usually grows at the rear of the lizard's head).

Cassette

A device used for cross flow filtration, typically in a rectangular form, comprised of stacked flat sheets of membrane integrally bonded together. Most cassettes are typically designed to fit into a standard cassette holder where the feed, permeate, and any retentate ports mate with appropriate fittings on the cassette holders.

Cast

Type of fossil preservation where the original material of the fossil has decayed and been replaced later by another material, much the way a plaster cast is made in a mold.

Catabolic reactions

Reactions in cells in which existing chemical bonds are broken and molecules are broken down; generally produce energy, involve oxidation, and lead to a decrease in atomic order.

Cataphyll

In cycads, a scale-like modified leaf which protects the developing true leaves.

Catastrophism

Once-popular belief that events in earth history had occurred in the past a sudden events and by processes unlike those operating today. Periods of catastrophic change were followed by long periods of little change. A subgroup, the Diluvialists, contended that Noah's Flood was the last of many floods which had occurred throughout earth history.

Cathaysian terranes

A set of small landmasses that developed in tropical to subtropical latitudes on the eastern side of Pangea during the Permian and Triassic, includes modern North China (Sino-Korea), South China (Yangtze), Eastern Qiangtang, Tarim, and Indochina.

Cathodoluminescence

An analytical technique used in geology and paleontology to analyze the different minerals in a sample, or diagenetic history of a sample how crystals grew, were deformed, and were replaced. A beam of electrons is fired at a sample to produce visible light, which can then be used to interpret the mineralogical and diagenetic history of the sample.

Cell

Fundamental structural unit of all life. The cell consists primarily of an outer plasma membrane, which separates it from the environment; the genetic material (DNA), which encodes heritable information for the maintainance of life; and the cytoplasm, a heterogeneous assemblage of ions, molecules, and fluid.

Cell body

In a neuron, the part that contains the nucleus and most of the cytoplasm and the organelles.

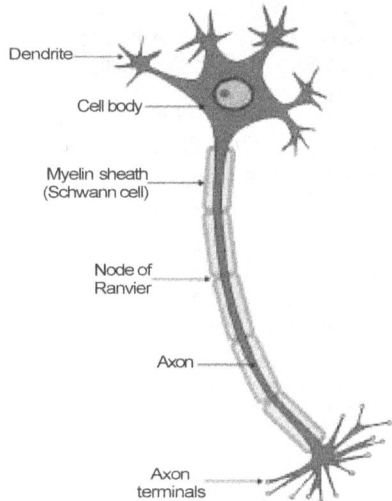

Cell cycle

Complete sequence of steps which must be performed by a cell in order to replicate itself, as seen from mitotic event to mitotic event. Most of the cycle consists of a growth period in which the cell takes on mass and replicates its DNA. Arrest of the cell cycle is an important feature in the reproduction of many organisms, including humans.

Cell harvesting

The process of concentrating (dewatering) the cell mass after fermentation. Cell slurries in excess of 70% wet cell weight are achievable. The cells may also be washed to prepare them for further processing, such as freezing or lysing. Unlike clarification processing, with cell harvesting, the cells are the target material.

Cell membrane

The outer membrane of a cell, which separates it from the environment. Also called a plasma membrane or plasmalemma.

Cell plate

In plants, a membrane-bound space produced during cytokinesis by the vesicles of the Golgi apparatus. The cell plate fuses with the plasma membrane, dividing the cell into two compartments.

Cytokinesis in Plant Cells
Cell Plate Formation

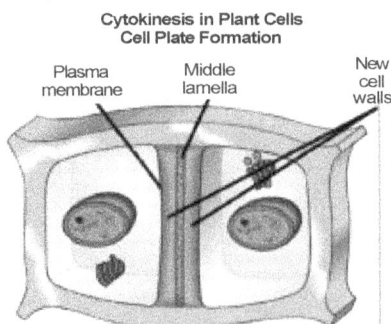

Cell theory

One of the four (or five) unifying concepts in biology. The cell theory states that all living things are composed of at least one cell and that the cell is the fundamental unit of function in all organisms. Corollaries: the chemical composition of all cells is fundamentally alike; all cells arise from preexisting cells through cell division.

Cell wall

Rigid structure deposited outside the cell membrane. Plants are known for their cell walls of cellulose, as are the green algae and certain protists, while fungi have cell walls of chitin.

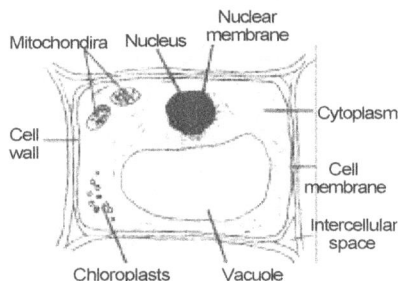

Cell-mediated immunity

Immune reaction directed against body cells that have been infected by viruses and bacteria; controlled by T cells.

Cellular respiration

The transfer of energy from various molecules to produce ATP; occurs in the mitochondria of eukaryotes, the cytoplasm of prokaryotes. In the process, oxygen is consumed and carbon dioxide is generated.

Cellulose

carbohydrate polymer of the simple sugar glucose. It is found in the cell walls of plants and green algae, as well as dinoflagellates. Cellulose is the most abundant compound on earth that is manufactured by living things.

Cenote
Mayan word for a sinkhole formed when fresh water dissolves limestone below the surface and the overlying rocks collapse.

Cenozoic era
The period of geologic time beginning after the end of the Mesozoic Era 65 million years ago and encompassing the present. Commonly referred to as the age of mammals.

Central nervous system
The part of an animal's nervous system that is made up of interneurons and exerts some control over the rest of the nervous system.

Centrifugal tail molt
The shedding and replacement of a bird's tail feathers that begins with the innermost pair of feathers being replaced first and then proceeding from the centre outward.

Centrifugation
From centrifuge, a rotating device for separating liquids of different specific gravities; the act of using a centrifuge to separate substances.

Centriole
A centriole is a barrel-shaped cell structure found in most animal eukaryotic cells, though it is absent in higher plants and most fungi. The walls of each centriole are usually composed of nine triplets of microtubules (protein of the cytoskeleton). Centrioles are a very important part of centrosomes, which are involved in organizing microtubules in the cytoplasm. The position of the centriole determines the position of the nucleus and plays

a crucial role in the spatial arrangement of the cell.

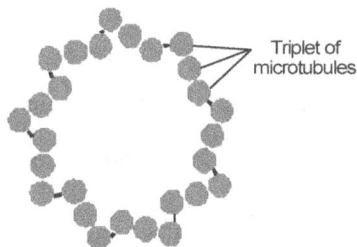

Cross section of centriole - Schema

Centromere
A specialized region on each chromatid to which kinetochores and sister chromatids attach.

Cephalization
The localization of neural control and sensory organs at the anterior end of an animal's body.

Cephalon
In trilobites, the head shield bearing the eyes, antennae, and mouth.

Cere
In birds (especially raptors), a raised and fleshy patch located at the base of the upper mandible (maxilla).

Cerebellum
That part of the brain concerned with fine motor coordination and body movement, posture, and balance; is part of the hindbrain and is attached to the rear portion of the brain stem.

Cerebral cortex
The outer layer of gray matter in the cerebrum; consists mainly of neuronal cell bodies and dendrites in humans; associated with higher functions, including language and abstract thought.

Cerebrum
The cerebrum or telencephalon, together with the diencephalon,

constitutes the forebrain. The cerebrum is the most anterior (or, in humans, most superior) region of the vertebrate central nervous system. Telencephalon refers to the embryonic structure, from which the mature cerebrum develops. In mammals, the dorsal telencephalon, or pallium, develops into the cerebral cortex, and the ventral telencephalon, or subpallium, becomes the basal ganglia. The cerebrum is also divided into approximately symmetric left and right cerebral hemispheres.

Cervix
The lower neck of the uterus that opens into the vagina.

Cetaceans
The order of marine mammals that includes toothed whales and toothless, filter-feeding (baleen) whales.

Chaetae
Stiff bristles characteristic of annelids.

Chalk
A soft compact calcite, CaCO3, with varying amounts of silica, quartz, feldspar, or other mineral impurities, generally gray-white or yellow-white and derived chiefly from fossil seashells.

Channel height
The path height that the feed/retentate solution must pass through in a flat sheet membrane cassette.

Channel length
The total length that the feed solution must travel along a cross flow membrane filter to reach the retentate outlet.

Channels
Transport proteins that act as gates to control the movement of sodium and potassium ions across the plasma membrane of a nerve cell.

Chaperones
Proteins that help other proteins fold or escort other proteins throughout the cell.

Character
Heritable trait possessed by an organism; characters are usually described in terms of their states, for example: "hair present" vs. "hair absent," where "hair" is the character, and "present" and "absent" are its states.

Character displacement
The divergence of adaptations or other characteristics in two similar species in locations where the animals share habitat.

Chargaff's rules
named for biochemist Erwin Chargaff, these rules describe the relationship of the amounts of the four nitrogenous bases which are found in DNA molecules. Specifically, Chargaff's rules state that the amount of adenine equals the amount of thymine, and that the amount of guanine equals the amount of cytosine in any DNA molecule.

Chela
The claw of an arthropod.

Chelicera
The first pair of appendages of a chelicerate arthropod. Originally a short clawed appendage, the chelicerae of many arachnids are highly modified for feeding; in spiders, for instance, they are modified into poisonous fangs.

Chemical compatibility
The ability of the components of a filter to resist chemicals that can

influence the filter's performance. For example, some chemicals could cause the filter to shed particles, swell, or dissolve filter components. Repeatable performance requires that filters are resistant to all the chemicals that they are exposed to at a given concentration, temperature, and total exposure time.

Chemical equilibrium
The condition when the forward and reverse reaction rates are equal and the concentrations of the products remain constant.

Chemical shift
An atomic property that varies depending on the chemical and magnetic properties of an atom and its arrangement within a molecule. Chemical shifts are measured by NMR spectroscopists to identify the types of atoms in their samples.

Chemiosmosis
The process by which ATP is produced in the inner membrane of a mitochondrion. The electron transport system transfers protons from the inner compartment to the outer; as the protons flow back to the inner compartment, the energy of their movement is used to add phosphate to ADP, forming ATP.

Chemotrophs
Organisms (usually bacteria) that derive energy from inorganic reactions; also known as chemosynthetic.

Chert
Hard, dense sedimentary rock, composed of interlocking quartz crystals and possibly amorphous silica (opal). The origin of the silica is normally biological, from diatoms, radiolaria or sponge spicules.

Chiasma
The site where the exchange of chromosome segments between homologous chromosomes takes place (crossing-over) (pl.: chiasmata).

Chitin
A carbohydrate polymer found in the cell walls of fungi and in the exoskeletons of arthropods, which provides strength for support and protection.

Chlamydia
A sexually transmitted disease caused by a parasitic bacterium that lives inside cells of the reproductive tract.

Chlorofluorocarbons
Chemical substances used in refrigerators, air conditioners, and solvents that drift to the upper stratosphere and dissociate. Chlorine released by CFCs reacts with ozone, eroding the ozone layer.

Chlorophyll
The green-coloured pigment that absorbs light during photosynthesis, often found in plants, algae, and some bacteria; it includes a porphyrin ring, and often has a long hydrophobic tail.

Chlorophyll a
The green photosynthetic pigment common to all photosynthetic organisms.

Chlorophyll b
An accessory chlorophyll found in green algae and plants.

Chlorophyll c
An accessory chlorophyll found in some protistans.

Chlorophyta
The taxonomic division that contains what are commonly called the green algae.

Chloroplasts
Disk-like organelles with a double membrane found in eukaryotic plant cells; contain thylakoids and are the site of photosynthesis. ATP is generated during photosynthesis by chemiosmosis.

Cholecystokinin
A hormone secreted in the duodenum that causes the gallbladder to release bile and the pancreas to secrete lipase.

Chordate
An animal with a notochord (a cartilaginous rod that extends the length of the body), dorsal hollow nerve cord (a fluid-filled tube that runs the length of the body), gill slits or pouches, and a tail at some stage in its life cycle.

Chorion
The two-layered structure formed from the trophoblast after implantation; secretes human chorionic gonadotropin.

Chorionic villi sampling (CVS)
A method of prenatal testing in which fetal cells from the fetal side of the placenta (chorionic villi) are extracted and analyzed for chromosomal and biochemical defects.

Chromatid
Generally refers to a strand of a replicated chromosome; consists of DNA and protein.

Chromatin
A complex of DNA and protein in eukaryotic cells that is dispersed throughout the nucleus during interphase and condensed into chromosomes during meiosis and mitosis.

Chromosome
The structures found in the nucleus of a cell, which contain the genes. Chromosomes come in pairs, and a normal human cell contains 46 chromosomes, 22 pairs

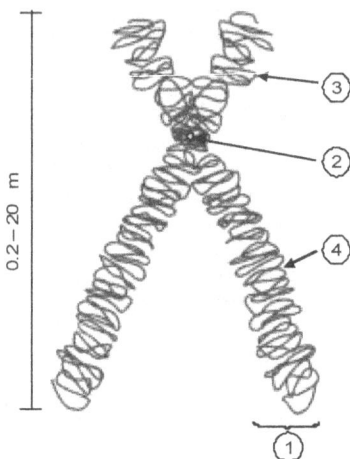

Chromosome theory of inheritance
Holds that chromosomes are the cellular components that physically contain genes; proposed in 1903 by Walter Sutton and Theodore Boveri.

Chronobiology
The field of biology that examines the rhythms (timing and duration) of biological activity or phenomena (eating, sleeping, mating, migration, cellular regeneration, etc.).

Chrysophytes
Protistan division that is referred to as the golden brown algae; includes the diatoms.

Chytridiomycosis
Chytridiomycosis is a leathal skin disease that affects amphibians. Chytridiomycosis is caused by the

chytrid fungus Batrachochytrium dendrobatidis.

Cilia
Hair-like organelles extending from the membrane of many eukaryotic cells; often function in locomotion (sing.: cilium).

Ciliated or ciliate
Type of leaf margin having little hairs.

Cimmerian terranes
An archipelago of small landmasses that developed in tropical and subtropical latitudes on the eastern side of Pangea during the Triassic, blocks that comprised it include modern Turkey, Iran, Afghanistan, Tibet, and Malaysia; also called Cimmeria.

Circadian rhythms
Biorhythms that occur on a daily cycle.

Circulatory system
One of eleven major body organ systems in animals; transports oxygen, carbon dioxide, nutrients, and waste products between cells and the respiratory system and carries chemical signals from the endocrine system; consists of the blood, heart, and blood vessels.

Circulatory system, closed
A system that uses a continuous series of vessels of different sizes to deliver blood to body cells and return it to the heart; found in echinoderms and vertebrates.

Circulatory system, open
A system in which the circulating fluid is not enclosed in vessels at all times; found in insects, crayfish, some mollusks, and other invertebrates.

Clade
A monophyletic taxon; a group of organisms which includes the most recent common ancestor of all of its members and all of the descendants of that most recent common ancestor. From the Greek word "klados", meaning branch or twig.

Cladistics
The area of study concerned with depicting phylogeny.

Cladode
Type of stem. The cladodes are leaflike stems. They appear because the real leaves are very small, therefore non functional. The prickly pear is an example.

Cladogenesis
The development of a new clade; the splitting of a single lineage into two distinct lineages; speciation.

Cladogram
A diagram, resulting from a cladistic analysis, which depicts a hypothetical branching sequence of lineages leading to the taxa under consideration. The points of branching within a cladogram are called nodes. All taxa occur at the endpoints of the cladogram.

Clambering
Type of stem. Elastic stems that wind around other plants or structures, like beans, for example.

Clappering
In birds (especially storks), a non-vocal form of communication expressed by the slapping together of the upper and lower parts of the bill together.

Classes
Taxonomic subcategories of phyla.

Clast
An individual grain or constituent of a rock; Describes a rock or sediment composed mainly of fragments of

preexisting rocks or minerals that have been transported some distance from their place of origin, e.g., sandstone, shale.

Clavicle
The collar bone.

Clean air act
The Clean Air Act was first enacted in 1970 and authorized the establishment of federal and state regulations that limit emissions stationary and mobile sources of air pollutants.

Clean water act
The Federal Water Pollution Control Act, also known more commonly as the Clean Water Act, came into effect in 1972. This Clean Water Act is the primary legislation concerning water pollution and its regulation.

Clean-in-place, (CIP)
The process of cleaning a filtration device without removing it from its filtration system.

Cleavage furrow
A constriction of the cell membrane at the equator of the cell that marks the beginning of cytokinesis in animal cells. The cell divides as the furrow deepens.

Climax
The point at which an ecological community has completed a successional sequence, or sere and has reached a steady state within a particular set of environmental conditions.

Climax community
The stage in community succession where the community has become relatively stable through successful adjustment to its environment.

Climbing
Type of stem. Stems provided with aerial roots to hold the plant to different surfaces, like the ivy. (Type of plant) It is said of plants that grip themselves to some kind of support to keep erect like ivy.

Climograph
A graph that depicts the annual cycle of temperature and rainfall for a geographical locations.

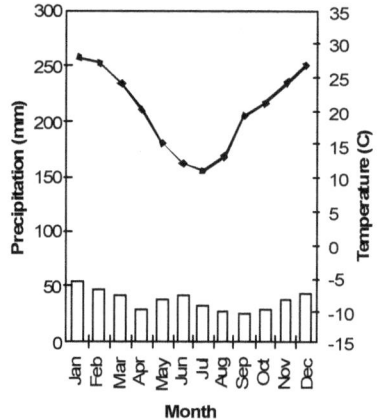

Clinical trials
The research studies that involve patients. Each study is designed to find better ways to prevent, detect, diagnose, or treat disease.

Clitellum
In annelids, a swelling of the body towards the head of the animal, where the gonads are located. Both oligochaetes and leeches have a clitellum.

Clitoris
The clitoris is a sexual organ that is present only in female mammals. In humans, the visible button-like portion is located near the anterior junction of the labia minora, above the opening of the urethra and vagina.

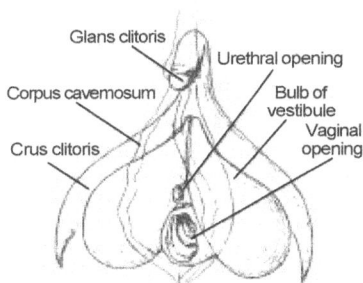

Glans clitoris
Urethral opening
Corpus cavernosum
Bulb of vestibule
Vaginal opening
Crus clitoris

Cloacal spur
A spur or claw in boas and pythons that is a remnant of the pelvic girdle or hind limb and is used by the male snake in courtship.

Clogging
Blockage of filter pores by solids in the process of being removed by the filter; generally results in increased differential pressure.

Clone
An identical copy of an organism. Most plants, fungi, algae, and many other organisms naturally reproduce by making clones of themselves as a form of asexual reproduction.

Closed community
A community in which populations have similar range boundaries and density peaks; forms a discrete unit with sharp boundaries.

Clutch
A group of eggs (and the resulting group of young) produced by a female for a single breeding attempt.

Cnidaria
The taxonomic group (phylum) of animals whose members are characterized by radial or biradial symmetry, diploblastic organization, and possess a gastrovascular cavity and nematocysts.

Cnidocyst
The "stinging cell" of a cnidarian.

Codominance
A type of inheritance in which heterozygotes fully express both alleles.

Codon
A sequence of three nucleotides in messenger RNA that codes for a single amino acid.

Coelenterates
A group of primitive aquatic animals that includes jellyfish, corals, and sea anemones.

Coelom
Fluid-filled cavity within the body of an animal; usually refers to a cavity lined with specialized tissue peritoneum in which the gut is suspended. The structure and development of the coelom is an important character for recognizing major groups of animals.

Coelomates
Animals that have a coelom or body cavity lined with mesoderm.

Coenocytic
Condition in which an organism consists of filamentous cells with large central vacuoles, and whose nuclei are not partitioned into separate compartments. The result is a long tube containing many nuclei, with all the cytoplasm at the periphery.

Coenzymes
Chemicals required by a number of enzymes for proper functioning; also known as enzyme cofactors.

Cohesion
The force that holds molecules of the same substance together.

Cohesion-adhesion theory

Describes the properties of water that help move it through a plant. Cohesion is the ability of water molecules to stick together (held by hydrogen bonds), forming a column of water extending from the roots to the leaves; adhesion is the ability of water molecules to stick to the cellulose in plant cell walls, counteracting the force of gravity and helping to lift the column of water.

Collagen

Long proteins whose structure is wound into a triple helix. The resulting fibres have a high tensile strength. Collagen is a primary component of mammalian hair.

Collar

A narrow band of pigment (in reptiles) that extends across the nape of the neck.

Collenchyma

One of the three major cell types in plants; are elongated and have thicker walls than parenchyma cells and are usually arranged in strands; provide support and are generally in a region that is growing.

Colonial

Condition in which many unicellular organisms live together in a somewhat coordinated group. Unlike true multicellular organisms, the individual cells retain their separate identities, and usually, their own membranes and cell walls.

Coltan

Columbite-tantalite or 'coltan' is a metallic ore found in Australia, Canada, Brazil, and central Africa.

Columella

A small column of tissue which runs up through the centre of a spore capsule. It is present in hornworts, mosses, and some rhyniophytes.

Commensalism

A symbiotic relationship in which one species benefits and the other is not affected.

Community

All species or populations living in the same area.

Community age

One of the factors that helps cause the latitudinal diversity gradient. Tropical communities have had more time to evolve because they have been less disrupted by advancing ice sheets and other relatively recent climatic changes.

Community simplification

The reduction of overall species diversity in a community; generally caused by human activity.

Community succession

The sequential replacement of species in a community by immigration of new species and by local extinction of old ones.

Compact bone

The outer dense layer that forms the shaft of the long bones; made up of concentric layers of mineral deposits surrounding a central opening.

Compactions

Fossils that have undergone some degree of flattening of their three-dimensional structure.

Companion cells

Specialized cells in the phloem that load sugars into the sieve elements and help maintain a functional plasma membrane in the sieve elements.

Competition

In ecology terms, competition arises when two or more individuals (or populations) rely on the same limited resource. In doing so, both parties are impacted negatively.

Competitive exclusion

Competition between species that is so intense that one species completely eliminates the second species from the area.

Competitive release

Occurs when one of two competing species is removed from an area, thereby releasing the remaining species from one of the factors that limited its population size.

Complement system

A chemical defense system that kills microorganisms directly, supplements the inflammatory response, and works with, or complements, the immune system.

Complementary nucleotides

The bonding preferences of nucleotides, Adenine with Thymine, and Cytosine with Guanine. Also referred to as complementary base pairing.

Complete dominance

The type of inheritance in which both heterozygotes and dominant homozygotes have the same phenotype.

Complete flower

Condition in which all flower parts are present. Example: lily.

Composite membrane

A membrane that is made up of two or more layers that are usually chemically or structurally different.

Compound

Type of leaf. Leave with a fragmented blade, with divisions reaching the midrib . Sometimes each one of these fragments is similar to a single leaf. They are called leaflets.

Compound eye

Found in many but not all arthropods, a compound eye is composed of a large number of small, closely packed simple eyes (ommatidia), each with its own lens and nerve receptors.

Compound leaf

A leaf in which the blade forms small leaflets. Compound leaves that have several small leaflets originating from a central axis are termed pinnately compound; example: rose. Compound leaves that have their leaflets originating from a common point are termed palmately compound; example: palm.

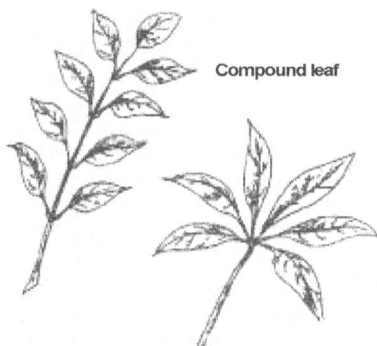

Compound leaf

Compound leaves

Leaves with two or more leaflets attached to a single leaf stem.

Compression

Fossil formed when an organism is flattened (compressed) and a thin film of organic material from its body is left in the rock.

Concentrate

The part of the process solution that does not pass through a cross flow membrane filter.

Concentration

Cross flow filtration process in which the components that do not pass through the membrane remain in the feed loop and therefore increase in concentration as filtrate leaves the system.

Concentration factor

The concentration factor equals the ratio of the initial feed volume to retentate volume after separation. For example, if the initial feed volume is 100 l and the final retentate volume is 20 l, the concentration factor is 5x.

Concentration polarization

The buildup of molecules of dissolved substances (solutes) on the surface of the filter membrane during filtration. The concentration polarization layer increases resistance to filtrate flow and reduces the permeate flux rate, thus decreasing filtration efficiency.

Concretion

A hard, rounded mass, commonly of silica, calcite, dolomite, iron oxide, pyrite, or gypsum, that formed within a rock from the precipitation of these minerals around a nucleus, such as a leaf, bone, shell, or fossil, and ranging in diameter from centimetres to metres.

Conditioned response

The response to a stimulus that occurs when an animal has learned to associate the stimulus with a certain positive or negative effect.

Conditioning

A type of learning in which associations are made. Learning can be acquired through stimulus-response or reward-punishment reinforcement.

Cones

Light receptors in primates' eyes that operate in bright light; provide colour vision and visual acuity.

Conglomerate

A coarse-grained sedimentary rock, with clasts larger than 2 mm.

Congo craton

A separate continental plate that rifted from the supercontinent Rodinia in the Late Precambrian; contained a large part of north-central Africa.

Conifers

Group of gymnosperms that reproduce by cones and have needle-like leaves (in general); includes the pines.

Connective tissue

Animal tissue composed of cells embedded in a matrix (gel, elastic fibres, liquid, or inorganic minerals). Includes loose, dense, and fibrous connective tissues that provide strength (bone, cartilage), storage (bone, adipose), and flexibility (tendons, ligaments).

Conservation

Conservation is the artificial control man imposes upon ecological relationships in a habitat, community, or ecosystem in order to sustain balance among the species it supports.

Constriction

A method many non-venomous snakes used to kill prey that involves the snake coiling around its prey and tightening its grip to suffocate the prey.

Consumers
The higher levels in a food pyramid; consist of primary consumers, which feed on the producers, and secondary consumers, which feed on the primary consumers.

Contamination
undesired foreign matter or organisms in a product or on an object.

Continental crust
The Earth's crust that includes both the continents and the continental shelves.

Continental margin
The ocean floor from the shore of continents to the abyssal plain.

Continental rise
Part of the continental margin; the ocean floor from the continental slope to the abyssal plain. The continental rise generally has a gentle slope and smooth topography.

Continental shelf
The part of the continental margin from the coastal shore to the continental slope; usually extending to a depth of about 200 metres and with a very slight slope, roughly 0.1 degrees; includes continental and oceanic sediments down to the ocean floor.

Continental slope
Part of the continental margin; the ocean floor from the continental shelf to the continental rise or oceanic trench. Usually to a depth of about 200 metres. The continental slope typically has a relatively steep grade, from three to six degrees.

Continuous variation
Occurs when the phenotypes of traits controlled by a single gene cannot be sorted into two distinct phenotypic classes, but rather fall into a series of overlapping classes.

Contour feathers
The outer layer of feathers that cover a bird's body, wings, and tail and give the bird its characteristic appearance.

Contractile vacuole
In many protists, a specialized vacuole with associated channels designed to collect excess water in the cell. Microtubules periodically contract to force this excess water out of the cell, regulating the cell's osmotic balance.

Contrast
In relation to microscopes, the ability to distinguish different densities of structures.

Convention on international trade in endangered species (CITES)
A convention established in 1973 that regulates or prohibits the international trade of plant and animal species that are believed to be harmed by or that may be harmed by international trade.

Convergence
Similarities which have arisen independently in two or more organisms that are not closely related. Contrast with homology.

Convergent evolution
The development of similar structures in distantly related organisms as a result of adapting to similar environments and/or strategies of life. Example: wings of birds and insects, the body shape of dolphins, sharks, and the extinct marine reptiles known as ichthyosaurs.

Convergent plate boundary
The boundary between two plates that are moving toward one another.

Copal
Brittle aromatic yellow to red resins of recent or fossil origin, obtained from tropical trees.

Coral berry
(Genus of plants) Evergreen trees and shrubs of Mirsinaceae Family very well know because of their decorative fruits (berries) There are about 400 species scattered in Tropical and subtropical Asia, América and Oceania.

Corallum
The skeleton of a colonial coral which, in turn, consists of individual corallites.

Cordate
(Type of leave), heart-shaped. More extended at the base than the ovate type and with a notch.

Core
That portion of the interior of the Earth that lies beneath the mantle, and goes all of the way to the centre. The Earth's core is very dense, rich in iron and the source of the magnetic field.

Coriaceous
Of fruits or leaves. It is said when the object presents a texture like leather.

Cork
The outer layer of the bark in woody plants; composed of dead cells.

Cork cambium
A layer of lateral meristematic tissue between the cork and the phloem in the bark of woody plants.

Corolla
The corolla or coloured section of the flower, where the petals , or coloured pieces, can be found. They are meant to attract the pollen carriers, so they contain perfume and nectar.

Coronary arteries
Arteries that supply the heart's muscle fibres with nutrients and oxygen.

Corpus callosum
Tightly bundled nerve fibres that connect the right and left hemispheres of the cerebrum.

Corpus luteum
A structure formed from the ovulated follicle in the ovary; secretes progesterone and estrogen.

Cortex
1) The outer part of an organ, e.g., the adrenal cortex, which produces several steroid hormones;
2) In plants, the region of the stem or root between the epidermis and the vascular bundle(s).

Cortisol
The primary glucocorticoid hormone; released by the adrenal cortex.

Corymb
Type of inflorescence. In a corymb all the florets are arranged along a floral

peduncle but , differently to racemes, stems have different length in such a way that all the florets appear at the same flat round level.

Costal grooves
A set of parallel, vertical grooves present on the sides of some salamanders, newts, and their larvae.

Cotyledon
Part of the seed. The first leaf or leaves of the embryo. According to the number of cotyledons, we classify plants in two groups— monocotyledons or monocots and dicotyledons or dicots. In the first group we find so important plants as cereals, palms, lilies, tulips or orchids. The members of the second group are more numerous and comprises most of the trees and flowers.

Countercurrent flow
An arrangement by which fish obtain oxygen from the water that flows through their gills. Water flows across the respiratory surface of the gill in one direction while blood flows in the other direction through the blood vessels on the other side of the surface.

Countershading
A colouration pattern in the plumage of some birds in which the underparts of a bird are light in colour while the upper parts of the bird are darker.

Courtship behaviour
Behavioural sequences that precede mating.

Covalent bond
A covalent bond is a form of chemical bonding that is characterized by the sharing of pairs of electrons between atoms. The stable balance of attractive and repulsive forces between atoms

when they share electrons is known as covalent bonding.

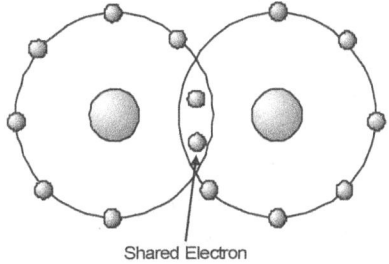

Shared Electron

COX-1 (cyclooxygenase-1)
An enzyme made continually in the stomach, blood vessels, platelet cells, and parts of the kidney. It produces prostaglandins that, among other things, protect the lining of the stomach from digestive acids. Because NSAIDs block COX-1, they foster ulcers.

COX-2 (cyclooxygenase-2)
An enzyme found in only a few places, such as the brain and parts of the kidney. It is made only in response to injury or infection. It produces prostaglandins involved in inflammation and the immune response. NSAIDs act by blocking COX-2. Because elevated levels of COX-2 in the body have been linked to cancer, scientists are investigating whether blocking COX-2 may prevent or treat some cancers.

Craniate
Craniates are a group of chordate animals that include hagfish, lampreys, and the jawed vertebrates such as cartilaginous fishes, bony fishes, and tetrapod vertebrates.

Cranium
The braincase; composed of several bones fitted together at immovable joints.

Craton

A part of the Earth's crust that has attained stability and has been little deformed for a long period of time, refers only to continents.

Creche

A group (flock) of unrelated young birds gathered together for protection.

Cretaceous period

The geologic period between the Jurassic Period (140 milliojn years ago) and the Tertiary Period (beginning 65 million years ago). The Cretaceous was marked by a mass extinction that closed the period along with the reign of the nonavian dinosaurs.

Cretaceous western interior seaway

The epicontinental sea that formed as marine waters from the north spread over North America from around 130 to 70 million years ago (Ma), at its peak in the Middle Cretaceous (~ 90 Ma) it extended from present-day Utah to the Appalachians and from the Arctic to the Gulf of Mexico; also refered to as the Western Interior Seaway

Cristae

Structures formed by the folding of the inner membrane of a mitochondrion.

Critical habitat

Areas of habitat that are crucial to the survival of a species and essential for its conservation and that have been formally designated as such by rule published in the Federal Register.

Crocodile

A crocodilian that inhabits tropical regions. A crocodile differs from an alligator in that it has a narrower snout.

Crop

An expandable pouch in the esophagus of some birds (members of the Order Gruiformes do not have a crop).

Cross flow filtration

In cross flow filtration, the feed solution flows parallel to the surface of the membrane. Driven by pressure, some of the feed solution passes through the membrane filter. Most of the solution is circulated back to the feed tank. The movement of the feed solution across the membrane surface helps to remove the buildup of materials on the surface. In direct (normal) flow filters, the liquid flows perpendicular to the filter surface, and all the feed passes through the filter.

Cross flow rate

Also called retentate flow rate. The flow rate of solution that remains in the feed loop as measured in the retentate line.

Cross-bedding

The arrangement of sedimentary beds tilted at different angles to each other, indicating that the beds were deposited by wind or flowing water.

Crossing-over

During the first meiotic prophase, the process in which part of a chromatid is physically exchanged with another chromatid to form chromosomes with new allele combinations.

Crossopterygians

A type of lobe-finned fish with lungs that were ancestral to amphibians.

Croton

Name of plants . Herbaceous or shrubby plants belonging to "Codiaeum" genus from Euphorbiaceae family. There are about 400 species, scattered in warm countries. Very appreciated in gardening as indoor plants because of their leaves, covered with painted designs.

Crown group
All the taxa descended from a major cladogenesis event, recognized by possessing the clade's synapomorphy.

Crust
The outermost layer of the Earth, varying in thickness from about 10 kilometres (6 miles) below the oceans, to 65 kilometres (about 40 miles) below the continents; represents less than 1 percent of the Earth's volume.

Crustaceans
A large taxonomic class of arthropods that includes lobsters, shrimps, and crabs.

Cryptic
Pertaining to characteristics that serve to conceal an animal.

Cuticle
1) In animals, a multilayered, extracellular, external body covering, usually composed of fibrous molecules such as chitin or collagen, and sometimes strengthened by the deposition of minerals such as calcium carbonate.
2) A waxy layer which seals the outer surface of land plants, helping to retain moisture.

Cyanobacteria
Blue-green bacteria; unicellular or filamentous chains of cells that carry out photosynthesis.

Cycadeoids
A group of gymnosperm seed plants not closely rated to, but superficially similar to, the cycads. Cycads and cycadeoids were dominant floristic elements of early and middle Mesozoic landscapes. This groupo is also known as the Bennettitaleans.

Cycads
Group of gymnosperm seed plants that have large fern-like leaves and reproduce by cones but not flowers.

Cyclamen
Genus of plants. Plants of the Primulaceae Family with cordate leaves and distinctive single flowers and tuberous roots. There are about 20 species mainly in the Mediterranean area.

Cycle
A recurring sequence of events; e. g., the secretion of certain hormones at regular intervals.

Cyclin
A protein found in the dividing cells of many organisms that acts as a control during cell division.

Cyclooxygenases
Enzymes that are responsible for producing prostaglandins and other molecules in the body.

Cyst
A small, capsule-like sac that encloses an organism in its resting or larval stage, e.g., a resting spore of an alga.

Cystic fibrosis
An autosomal recessive genetic disorder that causes the production of mucus that clogs the airways of the lungs and the ducts of the pancreas and other secretory glands.

Cytokinesis
The division of the cytoplasm during cell division.

Cytokinins

A group of hormones that promote cell division and inhibit aging of green tissues in plants.

Cytology

The branch of biology dealing with cell structure.

Cytoplasm

The viscous semiliquid inside the plasma membrane of a cell; contains various macromolecules and organelles in solution and suspension.

Cytosine

One of the pyrimidine nitrogenous bases occurring in both DNA and RNA.

Cytoskeleton

Integrated system of molecules within eukaryotic cells which provides them with shape, internal spatial organization, motility, and may assist in communication with other cells and the environment. Red blood cells, for instance, would be spherical instead of flat if it were not for their cytoskeleton.

Cytoxic T cells

T cells that destroy body cells infected by viruses or bacteria; also attack bacteria, fungi, parasites, and cancer cells and will kill cells of transplanted organs if they are recognized as foreign; also known as killer T cells.

D

Dark reactions
The photosynthetic process in which food (sugar) molecules are formed from carbon dioxide from the atmosphere with the use of ATP; can occur in the dark as long as ATP is present.

Dead-ended filtration
Also called normal flow filtration. In deadended filtration, liquid flows perpendicular to the filtration media, and all of the feed passes through.

Death rate
The ratio between deaths and individuals in a specified population at a particular time.

Debris
Remains of anything broken down: ruins, decayed matter, parts of stone or organisms.

Decay series
Most radioisotopes do not decay into a stable daughter element in one single decay, but rather through a series of radioactive intermediaries.

Deciduous
Deciduous means "falling off at maturity" or "tending to fall off", and is typically used in reference to trees or shrubs that lose their leaves seasonally, and to the shedding of other plant structures such as petals after flowering or fruit when ripe. In a more specific sense, deciduous means the dropping of a part that is no longer needed, or falling away after its purpose is finished.

Decomposer
An organism that breaks down the tissue and/or structures of dead organisms.

Decomposition
The breakdown of dead organic material by detrivores or saprophytes.

Decumbent
Type of stem. Stem that runs along the ground but stands up at the end.

Definitive plumage
The mature plumage of a bird attained after the molting of all immature plumages. Definitive plumage does not change as the bird ages and is renewed after each molt with identically marked plumage.

Dehiscent
Types or dry fruits. They are fruits that open when they grow up and let their seeds go away. There are different types like follicles, pods, siliques, capsules etc.

Delayed plumage maturation
The delayed development of a bird's definitive plumage such that the bird reaches sexual maturity before its replaces its immature plumage has been replaced. It occurs more frequently in the males of a species.

Deletion

The loss of a chromosome segment without altering the number of chromosomes.

Delist

To remove an animal or plant species from the list of endangered and threatened wildlife and plants.

Delphinidae

A taxonomic group of marine mammals that includes dolphins and their relatives. The delphinidae, or Family Delphinidae, belong to the Order Cetacea and is the most diverse of all groups of cetaceans.

Delta

A low, nearly flat accumulation of sediment deposited at the mouth of a river or stream, commonly triangular or fan-shaped.

Delta P, ΔP

In filtration, the pressure drop across the membrane. See Pressure drop.

Deme

A breeding population or local population that occurs in nature and which consists of similar organisms that interbreed more or less at random.

Demographic

A characteristic used to describe some aspect of a population and that can be measured for that population, such as growth rate, age structure, birth rate, and gross reproduction rate.

Dendrites

Small branching patterns on rocks made of iron and manganese oxides that show the passage of fluids through the rock.

Dendrochronology

The process of determining the age of a tree or wood used in structures by counting the number of annual growth rings.

Density

Referring to a population, the number of individuals per unit area or volume; referring to a substance, the weight per unit volume.

Density compensation

Increase in population size in response to reduction in the number of competing populations; often observed on islands.

Density dependent

Having influence on individuals in a population that varies with the degree of crowding within the population.

Density independent

Having influence on individuals in a population that does not vary with the degree of crowding.

Dentate

Type of leave. Dentate leaves have little teeth at the margin.

Deoxyribonucleic acid

Also known as "DNA." The molecule which contains the hereditary information of most living organisms. This information is encoded in the sequence of bases arrayed along the length of the DNA molecule. DNA is a double helix, coiled around a central axis. The DNA backbones are composed of alternating sugar and phosphate subunits, while the interior portion of the molecule is composed of pairs of nitrogenous bases. The helix has a radius of 1 nm, and completes one 360 degree turn every 3.4 nm. The base pairs are 0.34 nm apart from each other. The two strands which make up the DNA molecule are anti-parallel—that is they run in opposite directions from each other.

The Structure of DNA

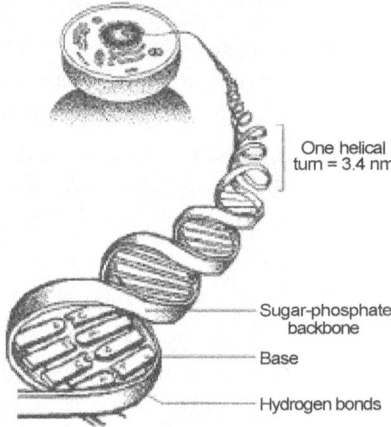

One helical turn = 3.4 nm

Sugar-phosphate backbone

Base

Hydrogen bonds

Deoxyribose
Five-carbon sugar found in nucleotides of DNA.

Deposition
Any accumulation of material, by mechanical settling from water or air, chemical precipitation, evaporation from solution, etc.

Depth diversity gradient
The increase in species richness with increasing water depth until about 2000 metres below the surface, where species richness begins to decline.

Depth filter
A thick filter that captures contaminants within its pore structure using entrapment and adsorption.

Depyrogenate
The removal or decomposition of pyrogens (lipopolysaccharides) from a process solution.

Derived
It refers to a character or feature found within a single lineage of a larger group; it is not shared with all organisms in the larger group. Derived characters are used to infer evolutionary relationships, as derived characters evolved after primitive characters. In comparing humans and apes, it can be said that an upright stance in humans is a derived character.

Dermal system
Plant organ system that provides the covering for the plant.

Dermis
The dermis is a layer of skin between the epidermis (with which it makes up the cutis) and subcutaneous tissues, and is composed of two layers, the papillary and reticular dermis. Structural components of the dermis are collagen, elastic fibres, and extrafibrillar matrix (previously called ground substance).

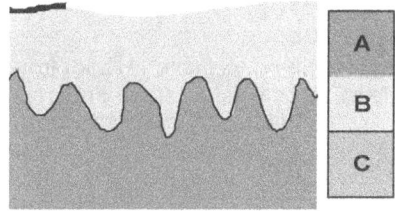

Descent with Modification
Descent with modification refers to the passing on of traits from parent organisms to their offspring.

Desert biome
Characterized by dry conditions and plants and animals that have adapted to those conditions; found in areas where local or global influences block rainfall.

Desiccation
The process of drying out. In biology, moisture loss in organisms.

Desmosome
A circular region of membrane cemented to an adjacent membrane by a molecular glue made of polysaccharides; found in tissues that undergo stretching.

Destruction or adverse modification of critical habitat
A direct or indirect alteration that appreciably diminishes the value of critical habitat for both the survival and recovery of a listed species.

Deterministic
It is referring to the outcome of a process that is not subject to stochastic (random) variation.

Detritivore
An organism that feeds on freshly dead or partially decomposed organic matter.

Detritus
Accumulated organic debris from dead organisms, often an important source of nutrients in a food web.

Detrivore
Detritivores, also known as detritophages or detritus feeders or detritus eaters or saprophages, are heterotrophs that obtain nutrients by consuming detritus (decomposing plant and animal parts as well as organic fecal matter). By doing so, they contribute to decomposition and the nutrient cycles. They should be distinguished from other decomposers, such as many species of bacteria, fungi and protists, which are unable to ingest discrete lumps of matter, but instead live by absorbing and metabolizing on a molecular scale.

Deuterostomes
Animals in which the first opening that appears in the embryo becomes the anus while the mouth appears at the other end of the digestive system. Main groups include chordates and echinoderms.

Development
The process by which a multicellular organism is produced from a single cell.

Developmental response
Physiological and morphological characteristics an organism develops in response to prolonged exposure to environmental conditions.

Devonian
Period of geologic time from 410 - 360 million years before the present. Life on land diversified, with the amphibians appearing late in this period. Plants underwent major changes, including the development of forests and seeds. In the water, fish diversified into all modern groups as well as numerous now-extinct forms.

Devonian period
The Devonian Period (408-360 Myr BP) is the fourth of six periods that make up the Paleozoic Era. It is preceded by the Silurian Period and followed by the Carboniferous Period.

Diabetes mellitus, Types I & II
A disorder associated with defects in insulin action. Type I diabetes is characterized by inadequate insulin secretion; Type II diabetes is characterized by impaired insulin secretion in response to elevated blood glucose levels or by loss of sensitivity to insulin by target cells.

Diafiltration

Diafiltration is a unit operation that incorporates ultrafiltration membranes to remove salts or other microsolutes from a solution. Small molecules are separated from a solution while retaining larger molecules in the retentate. Microsolutes are generally so easily washed through the membrane that, for a fully permeated species, about three volumes of diafiltration water will eliminate 95-99% of the microsolute.

Diagenesis

Any sort of chemical, physical, or biogenic change that occurs in fossils and sediments after their deposition. Physical erosion of a shell in a river, dissolution of carbonate in acidic conditions, and microbial invasion of a bone are all forms of diagenesis.

Dialysis

The removal of small molecules from a solution of macromolecules by allowing them to diffuse through a semipermeable membrane into water or a buffer solution. This pressure separations method is controlled by the concentration gradient of salts across the membrane.

Diapause

Temporary interruption in the development of insect eggs or larvae, usually associated iwth a dormant period.

Diaphragm

A dome-shaped muscle that separates the thoracic and abdominal cavities. The diaphragm functions in breathing. During inhalation, the diaphragm contracts, thus enlarging the thoracic cavity (the external intercostal muscles also participate in this enlargement). This reduces intra-thoracic pressure: In other words, enlarging the cavity creates suction that draws air into the lung, or lungs.

Diapsid

A vertebrate distinguished by a skull with two pairs of openings in the side behind the eyes, e.g., lizards, snakes, crocodiles, dinosaurs, and pterosaurs.

Diastole

The filling of the ventricle of the heart with blood.

Diatomaceous earth

Fossilized deposits of diatoms; used for abrasives, polishes and as a filtering agent.

Diatomite

Diatomite, or diatomaceous earth, is a siliceous sedimaentary rock formed from the accumulations of diatoms or other nanoplankton.

Dicots

One of the two main types of flowering plants; characterized by having two cotyledons, floral organs arranged in cycles of four or five, and leaves with reticulate veins; include trees (except conifers) and most ornamental and crop plants.

Dictyosomes

Organelles in plant cells composed of a series of flattened membrane sacs that sort, chemically modify, and package proteins produced on the rough endoplasmic reticulum. Also known as the Golgi Apparatus.

Diencephalon

Part of the forebrain; consists of the thalamus and hypothalamus.

Differential pressure

In cross flow filtration, the pressure drop along the membrane between the feed (inlet) port and the retentate (outlet) port.

Differential pressure gauge

Instrumentation capable of showing or recording differential pressure readings between two points.

Differentiation

In cancer, refers to how mature (developed) the cancer cells are in a tumour. Differentiated tumour cells resemble normal cells and grow at a slower rate than undifferentiated tumour.

Diffuse coevolution

The evolution of traits influencing species interactions, subject to selection from a wide variety of species interacting with different intensities.

Diffuse competition

The sum of weak competitive interactions with species that are ecologically distantly allied.

Diffusion

Movement of particles of gas or liquid from regions of high to low concentration by means of their own spontaneous motion.

Digestion

The process of breaking down food into its molecular and chemical components so that these nutrient molecules can cross plasma membranes.

Digestive system

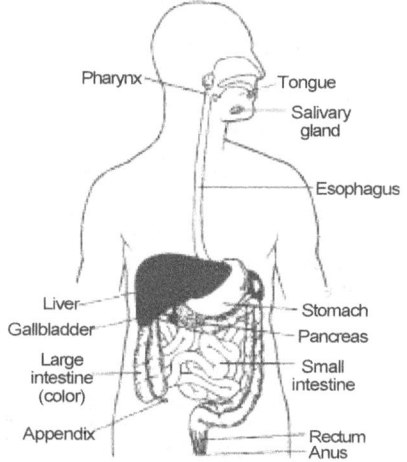

One of eleven major body organ systems in animals; converts food from the external environment into nutrient molecules that can be used and stored by the body and eliminates solid wastes; involves five functions: movement, secretion, digestion, absorption, and elimination.

Digestive System

Dihybrid cross

In genetics, a cross that involves two sets of characteristics.

Dikaryotic

Having two different and distinct nuclei per cell; found in the fungi. A dikaryotic individual is called a dikaryon.

Dimorphism

Occurrence of two forms of individuals within a population.

Dinoflagellates

Single-celled to colonial protistans characterized by two flagella, one girdling the cell and the other trailing the cell. Some dinoflagellates exist in coral, in a symbiotic relationship.

These dinoflagellates are termed the zooxanthellae. Other dinoflagellates occur in such high numbers that the water is coloured red, a phenomenon known as a red tide.

Dinosaurs
Any of the Mesozoic diapsids (once considered to be reptiles) belonging to the groups designated as ornithischians and saurischians.

Dinosteranes/dinosteroids
Chemicals found in dinoflagellates, which have been useful in documenting their existence early in the fossil record.

Dioctal phthalate test, (dop)
Test for evaluation of filtration efficacy that counts the number of controlled-size, 3 im particles (dioctal phthalate aerosol) entering and emerging from a filter. According to ASTM:D2986-71), a HEPA (High Efficiency Particulate Air) filter must retain at least 99.97% of 0.3 im DOP droplets. Particles of 0.3 im were chosen because for many air filters, this size is the most difficult to retain.

Dioecious
Possessing either male or female organs. Describes a group of organisms in which male and femal organs are in different individuals.

Diorite
Igneous plutonic rock, less mafic than gabbro, but more mafic than granite and granodiorite; rough plutonic equivalent of andesite.

Dip
The angle that a bedding plane or fault makes with the horizontal when measured perpendicular to the strike of the bedding plane or fault.

Diploblastic
Having body parts derived from two layers during embryologic development.

Diploid
Cells that contain homologous chromosomes. The number of chromosomes in the cells is the diploid number and is equal to 2n (n is the number of homologous pairs).

Diploid life cycle
Occurs when the only multicellular stage in an organism's life cycle is diploid.

Direct flow filtration
Filtration process where the entire feed stream flows through the filter's media. Also called normal flow filtration or dead ended filtration.

Directional selection
A process of natural selection that tends to favor phenotypes at one extreme of the phenotypic range.

Disaccharides
1. Sugars made up of two monosaccharides held together by a covalent bond; e.g., sucrose and lactose.
2. Type of sugar (saccharide) composed of two sugar molecules bonded together with an ester (covalent) bond examples include sucrose, maltose, and lactose.

Discontinuous variation
Occurs when the phenotypes of traits controlled by a single gene can be sorted into two distinct phenotypic classes.

Disease
Organisms suffer from disease when their normal function is impaired by some genetic disorder, or more often

from the activity of a parasite or other organism living within them. Many diseases are caused by viruses, bacteria, or fungi.

Dispersal

The scattering of organisms of a species, often following a major reproductive event. Spores and larvae are commonly dispersed into the environment. Pollen or gametes may also be dispersed, but in this case the intent is to target another individual so that reproduction may occur. Organisms may disperse as spores, seeds, eggs, larvae, or adults.

Disruptive selection

A process of natural selection that favors individuals at both extremes of a phenotypic range.

Distal

An anatomical directional term that means further from the mid-point of the body or further from the point where a limb attaches to the body.

Distal tubule

The section of the renal tubule where tubular secretion occurs.

Distinct population segment (DPS)

A subdivision of a vertebrate species that is treated as a species for purposes of listing under the Endangered Species Act.

Divergent evolution

The divergence of a single interbreeding population or species into two or more descendant species.

Divergent plate boundary

Divergent plate boundary (also known as a constructive boundary or an extensional boundary) is a linear feature that exists between two tectonic plates that are moving away from each other. Divergent boundaries within continents initially produce rifts which produce rift valleys. Most active divergent plate boundaries occur between oceanic plates and exist as mid-oceanic ridges. Divergent boundaries also form volcanic islands which occur when the plates move apart to produce gaps which molten lava rises to fill.

Diversity

Term used to describe numbers of taxa, or variation in morphology.

Diving reflex

A set of complex physiological adaptations some marine mammals have evolved that enables them to dive to great depths for extended periods of time.

DNA (deoxyribonucleic acid)

The substance of heredity. A long, usually double-stranded chain of nucleotides that carries genetic information necessary for all cellular functions, including the building of proteins. DNA is composed of the sugar deoxyribose, phosphate groups, and the bases adenine, thymine, guanine, and cytosine.

DNA cloning

Facilitates isolation and manipulation of fragments of an organism's genome by replicating them as part of an independent vector.

DNA double helix

Most common form of DNA. Two separate and antiparallel chains of DNA are wound around each other in a right - handed helical path, with sugar phosphate backbones on the outside and bases connected by hydrogen bonds on the inside. A (Adenine) pairs with T (Thymine); G

(Guanine) pairs with C (Cytosine). The two chains are complementary.

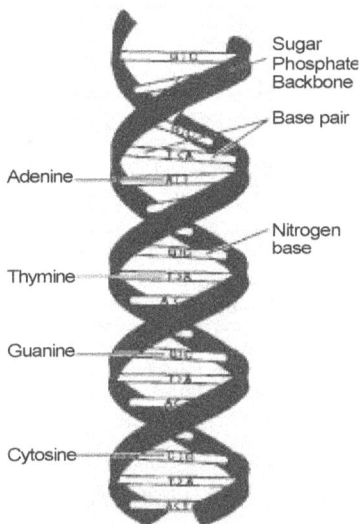

Sugar Phosphate Backbone

Base pair

Adenine

Nitrogen base

Thymine

Guanine

Cytosine

DNA fingerprinting
Hybridizing Southern blots of genomic DNA with probes that recognise simple nucleotide repeats gives a pattern that is unique to the individual and can be used as a fingerprint.

DNA hybridization
The formation of hybrid DNA molecules that contain a strand of DNA from two different species. The number of complementary sequences in common in the two strands is an indication of the degree of relatedness of the species.

DNA libraries
It consist of sets of random cloned fragments of either genomic or cDNA, each in a separate vector molecule. Are used in isolation of unknown genes.

DNA ligase
In recombinant DNA technology, an enzyme that seals together two DNA fragments from different sources to form a recombinant DNA molecule.

DNA polymerase
In DNA replication, the enzyme that links the complementary nucleotides together to form the newly synthesized strand.

DNA sequencing
The widely used Sanger's enzymic method uses dideoxynucleotide's as chain terminators to produce a ladder of molecule's generated by polymerase extension of a primer.

DNA/RNA sequence
A nucleic acid sequence of bases A, C,G,T/U in the DNA/RNA chain. Usually written from 5' to 3' end of molecule e.g. 5'-ATAAGCTC-3' (DNA) or 5'-AUAGCUUGA-3' (RNA).

Dolomite
A carbonate sedimentary rock composed of more than 50 percent of the mineral calcium-magnesium carbonate $CaMg(CO_3)_2$.

Dominance
The property of one of a pair of alleles that suppresses the expression of the other member of the pair in heterozygotes.

Dominance hierarchy
A social structure among a group of animals in which one is dominant and the others have subordinate nonbreeding positions.

Dominant
Refers to an allele of a gene that is always expressed in heterozygotes.

Dormancy
A period of suspended growth and metabolic activity. Many plants, seeds, spores, and some invertebrates

become dormant during unfavorable conditions.

Dorsal
Pertaining to the back.

Double fertilization
A characteristic of angiosperms in which a pollen tube carries two sperm cells to the female gametophyte in the ovule. One sperm cell fuses with the egg cell and gives rise to a diploid embryo The other sperm cell fuses with the two polar cells to form a triploid cell that develops into the endosperm.

Double membrane
In mitochondria and plastids, there is a two-layered membrane which surrounds the organelle. This is believed to be the result of endosymbiosis, with the outer membrane coming from the eukaryotic cell, and the inner membrane belonging to the original prokaryote which was "swallowed".

Downstream processing
Starting with a feed stream free of cells and cell debris, the purification sequences involving chromatography and membrane separations to achieve final product purity.

Dracaena
Genus of plants. Perennial trees and shrubs of the Liliaceae family. They live in equatorial zones. Very appreciated because of their leaves as indoor plants.

Drag
A force that works in opposition to the direction of movement.

Drain
Connection on a filter, generally fitted with a valve, at a low point to allow outflow of liquid.

Drain valve
A device for controlling the flow of material in a filter housing, generally at the lowest point.

Drill core
A column of material (e.g., mud, ice, rock) removed from the earth by drilling. Often used as a tool for exploration of natural resources.

Drug
Any chemical compound that may be used on humans to help in diagnosis, treatment, cure, mitigation, or prevention of disease or other abnormal conditions.

Drumlin
Elongated mound of glacial sediment deposited parallel to ice flow.

Drupe or stone
(Type of fruit) Drupes or stones are fruits with soft mesocarp and a coriaceous endocarp . They become from an inferior ovary. For example, peaches, plums or olives.

Dry
Type of fruit. Dry fruits are those fruits showing a hard texture. They bear a wood-like leathery appearance and when we press on them we feel they are not soft.

Dummy nest
A decoy nest that is built in order to attract females, reduce predation, or reduce nest parasitization. If eggs are disturbed in the primary nest, they can be moved to the alternate nest if needed.

Dung
The solid excrement of animals: feces, droppings, manure, bowel movement, scat.

Duodenum
The upper part of the small intestine.

Duplication
An extra copy of a chromosome segment without altering the number of chromosomes.

Dycotiledon or dico
Type of plant according to the cotyledons. Plants with two cotyledons in the seed. The members of this group are more numerous than the monocotyledons and comprise most of the trees and flowers.

Dystrophin
Protein making up only 0.002% of all protein in skeletal muscle but which appears vital for proper functioning of the muscle. Sufferers of muscular dystrophy appear to lack dystrophin.

E

E. Coli
Common bacterium that has been studied intensively by geneticists because of its small genome size, normal lack of pathogenicity, and ease of growth in the laboratory.

Eccrine glands
Sweat glands that are linked to the sympathetic nervous system and are widely distributed over the body surface.

Ecolocation
A method of sensing surrounding objects that employs pulses of high-frequency sound.

Ecological efficiency
A measure of the amount of energy in the biomass that is produced by one trophic level and is incorporated into the biomass produced by the next (higher) trophic level.

Ecological isolation
The isolation of competing species of organisms made possible by differences in each species food resources, habitat use, activity period, or geographical range.

Ecological niche
The role an organism occupies and the function it performs in an ecosystem; closely associated with feeding.

Ecological release
The expansion of habitat and resource usage by populations into areas of lower species diversity. Ecological release results from lower levels of interspecific competition.

Ecological time
A timescale that focuses on community events that occur on the order of tens to hundreds of years.

Ecology
The study of the ecosystems, communities, habitats, and other elements of the natural environment that examines the relationships among organisms as well as relationships between organisms and their environment.

Ecomorphology
The study of the relationship between the ecological role of an individual and its morphological adaptations.

Ecosystem
All the organisms in a particular region and the environment in which they live. The elements of an ecosystem interact with each other in some way, and so depend on each other either directly or indirectly.

Ecosystem approach
An approach to resource management that recognizes that all

components of an ecosystem (function, structure, and species composition) are interrelated and must be considered when protecting and restoring natural balances.

Ecotone

A habitat created by the juxtaposition of distinctly different habitats; an edge habitat; a zone of transition between habitat types.

Ecotype

A subdivision of a species; a stage in the formation of a species such that reproductive isolation has occurred.

Ectoderm

The outer basic layer of tissue in those animals with true tissues. In vertebrates, for instance, the embryonic ectoderm differentiates into the skin and also the nervous system.

Ectoparasite

A parasite, for example, a tick, that lives on, or attached to the host's surface.

Ectotherms

Animals with a variable body temperature that is determined by the environment. Examples: fish, frogs, and reptiles.

Ectothermy

Capcity to maintain body temperature by gaining heat from the environment, either by conduction or by absorming radiation.

Edge

Part of the leaf. The verge of the leaf.

Effective area, effective filtration area, EFA

In a membrane separations device, the active area of the membrane exposed to flow. It represents the area available for filtration, not the total area of material used to make the filter, some of which is occluded by seals, joints, and so on.

Effective population size

The average size of a population expressed in terms of individuals assumed to contribute genes equally to the next generation; generally smaller than the actual size of the population, depending on the variation in the reproductive success among individuals.

Effector

In a closed system, the element that initiates an action in response to a signal from a sensor. In human systems, a muscle or gland often serves as an effector.

Effluent

Fluid that has passed through a filter. Opposite of affluent.

Egestion

Elimination of undigested food material.

Egg

(1) A large gamete without flagellae that is fertilized by a sperm cell. An egg cell is also called an ovum.
(2) A complex multicellular structure in which an animal embryo develops.

Egg dumping

The practice of placing eggs in a nest built by another bird.

Ejaculatory duct

The ejaculatory ducts (ductus ejaculatorii) are paired structures in male anatomy. Each ejaculatory duct is formed by the union of the vas deferens with the duct of the seminal vesicle. They pass through the prostate, and open into the urethra at the Colliculus seminalis. During ejaculation, semen passes through the prostate gland, enters the urethra and exits the body via the tip of the penis.

Elater

A cell or part of a cell which assists in dispersing spores. The elaters change shape as they lose or acquire water, and they will then push against surrounding spores.

Electromagnetic radiation

Electromagnetic radiation (often abbreviated E-M radiation or EMR) is a form of energy that exhibits wave-like behaviour as it travels through space. EMR has both electric and magnetic field components, which oscillate in phase perpendicular to each other and perpendicular to the direction of energy propagation.

Electromagnetic Radiation

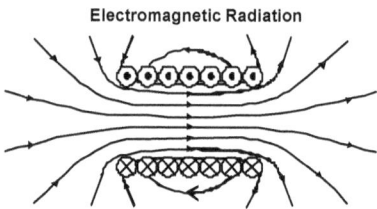

Electromagnetic radiation is classified according to the frequency of its wave. The electromagnetic spectrum, in order of increasing frequency and decreasing wavelength, consists of radio waves, microwaves, infrared radiation, visible light, ultraviolet radiation, X-rays and gamma rays. The eyes of various organisms sense a small and somewhat variable window of frequencies called the visible spectrum. The photon is the quantum of the electromagnetic interaction and

the basic "unit" of light and all other forms of electromagnetic radiation and is also the force carrier for the electromagnetic force.

Electron

A subatomic particle with a negative charge. Electrons circle the atom's nucleus in regions of space known as orbitals.

Electron accepter

A molecule that forms part of the electron transport system that transfers electrons ejected by chlorophyll during photosynthesis. Part of the energy carried by the electrons is transferred to ATP, part is transferred to NADPH, and part is lost in the transfer system.

Electron transport

1) A series of coupled oxidation/reduction reactions where electrons are passed like hot potatoes from one membrane-bound protein/enzyme to another before being finally attached to a terminal electron acceptor (usually oxygen or NADPH). ATP is formed by this process.
2) Coupled series of oxidation/reduction reactions during which ATP is generated by energy transfer as electrons move from high reducing state to lower reducing state.

Electrostatic attraction

The attraction between atoms of opposite charge that holds the atoms together in ionic bonds.

Element

A filter element consists of filter media and any hardware and supporting materials, installed as a single unit. Examples: filter cartridge, filter capsule.

Elliptic

Type of leaf. Leaf remembering to ellipse. 2 or 3 times longer than wider.

Elliptical

Egg shape equally rounded at both ends and broadest in the middle.

Elongated taproot

Type of root. They offer a very fat primary root because they accumulate food it. like in turnips.

Elongation

During protein synthesis, the growth of the polypeptide chain through the addition of amino acids; the second step in translation.

Embrio

Part of the seed. It is the little plant in embryonic state. When conditions are favorable (suitable humidity, warm and oxygen) it develops into a new plant.

Embryo

The earliest stage of development in an animal or plant. An embryo begins to form following the fusion of egg and sperm (a zygote).

Embryo sac

Alternate term applied to the angiosperm female gametophyte contained within a megaspore.

Embryophyte

Synonym for the Plantae, as here defined. It includes all green photosynthetic organisms which begin the development of the sporophyte generation within the archegonium.

Emigration

Movement of individuals out of a population.

Emphysema

Lung disease characterized by shortness of breath, often associated with smoking.

Enations

Flaps of tissue such as those found on psilophytes.

Endangered animals

Endangered animals are species or populations that are at risk of becoming extinct.

Endangered species

An animal or plant species in danger of extinction throughout all or a significant portion of its range.

Endergonic

Chemical reactions that require energy input to begin.

Endocarp

Part of the fruit. It is the inner covering, in many cases the stiffened part normally covering the seed. In a plum, for example, what we commonly know as the "stone".

Endochondral ossification

The process by which human bones form from cartilage.

Endocrine

The endocrine system is a system of glands, each of which secretes a type of hormone directly into the bloodstream to regulate the body. The endocrine system is in contrast to the exocrine system, which secretes its chemicals using ducts. It derives from the Greek words "endo" meaning inside, within, and "crinis" for secrete. The endocrine system is an information signal system like the nervous system, yet its effects and mechanism are classifiably different.

The endocrine system's effects are slow to initiate, and prolonged in their response, lasting for hours to weeks. The nervous system sends information very quickly, and responses are generally short lived. Hormones are substances (chemical mediators) released from endocrine tissue into the bloodstream where they travel to target tissue and generate a response. Hormones regulate various human functions, including metabolism, growth and development, tissue function, and mood. The field of study dealing with the endocrine system and its disorders is endocrinology, a branch of internal medicine.

Endocrine system

One of eleven major body organ systems in animals; a system of glands that works with the nervous system in controlling the activity of internal organs, especially the kidneys, and in coordinating the long-range response to external stimuli.

Endocytosis

The incorporation of materials from outside the cell by the formation of vesicles in the plasma membrane. The vesicles surround the material so the cell can engulf it.

Endoderm

The inner layer of cells in embryonic development that gives rise to organs and tissues associated with digestion and respiration. Also, the inner tissue layer in þatworms.

Endodermis

Literally "inner skin", this is a layer of cells which surrounds the central core of vascular tissue, and which helps to regulate the flow of water and dissolved substances.

Endometrium

The inner lining of the uterus.

Endoparasite

A parasite that lives within the tissues or bloodstream of its host.

Endoplasmic reticulum (ER)

A network of membranous tubules in the cytoplasm of a cell; involved in the production of phospholipids, proteins, and other functions. Rough ER is studded with ribosomes; smooth ER is not.

Endoskeleton

An internal supporting skeleton with muscles on the outside; in vertebrates, consists of the skull, spinal column, ribs, and appendages.

Endosperm

A food storage tissue that provides nutrients to the developing embryo in angiosperms; formed from the triploid cell produced when a sperm cell fertilizes the central cell. Some endosperm is solid (as in corn), some is liquid (as in coconut).

Endosymbiosis

Theory that attempts to explain the origin of the DNA-containing mitochondria and chloroplasts in early eukaryotes by the engulfing of various types of bacteria that were not digested but became permanent additions to the ancestral "eukaryote".

Endothermic

A reaction that gives off energy. The product is in a lower energy state than the reactants.

Endotherms

Animals that have the ability to maintain a constant body temperature over a wide range of environmental conditions.

Endothermy

The internal control of body temperature; the ability to generate and maintain internal body heat.

Endotoxin

The outer cell wall of gram-negative bacteria, also known as lipopolysaccharides (LPS) & pyrogens.

Energy

The ability to bring about changes or to do work.

Energy flow

The movement of energy through a community via feeding relationships.

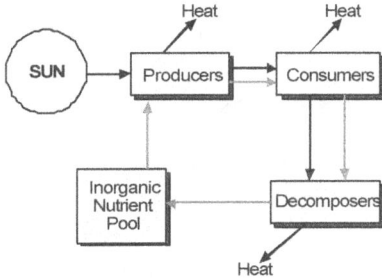

Energy of activation

The minimum amount of energy required for a given reaction to occur; varies from reaction to reaction.

Enhancement of Survival Permit

A type of permit issued by the US Fish and Wildlife Service under the authority of the Endangered Species Act.

Entire

Type of leaf. An entire leaf has a smooth, individed margin.

Entomology

the study of insects. Entomolgists are scientists who study insects.

Entomophily

Seed plants which are pollinated by insects are said to be entomophilous.

Entropy

The degree of disorder in a system. As energy is transferred from one form to another, some is lost as heat; as the energy decreases, the disorder in the system & —;and thus the entropy & — ;increases.

Environment

The place in which an organism lives, and the circumstances under which it lives. Environment includes measures like moisture and temperature, as much as it refers to the actual physical place where an organism is found.

Enzyme

A substance, usually a protein, that speeds up, or catalyzes, a specific chemical reaction without being permanently altered or consumed. Some RNA molecules can also act as enzymes.

Eon

The longest unit of geological time.

Epicentre

Point on the Earth's surface directly above the focus of an earthquake.

Epidermis

1. The outermost layer of skin consisting of several layers of epithelial cells&emdash;notably, keratinocytes&emdash;and, in the inner layer of the epidermis, basal cells and melanocytes.
2. The outer layer of cells in the plant body, often covered by a waxy cuticle.

Epididymis

A long, convoluted duct on the testis where sperm are stored.

Epigeous
Type of germination. In germination when cotyledons are raised above ground level.

Epiglottis
A þap of tissue that closes off the trachea during swallowing.

Epinephrine
Epinephrine (also known as adrenaline) is a hormone and a neurotransmitter. It increases heart rate, constricts blood vessels, dilates air passages and participates in the fight-or-flight response of the sympathetic nervous system. In chemical terms, adrenaline is one of a group of monoamines called the catecholamines. It is produced in some neurons of the central nervous system, and in the chromaffin cells of the adrenal medulla from the amino acids phenylalanine and tyrosine.

Epiphyte
A plant which grows upon another plant. The epiphyte does not "eat" the plant on which it grows, but merely uses the plant for structural support, or as a way to get off the ground and into the canopy environment.

Epistasis
The masking of the effects of one gene by the action of another, example: widow's peak masked by the baldness gene.

Epithelial tissue
Cells in animals that are closely packed in either single or multiple layers, and which cover both internal and external surfaces of the animal body. Also referred to as epithelium.

Epithelium
Layer of cells which lines a body cavity; cells may be ciliated or unciliated, and may be squamous (flat, scale-shaped), cuboidal (cube-shaped), or columnar (column-shaped). Your stomach and cheeks are lined with epithelium.

Epoch
Subdivision of a geological period.

Eras
One of the major divisions of the geologic time scale.

Erosion
The processes by which materials of the Earth's crust are worn away, loosened, or dissolved while being transported from their place of origin.

Erratic
A large, isolated boulder left behind by a glacier.

Erythrocytes
Red blood cells; doubly concave, enucleated cells that transport oxygen in the blood.

Escarpment
A steep or vertical cliff, either above or below sea level.

Esker
A ridge of glacial sediment deposited by a stream flowing in and under a melting glacier.

Esophagus
The esophagus (or oesophagus) is an organ in vertebrates which consists of a muscular tube through which food passes from the pharynx to the stomach. During swallowing, food passes from the mouth through the pharynx into the esophagus and travels via peristalsis to the stomach. The word esophagus is derived from the Latin œsophagus, which derives from the Greek word oisophagos , lit. "entrance for eating." In humans the esophagus is continuous with the

laryngeal part of the pharynx at the level of the C6 vertebra. The esophagus passes through posterior mediastinum in thorax and enters abdomen through a hole in the diaphragm at the level of the tenth thoracic vertebrae (T10). It is usually about 25–30 cm long depending on individual height. It is divided into cervical, thoracic and abdominal parts.

Estivation
A temporary state of inactivity during a time that the animal is usually active (for example, snails go into estivation in summer months if it is too hot or too dry).

Estrogen
A female sex hormone that performs many important functions in reproduction.

Estuary
An area where fresh water comes into contact with seawater, usually in a partly enclosed coastal body of water; a mix of fresh and salt water where the current of a stream meets the tides.

Ethylene
A gaseous plant hormone that stimulates fruit ripening and the dropping of leaves.

Ethylene oxide sterilization, (ETO)
A sterilization process still common for biomedical products, in which product is subjected to steam and highly toxic ethylene oxide gas. Because many materials change properties when exposed to moisture and EtO byproducts, products destined for this process must be specially engineered for EtO sterilization.

Etiology
The study of the causes of abnormal condition or disease.

Eubacteria
The subunit of the Monera that includes the true bacteria such as E. coli. One of the three major groups of prokaryotes in the Kingdom Monera. The eubacteria have cell walls containing peptidoglycan.

Eucaryotic cell
A cell containing a distinct membrane-bounded nucleus, characteristic of all organisms except bacteria.

Euglenoids
Term applied to a division of protozoans that have one long flagellum, no cell wall, and which may have chloroplasts.

Eukaryote
A type of cell found in many organisms including single-celled protists and multicellular fungi, plants, and animals; characterized by a membrane-bounded nucleus and other membraneous organelles; an organism composed of such cells. The first eukaryotes are encountered in rocks approximately 1.2-1.5 billion years old.

Euphotic zone
The upper part of the marine biome where light penetrates and photosynthesis occurs; usually extends to about 200 metres below the water surface.

Euramerica
A supercontinent that existed in the Late Silurian through Devonian, formed by the collision of Baltica, Laurentia, and Avalonia; included modern North America, Greenland, Scandinavia, and Europe; also called

the "Old Red Continent" for the red colour of its oxidized deposits.

Eustele
When a plant's vascular tissue develops in discrete bundles, it is said to have a eustele. See also protostele and siphonostele.

Eutrophication
"Runaway" growth of aquatic plants that occurs when agricultural fertilizers containing phosphorus and nitrogen run off into lakes and ponds; also ultimately increases the plant death rate with the result that the bacterial decomposition of the dead plants uses up oxygen, causing Þsh and other organisms to suffocate.

Evaporate
turn to vapour. Salt water absorbs heat and evaporates leaving a deposit of dry salt.

Evaporation
The part of the hydrologic cycle in which liquid water is converted to vapor and enters the atmosphere.

Evaporite
A deposit of salt minerals (e.g., halite, gypsum, anhydrite) left behind by the evaporation of seawater, usually forms within a restricted basin.

Evolution
1) The change in life over time by adaptation, variation, over-reproduction, and differential survival/reproduction, a process referred to by Charles Darwin and Alfred Wallace as natural selection.
2) Descent with modification.

Evolutionary tree
A diagram showing the evolutionary history of organisms based on differences in amino acid sequences.

Organisms with fewer differences are placed closer together while those with more differences are further apart.

Excretion
The process of removing the waste products of cellular metabolism from the body.

Excretory system
One of eleven major body systems in animals; regulates the volume and molecular and ionic constitution of internal body Þuids and eliminates metabolic waste products from the internal environment.

Exine
Outer covering of pollen grains, often containing sporopollenin, an acid-resistant polysaccharide that allows pollen grains to become fossils.

Exocarp
Part of the fruit. It is the outer covering of the pericarp. In an apple, for instance, it is what we know as the "skin".

Exocytosis
The process in which a membrane-enclosed vesicle Þrst fuses with the plasma membrane and then opens and releases its contents to the outside.

Exon
The DNA bases that code for an amino acid sequence. Exons are separated by introns that code for no amino acid sequences.

Exoskeleton
A hard, jointed, external covering that encloses the muscles and organs of an organism; typical of many arthropods including insects.

Exothermic

A reaction where the product is at a higher energy level than the reactants.

Expendables

Filter cartridges, elements and other media that require periodic replacement to maintain filtration efficacy. Expendables are additional to basic initial equipment or system hardware and piping configurations.

Experiment

A test, a trial, a tentative procedure, an effort to test an idea.

Exponential rate

An extremely rapid increase, e.g., in the rate of population growth.

Expression

In relation to genes, the phenotypic manifestation of a trait. Expression may be age-dependent (e.g., Huntington disease) or affected by environmental factors (e.g., dark fur on Siamese cats).

Extinction

The elimination of all individuals in a group, both by natural (dinosaurs, trilobites) and human-induced (dodo, passenger pigeon, liberals) means.

Extracellular digestion

A form of digestion found in annelids, crustaceans, and chordates including vertebrates; takes place within the lumen of the digestive system, and the resulting nutrient molecules are transferred into the blood or body fluid.

Extracellular matrix

(ECM) Region outside of metazoan cells which includes compounds attached to the plasma membrane, as well as dissolved substances attracted to the surface charge of the cells. The ECM functions both to keep animal cells adhered together, and well as buffering them from their environment.

Extracellular route

Path taken by water through the root in which water moves through the spaces between cell walls of the cortex parenchyma.

Extractables

Substances that may dissolve or leach from a membrane device during filtration and contaminate the process solution. For example, the leachates might include wetting agents in the membrane, membrane cleaning solutions, or substances from the materials used to encase the membrane.

Eyeshine

The shine that is present in the eyes of various birds (goatsuckers, owls, kiwis, and other night birds). Caused by reflection off of the tapetum, the vascular membrane of the retina within the eye.

Eyespot

1. A pigmented photoreceptor in euglenoids. The eyespot senses light and orients the cell for maximum rates of photosynthesis.
2. Term applied to a photosenstive area in starfish.

F

Fall overturn

The vertical mixing of the layers of the water in temperate lakes. This turnover occurs in autumn when temperatures start to change.

Fallout

Birds that are forced during migration to land in areas they would not normally inhabit in order to avoid harsh weather.

False negative

When a test wrongly shows an effect or condition to be absent (e.g., that a woman is not pregnant when, in fact, she is).

False positive

When a test wrongly shows an effect or condition to be present (e.g. that is woman is pregnant when, in fact, she is not).

Families

1. In taxonomy, term applied to subcategories within orders.
2. Term applied to a group of similar things, such as languages, chromosomes, etc.

Family

A taxonomic group used in the classification of living things. This group ranks below an order and is subdivided into one or more genera.

Fang

A long hollow tooth found in venomous snakes. The snakes inject their venom into prey through their fangs.

Fats

1. Triglycerides that are solid at room temperature.
2. A legendary pool player from Minnesota?

Fault

A fracture, or large crack, in the Earth's crust where one side moves up/down/sideways relative to the other; fault block-n. pieces of crust that have slipped into or alongside a fault; fault zone-n. an area with multiple faults.

Fauna

Term referring collectively to all animals in an area. The zoological counterpart of flora.

Feces

Semisolid material containing undigested foods, bacteria, bilirubin, and water that is produced in the large intestine and eliminated from the body. Frequently noted as "hitting the fan".

Fecundity

A measure of the rate at which an individual organism reproduces.

Feed
Material or solution that is introduced into a membrane separations system.

Feed pressure
The pressure measured at the separations device, such as a membrane cassette holder.

Felsic
Term used to describe the amount of light-coloured feldspar and silica minerals in an igneous rock.

Female
In organisms with separate sexes, the one which produces eggs.

Femur
The thigh bone in vertebrates that have four limbs or the third segment of the leg in insects.

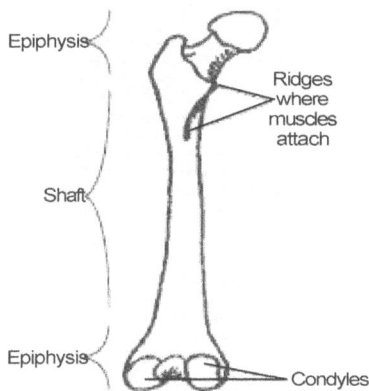

Feral
Pertaining to an animal that comes from domesticated stock and that has subsequently taken up life in the wild.

Fermentation
Action of microbes on substance in absence of air. Yeast ferments glucose to alcohol & CO_2. Yeast enzymes catalyse the change. Initially, enzymes were called ferments.

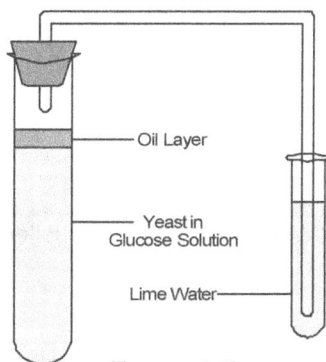

Fermentation

Fertilization
The fusion of two gametes (sperm and ovum) to produce a zygote that develops into a new individual with a genetic heritage derived from both parents. Strictly speaking, fertilization can be divided into the fusion of the cells (plasmogamy) and the fusion of nuclei (karyogamy).

Fetus
An embryo that is in the later stages of development but is still in the egg or uterus.

Fibre
Elongated and thickened cell found in xylem tissue. It strengthens and supports the surrounding cells.

Fibroblast
A term applied to a cell of connective tissue that is separated from similar cells by some degree of matrix material; fibroblasts secrete elastin and collagen protein fibres.

Fibrous
Type of root. Fibrous roots do not have a primary root. They show almost the same size and width, like in grasses.

Fibrous root
A root system found in monocots in which branches develop from the adventitious roots, forming a system in which all roots are about the same size and length.

Filament
(In a flower) Part of the statement like a stick, carrying on top of it a " little bag" (anthera) loaded with pollen.

Filly
A female horse that is four years or younger in age.

Filter
A device used to separate a liquid or gas from another liquid or gas; or to remove solid contaminate from a liquid or gas. The latter meaning is the most common in the industry. Types include membrane, centrifuge, baffle, pre-coat, leaf, edge, plate and frame, cyclone and replaceable filter.

Filter area
The surface area of filter media inside a separations device.

Filter efficiency
Filter efficiency represents the percentage of a given size particle removed from the fluid by the filter.

Filter feeder
An organism that filters food particles from its surrounding aqueous environment. It strains the water using sieve-like structures. Examples of filter feeders include clams and baleen whales.

Filter press
A filtration device typically consisting of carrier plates fitted with filter media or pads and clamped in series. The pads may contain absorbents. Also, "plate-and-frame" filter.

Filterability
Descriptive term expressing the ease or difficulty of filtering.

Filtrate
Also called permeate or effluent. The portion of the process fluid that passes through the membrane.

Filtration
The act of removing particles (normally solids) from a substance (generally fluids). These particles can be valuable products, or contaminants.

Fiord
A steep-sided, drowned coastal valley carved by glacial action. Also spelled 'fjord.'

First law of thermodynamics (conservation)
Energy is neither created nor destroyed, it changes from one form to another.

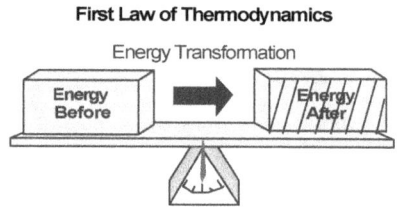
First Law of Thermodynamics

Fish
The term fish is used to refer to any aquatic vertebrate that has a skin covered with scales, two sets of paired fins, some unpaired fins, and a set of gills.

Fission
Division of single-celled organisms, especially prokaryotes, in which mitosis does not occur. Also used to refer to mitosis in certain unicellular fungi.

Fitness

A measure of an individual's ability to survive and reproduce; the chance that an individual will leave more offspring in the next generation than other individuals.

Flagella

Long, whip-like locomotion organelles found in both prokaryotic and eukaryotic cells; sing.: flagellum. Eukaryotic flagella have an internal arrangement of microtubules in a 9 + 2 array.

Flagellin

Protein which is the primary component of prokaryotic flagella.

Flagellum

Hair-like structure attached to a cell, used for locomotion in many protists and prokaryotes. The prokaryotic flagellum differs from the eukaryotic flagellum in that the prokaryotic flagellum is a solid unit composed primarily of the protein flagellin, while the eukaryotic flagellum is composed of several protein strands bound by a membrane, and does not contain flagellin. The eukaryotic flagellum is sometimes referred to as an undulipodium.

Flame cell

A specialized cell at the blind end of a nephridium that Þlters body Þuids.

Fledging

The development in young birds of the feathers necessary for flight.

Fledgling

A young bird that ahs left the nest but is not yet completely independent of parental care.

Fleshy

Type of fruit. Are those containing a more or less soft pericarp. In other words, those offering " fleshy material" around the " stone". Besides, they all derive from a single ovary,

Flight feathers

Collective name for the long feathers of the wings and tail.

Floodplain

The flat area on either side of an active river channel that can be covered in water when the river is in flood. When the channel is breached, sediment-laden waters spread across the floodplain. When the waters recede, a layer of sediment is left behind. When the floodplain is not covered with water, it commonly supports vegetation and soil formation.

Flora

Term collectively applied to all of the plants in an area. The botanical counterpart of fauna.

Floret

Each one of the flowers that form an inflorescence

Flower

Collection of reproductive structures found in flowering plants.

Flowpath length, nominal flowpath length

The total length that a feed solution travels from inlet to outlet. Flowpath length is an important parameter to consider when doing any process development, system design, or scale-up or scale-down experiments. The flowpath length and other fluid channel geometries, such as lumen diameter or channel height, can affect the fluid dynamics of the system and will directly affect pump requirements and differential pressure of the filtration step.

Fluid feeders

Animals such as aphids, ticks, and mosquitoes that pierce the body of a host plant or animal and obtain food from ingesting its þuids.

Fluid-mosaic

Widely accepted model of the plasma membrane in which proteins (the mosaic) are embedded in lipids (the fluid).

Flux

Flux represents the volume of solution flowing through a given membrane area during a given time. Expressed as LMH (litres per square metre per hour).

Foal

Refers to a horse, either male or female, up to six months in age.

Focus

The initial point within the Earth that ruptures in an earthquake, directly below the epicenter.

Folicle

(Type of deshiscent fruit) Folicles are fruits with a single carpel. Being ripe, they open one side.

Follicles (ovary)

Structures in the ovary consisting of a developing egg surrounded by a layer of follicle cells.

Follicles (thyroid)

Spherical structures that make up the thyroid gland; contain a gel-like colloid surrounded by a single layer of cells, which secrete thyroglobulin into the colloid.

Follicle-stimulating hormone (FSH)

A hormone secreted by the anterior pituitary that promotes gamete formation in both males and females.

Fontanels

Membranous areas in the human cranial bones that do not form bony structures until the child is 14 to 18 months old; know as "soft spots."

Food chain

The simplest representation of energy flow in a community. At the base is energy stored in plants, which are eaten by small organisms, which in turn are eaten by progressively larger organisms; the food chain is an oversimplification in that most animals do not eat only one type of organism.

Food pyramid

A way of depicting energy flow in an ecosystem; shows producers (mostly plants or other phototrophs) on the Þrst level and consumers on the higher levels.

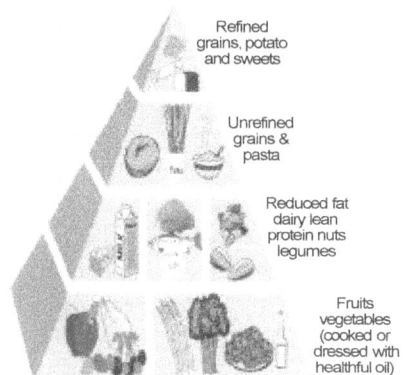

Refined grains, potato and sweets

Unrefined grains & pasta

Reduced fat dairy lean protein nuts legumes

Fruits vegetables (cooked or dressed with healthful oil)

Food web

All the interactions of predator and prey, included along with the exchange of nutrients into and out of the soil. These interactions connect the various members of an ecosystem, and describe how energy passes from one organism to another.

Foraminifera

Single-celled protists that secrete a shell or test. Accumulations of the shells of dead foraminifera and other microscopic sea creatures form chalk deposits.

Forebrain

The part of the brain that consists of the diencephalon and cerebrum.

Fossil

Any evidence of past life, including remains, traces, imprints as well as life history artifacts. Examples of artifacts include fossilized bird's nests, bee hives, etc.

Fossil fuels

Fuels that are formed in the Earth from plant or animal remains; e.g., coal, petroleum, and natural gas.

Fossil record

All of the fossils that have existed throughout life's history, whether they have been found or not.

Fouling

A buildup of material on the membrane surface that reduces the filtration rate. This material is not redeposited in the bulk stream by higher shear rates.

Founder effect

The difference in gene pools between an original population and a new population founded by one or a few individuals randomly separated from the original population, as when an island population is founded by one or a few individuals; often accentuates genetic drift.

Fovea

The area of the eye in which the cones are concentrated.

Fractionation

The separation of molecules in a solution based on differences in the molecular weight of the molecules.

Freezing

To preserve an organism without any significant alteration to its chemical composition by subjecting it to freezing temperatures.

Freshwater biome

The aquatic biome consisting of water containing fewer salts than the waters in the marine biome; divided into two zones: running waters (rivers, streams) and standing waters (lakes, ponds).

Frontal lobe

The lobe of the cerebral cortex that is responsible for motor activity, speech, and thought processes.

Frugivore

Animal which primarily eats fruit. Many bats and birds are frugivores.

Frugivorous

Fruit-eating. Relying on fruit as a sole source of food.

Fruit

In flowering plants, the structure which encloses the seeds. True fruits develop from the ovary wall, such as bananas and tomatoes, though not all fruits are edible, such as the dry pods of milkweed or the winged fruits of the maple.

Frustule

The mineral "skeleton" of a diatom or other unicellular organism.

Fucoxanthin

Yellowish-brown pigment found in some members of the Chromista, including kelps and diatoms.

Functional response

Change in the rate of exploitation of prey by an individual predator as a result of a change in prey density.

Fungi

None makes its own food; they use dead matter or living organisms. Includes molds, mildews, rusts, smuts, mushrooms, yeasts-have some differences.

Funnel-shaped or funnelform

Flowers similar to funnels, very wide at the top and narrower at the base.

Fused or synsepalous

Type of flowers. If the sepals are partially or wholly joined

G

Gabbro
Highly mafic igneous plutonic rock, typically dark in colour; rough plutonic equivalent of basalt.

Gaia
A hypothetical superorganism composed of the Earth's four spheres: the biosphere, hydrosphere, lithosphere, and atmosphere.

Gamete
Reproductive cells which fuse to form a zygote. Gametes are haploid, and may be differentiated into egg and sperm.

Gametophyte
The haploid stage in the life cycle of an organism undergoing alternations of generations. The gametophyte is multicellular and mitotically produces gametes. In plants, the gametophyte nourishes the zygote and young sporophyte.

Gamma sterilization
A type of sterilization process accomplished by bombarding the object to be sterilized with electron beam, x-ray, 60Co or 137Cs irradiators. All generate forms of gamma rays, radiant energy at short wavelength (0.1 nm or less). The governing standard is ISO 11137—Sterilization of Healthcare Products—Requirements for Validation and Routine Control—Radiation Sterilization. Because some product materials can be adversely affected by gamma radiation, objects destined for gamma sterilization must be engineered specifically for this process.

Ganglia
Clusters of neurons that receive and process signals; found in flatworms and earthworms.

Gap junctions
Junctions between the plasma membranes of animal cells that allow communication between the cytoplasm of adjacent cells.

Gaping
A foraging technique in which a bird thrusts its bill into the soil and forcibly opens the bill, creating an opening.

Gastric pits
The folds and grooves into which the stomach lining is arranged.

Gastrin
A hormone produced by the pyloric gland area of the stomach that stimulates the secretion of gastric acids.

Gastrodermis
In cnidarians, the endodermis which lines the gut cavity. The term is often used instead of endodermis since cnidarians only have two tissue layers instead of three.

Gastroesophageal sphincter

A ring of muscle at the junction of the esophagus and the stomach that remains closed except during swallowing to prevent the stomach contents from entering the esophagus.

Gastroliths

Fossilized gizzard stones, usually only applicable in the study of fossil reptiles.

Gel layer

During the filtration process, the thin layer of particles or molecules that may build up at the membrane surface. It is also referred to as the concentration polarization layer. Higher TMP can be the result of an increase in the thickness of the gel layer. Gel layer formation can negatively impact the filtration process by reducing flux and inhibiting passage though the membrane. Operating at a higher shear rate may reduce the thickness of the gel layer.

Gelding

A male horse that has been castrated.

Gene

A unit of inheritance; a working subunit of DNA. Each of the body's 50,000 to 100,000 genes contains the code for a specific product, typically, a protein such as an gene's coded information is translated into the structures present and operating in the cell (either proteins or RNAs).

Gene flow

Exchange of genetic traits between populations by movement of individuals, gametes, or spores.

Gene frequency

The proportion of a particular allele of a gene in the gene pool of a population.

Gene pool

The sum of all the genetic information carried by members of a population. Note: there is *no* diving in the deep end of the gene pool!

Gene therapy

The insertion of normal or genetically altered genes into cells through the use of recombinant DNA technology; usually done to replace defective genes as part of the treatment of genetic disorders.

Genera

Taxonomic subcategories within families (sing.: genus), composed of one or more species.

Generalist

Organism which can survive under a wide variety of conditions, and does not specialize to live under any particular set of circumstances.

Generation time

Average age at which a female gives birth to her offspring, or the average time for a population to increase by a factor equal to the net reproductive rate.

Genetic code

The linear series of nucleotides, read as triplets, that specifies the sequence of amino acids in proteins. Each triplet specifies an amino acid, and the same codons are used for the same amino acids in almost all life-forms, an indication of the universal nature of the code.

Genetic divergence

The separation of a population's gene pool from the gene pools of other populations due to mutation, genetic drift, and selection. Continued divergence can lead to speciation.

Genetic drift

Random changes in the frequency of alleles from generation to generation; especially in small populations, can lead to the elimination of a particular allele by chance alone.

Genetic feedback

Evolutionary response of a population to the adaptations of competitors, predators, or prey.

Genetic maps

Diagrams showing the order of and distance between genes; constructed using crossover information.

Genetic polymorphisms

It result from base changes (mutations) in a gene or a chromosomal locus that create multiple forms (polymorphs) of that locus. Common types are Single Nucleotide Polymorphism's (SNPs) and Simple Sequence Length Polymorphism's (SSLPs).

Genetic variance

Variation in a phenotypic value within a population due to the expression of genetic factors.

Genetically modified organisms

The introducing a foreign gene into an organism which can propagate creates a genetically modified organism.

Genetics

The scientific study of heredity how particular qualities or traits are transmitted from parents to offspring.

Genital herpes

A sexually transmitted disease caused by the herpes virus; results in sores on the mucus membranes of the mouth or genitals.

Genome

The cell's total complement of DNA: in eucaryotes, the nuclear and organelle chromosomes; in procaryotes, the major chromosome, episomes, and plasmids. In viruses and viroids, the total complement of DNA or RNA.

Genotype

All the genetic characteristics that determine the structure and function of an organism; often applied to a single gene locus to distinguish one allele, or combination of alleles, from another.

Genus

A group of species; Example: all oak species belong to the Oak genus Quercus.

Geographic isolation

Separation of populations of a species by geographic means (distance, mountains, rivers, oceans, etc.) that lead to reproductive isolation of those populations.

Geographic range

The total area occupied by a population.

Geologic maps

Maps that show the types and ages of rock of an area. These maps are used by paleontologists to find areas that are likely to contain fossils they are interested in.

Geologic province

A group of rocks that share a common history or event, for example, rocks that were formed in the same environment at the same time or that were folded and faulted by the same event.

Geological time

The span of time that has passed since the formation of the Earth and its physical structures; also, a timescale that focuses on events on the order of thousands of years or more.

Geotropism

Plants' response to gravity: roots grow downward, showing positive geotropism, while shoots grow upward in a negative response.

Germ cells

Collective term for cells in the reproductive organs of multicellular organisms that divide by meiosis to produce gametes.

Germination

Germination is the process in which a plant or fungus emerges from a seed or spore, respectively, and begins growth. The most common example of germination is the sprouting of a seedling from a seed of an angiosperm or gymnosperm. However the growth of a sporeling from a spore, for example the growth of hyphae from fungal spores, is also germination. In a more general sense, germination can imply anything expanding into greater being from a small existence or germ.

Gestation

Period of time between fertilization and birth of an animal. Commonly called pregnancy.

Gibberellins

A group of hormones that stimulate cell division and elongation in plants. Gibberellic acid (GA), the first of this class to be discovered, causes bolting (extreme elongation) of stems. GA is also applied to certain plants to promote larger fruits.

Gill

In aquatic animals, highly vascularized tissues with large surface area; these are extended out of the body and into the surrounding water for gas exchange.

Gill arches

Stiffenings which support the flesh between the gill slits of chordates. In most vertebrates, the first gill arches have been modified to form the jaw, and in tetrapods, the inner ear bones.

Gill slit

A slitlike or porelike opening connecting the pharynx of a chordate with the outside of the body. Gill slits may contain the gills and be used for gas exchange, as in most fish, but may also be used for filter-feeding, or may be highly modified in land-dwelling vertebrates.

Ginkgos

Group of seed plants today restricted to a single genus (Ginkgo biloba); ginkgos were more diverse during the Mesozoic Era.

Gizzard

A chamber of an animal's digestive tract specialized for grinding food.

Glabrous or hairless
It is said of the plant or part of it having no hairs.

Glandular
It is said of the part of a plant having glands

Glass
A non-crystaline rock that results from very rapid cooling of magma.

Glial cells
Nonconducting cells that serve as support cells in the nervous system and help to protect neurons.

Glomerulus
A tangle of capillaries that makes up part of the nephron; the site of þltration.

Glucagon
A hormone released by the pancreas that stimulates the breakdown of glycogen and the release of glucose, thereby increasing blood levels of glucose. Glucagon and insulin work together to maintain blood sugar levels.

Glucocorticoids
A group of steroid hormones produced by the adrenal cortex that are important in regulating the metabolism of carbohydrates, fats, and proteins.

Glucose
simple sugar, and the primary product of photosynthesis. It is polymerized to make cellulose and chitin.

Glycogen
Polysaccharide consisting of numerous monosaccharide glucoses linked together. The animal equivalent of starch.

Glycolipids
Polysaccharides formed of sugars linked to lipids, a part of the cell membrane.

Glycolysis
The universal cellular metabolic process in the cell's cytoplasm where 6-carbon glucose is split into two 3-carbon pyruvate molecules, and some ATP and NADH are produced. Glycolysis is a definite sequence of ten reactions involving ten intermediate compounds (one of the steps involves two intermediates). The intermediates provide entry points to glycolysis.

Glycoprotein
A membrane-bound protein which has attached branching carbohydrates. These may function in cell-cell recognition, such as in human blood groups and immune system response, as well as in resisting compression of cells.

Gnathobase
The expanded and hardened base of the appendage of many arthropods, notably trilobites, crustaceans, and marine cheliceramorphs. Used to macerate food items before ingestion.

Gnetales
Group of seed plants restricted to three genera today (Gnetum, Ephedra, and Welwitschia); the possible outgroup for flowering plants.

Golden brown algae
Common name applied to the protistan division Chrysophyta.

Golgi apparatus
Eukaryotic organelle which package cell products, such as enzymes and hormones, and coordinate their transport to the outside of the cell.

Golgi complex
Organelles in animal cells composed of a series of þattened sacs that sort, chemically modify, and package

proteins produced on the rough endoplasmic reticulum.

Gonadotropin-releasing hormone (GNRH)

A hormone produced by the hypothalamus that controls the secretion of luteinizing hormone.

Gonadotropins

Hormones produced by the anterior pituitary that affect the testis and ovary; include follicle-stimulating hormone and luteinizing hormone.

Gonads

The male and female sex organs.

Gondwana

Name applied to the ancient (Paleozoic-early Mesozoic) southern hemisphere supercontinent that rifted apart to form present-day Antarctica, India, Africa, Australia, and South America. The southern part of Pangaea.

Gonorrhea

A sexually transmitted disease that is caused by a bacterium that damages epithelial cells of the reproductive system.

Gorget

Iridescent throat patch on hummingbirds.

Gradualism

A model of evolution that assumes slow, steady rates of change. Charles Darwin's original concept of evolution by natural selection assumed gradualism. Contrast with punctuated equilibrium.

Grain

(1) The texture of wood, produced by the kinds of xylem cells present.
(2) The fruit of a member of the grasses.

Grana

A series of stacked thylakoid disks containing chlorophyll; found in the inner membrane of chloroplasts.

Granite

Highly felsic igneous plutonic rock, typically light in colour; rough plutonic equivalent of rhyolite. Granite is actually quite rare in the U.S.; often the term is applied to any quartz-bearing plutonic rock.

Granodiorite

Igneous plutonic rock, less felsic than granite, typically light in colour; rough plutonic equivalent of dacite.

Grassland

Region in which the climate is dry for long periods of the summer, and freezes in the winter. Grasslands are characterized by grasses and other erect herbs, usually without trees or shrubs.

Grasslands biome

Occurs in temperate and tropical regions with reduced rainfall or prolonged dry seasons; characterized by deep, rich soil, an absence of trees, and large herds of grazing animals.

Graywacke

Sandstone composed of poorly sorted angular clasts.

Green algae

Common name for algae placed in the division Chlorophyta.

Greenhouse effect

The heating that occurs when gases such as carbon dioxide trap heat escaping from the Earth and radiate it back to the surface; so-called because the gases are transparent to sunlight but not to heat and thus act like the glass in a greenhouse.

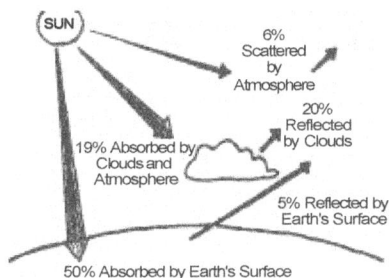

50% Absorbed by Earth's Surface

Gross production
The total energy or nutrients assimilated by an organism, a population, or an entire community.

Ground system
Plant tissue system, composed mainly of parenchyma cells with some collenchyma and sclerenchyma cells, that occupies the space between the epidermis and the vascular system; is involved in photosynthesis, water and food storage, and support; one of the four main tissue systems in plants.

Groundwater
Water found underground as a result of rainfall, ice and snow melt, submerged rivers, lakes, and springs. This water often carries minerals. These minerals can accumulate in the remains of buried organisms and eventually cause fossilization.

Group selection
Elimination of groups of individuals with a detrimental genetic trait, caused by competition with other groups lacking the trait; often called intergroup selection.

Growth hormone (GH)
A peptide hormone produced by the anterior pituitary that is essential for growth.

Growth rings
Features of woody stems produced by plants growing in areas with seasonal (as opposed to year-long) growth. The growth ring marks the position of the vascular cambium at the cessation of the previous year's growth.

Guanine
One of the nitrogenous bases in nucleic acids, guanine is one of the two purine bases.

Guano
Large deposits of bird feces that accumulate in sites that birds regularly use, such as breeding colonies.

Guard cells
Specialized epidermal cells that flank stomates and whose opening and closing regulates gas exchange and water loss.

Gular fluttering
A cooling behaviour in which birds rapidly flap membranes in the throat to increase evaporation; particularly obvious in cormorants, pelicans, and their relatives.

Gular pouch
A bare throat pouch that can be expanded to accommodate large prey; found in pelicans and their relatives.

Gut (enteron)
Body cavity formed between the mouth and anus in which food is digested and nutrients absorbed; it consists of the mouth, pharynx, esophagus, stomach, intestine, and anus, though some animals do not have all these regions.

Gymnosperms
Flowerless, seed-bearing land plants; the first seed plants; living groups include the pines, ginkgos, and cycads. Naked seeds.

Gynoecium

Gynoecium is most commonly used as a collective term for all carpels in a flower. A carpel is the ovule and seed producing reproductive organ in flowering plants. Carpels are derived from ovule-bearing leaves which evolved to form a closed structure containing the ovules.

Gynostemium

The central reproductive stalk of an orchid, which consists of a stamen and pistil fused together.

H

Habit
The general growth pattern of a plant. A plant's habit may be described as creeping, trees, shrubs, vines, etc.

Habitat
Place where an animal or plant normally lives, often characterized by a dominant plant form or physical characteristic (that is, the stream habitat, the forest habitat).

Habitat destruction
Habitat destruction is the process by which natural habitat is damaged or destroyed to such an extent that it no longer is capable of supporting the species and ecological communities that naturally occur there.

Habitat disruption
A disturbance of the physical environment in which a population lives.

Habitat patch
An area of distinct habitat type.

Habitat selection
Preference for certain habitats.

Hacking
A conservation and rehabilitation practice in which birds released into the wild are provisioned with food while they gradually become independent.

Hair bulb
The base of a hair; contains cells that divide mitotically to produce columns of hair cells.

Hair root
The portion of a hair that extends from the skin's surface to the hair bulb.

Hair shaft
The portion of a hair that extends above the skin's surface.

Half-life
The time required for one-half of an original unstable radioactive element to be converted to a more stable daughter element.

Halophile
Organism which lives in areas of high salt concentration. These organisms must have special adaptations to permit them to survive under these conditions.

Haploid
Cells that contain only one member of each homologous pair of chromosomes (haploid number = n). At fertilization, two haploid gametes fuse to form a single cell with a diploid number of chromosomes.

Haploid life cycle
Occurs when the only multicellular stage in an organism's life cycle is haploid.

Haploid-diploid life cycle

Occurs when a multicellular diploid phase, or sporophyte, alternates with a multicellular haploid phase, or gametophyte. Only plants and certain algae possess this kind of life cycle, which is also called "alternation of generations".

Haptonema

Peg-like structure unique to the Prymnesiophyta; its function is not known.

Hardwoods

Term applied to dicot trees, as opposed to softwoods, a term applied to gymnosperms.

Hastate

Halberd-shaped leaf. Remembering to that old fashioned weapon which was a combination between a spear and a battle-ax. Wider at the base but with lobes ending sharply.

Hatchling

Animal that has just emerged from an egg.

Haversian canal

Haversian canals (sometimes Canals of Havers, named after British physician Clopton Havers) are a series of tubes around narrow channels formed by lamellae. This is the region of bone called compact bone. Osteons are arranged in parallel to the long axis of the bone. The Haversian canals surround blood vessels and nerve cells throughout the bone and communicate with osteocytes in lacunae (spaces within the dense bone matrix that contain the living bone cells) through canaliculi. This unique arrangement is conducive to mineral salt deposits and storage which gives bone tissue its strength.

Head

In heads florets bearing no stem are gathered together on a platform-shaped peduncle. This is the inflorescence characteristic in the daisy family.

Heart

The multicellular, chambered, muscular structure that pumps blood through the circulatory system by alternately contracting and relaxing.

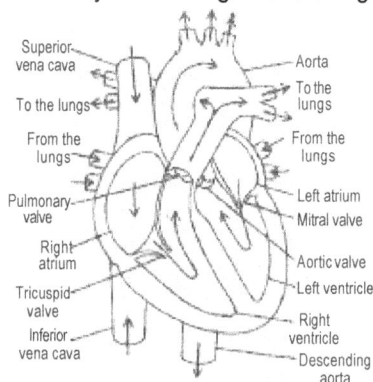

Heartwood

Inner rings of xylem that have become clogged with metabolic by-products and no longer transport water; visible as the inner darker areas in the cross section of a tree trunk.

Heat sensitive pit

Organ that helps certain snakes locate their warm-blooded prey. In boas and pythons, these border the mouth (labial pits); in pitvipers, they are between the nostri, the eye, and the moutn (loreal pits).

Heather

The heather family - ericaceae. It includes about 200 species of plants scattered throughout the world. They are mainly bushes or little trees.

Hedge

Group of bushes.

Helper T cells
A type of lymphocyte that stimulates the production of antibodies by activating B cells when an antigen is present.

Hemizygous
Having one or more genes that have no allele counterparts. Usually applied to genes on the male's X chromosome (in humans).

Hemoglobin
Protein complex found in the blood of most chordates and the roots of certain legumes. It binds oxgen molecules, and in chordates serves as the means by which the oxygen is supplied to the cells of the body.

Hemophilia
A human sex-linked recessive genetic disorder that results in the absence of certain blood-clotting factors, usually Factor VII. Hemophiliacs suffer from an inability to clot their blood.

Hepatitis B
A potentially serious viral disease that affects the liver; can be transmitted through sexual contact or through contact with infected blood.

Herb
Generally any plant which does not produce wood, and is therefore not as large as a tree or shrub, is considered to be an herb.

Herbaceous
Type of plant according to the stem. Herbaceous plants do not have developed ligneous stiffened structures. They are generally frail.

Herbivores
Term pertaining to a heterotroph, usually an animal, that eats plants or algae. Herbivores function in food chains and food webs as primary consumers.

Hermaphroditic
A type of animal in which each individual possesses both male and female reproductive organs.

Hesperidium
Type of fruit. Hesperidiums are fruits containing fleshy stuff between the endocarp and the seeds. Carpels are closed. For instance, lemons or oranges.

Heterodactyly
Arrangement of the toes in which the inner front toe is turned backward such that two toes point forward and two backward.

Heterogametic sex
The sex with two different chromosomes, such as males in humans and Drosophila.

Heterogeneity
The variety of qualities found in an environment (habitat patches) or a population (genotypic variation).

Heterosporangiate
Producing two different kinds of sporangia, specifically microsporangia and megasporangia.

Heterosporous
Producing two different sizes or kinds of spores. These may come from the same or different sporangia, and may produce similar or different gametophytes. Contrast with homosporous, and compare with heterosporangiate.

Heterotroph
An organism that utilizes organic materials as a source of energy and nutrients.

Heterotrophic
Refers to organisms, such as animals, that depend on preformed organic molecules from the environment (or another organism) as a source of nutrients/energy.

Heterotrophs
Organisms that obtain their nutrition by breaking down organic molecules in foods; include animals and fungi.

Heterozygous
Having two different alleles (one dominant, one recessive) of a gene pair.

Hibernation
State of winter dormancy associated with lowered body temperature and metabolism.

Hibiscus
Genus of plants. Shrub and trees of the Malvaceae family. Very well known because of their big and very distinctive flowers, with protuding stamens polinized by humming birds. There are more that 200 species.

Hierarchy
A series in which each element is categorized into successive ranks or grades with each level subordinate to the one above.

Histamine
A chemical released during the inflammatory response that increases capillary blood flow in the affected area, causing heat and redness.

Histology
The structure and arrangement of the tissues of organisms; the study of these.

Histone proteins
Proteins associated with DNA in eukaryote chromosomes.

Histones
Histones are highly alkaline proteins found in eukaryotic cell nuclei that package and order the DNA into structural units called nucleosomes. They are the chief protein components of chromatin, acting as spools around which DNA winds, and play a role in gene regulation. Without histones, the unwound DNA in chromosomes would be very long (a length to width ratio of more than 10 million to one in human DNA). For example, each human cell has about 1.8 metres of DNA, but wound on the histones it has about 90 micrometers (0.09 mm) of chromatin, which, when duplicated and condensed during mitosis, result in about 120 micrometers of chromosomes.

Histostructure
The organization and arrangement of tissue ("histo" is from the Greek word for tissue). Since eggshell is a tissue, eggshell histostructure describes the two- and three-dimensional organization of mineral crystals and shell components.

HIV protease
An HIV enzyme that is required during the life cycle of the virus. It is required for HIV virus particles to mature into fully infectious particles.

Holarctic
Relating to the boigeographic region that includes the northern parts of the Old and New Worlds, and that comprises the Nearctic and Palearctic regions.

Holdfast
Anchoring base of an alga.

Hold-up volume
Quantity of fluid remaining within the system after the filtration step is complete.

Hollow fibre

A tubular structure made from a membrane and sealed inside a cross flow cartridge. When in use, the feed stream flows into the inner diameter of one end of the hollow fibre and the retentate (the material that does not permeate through the walls of the hollow fibre) flows out the other end. The material that passes through the membrane (walls of the hollow fibre) is called the permeate.

Holotype

A single individual organism that is selected to represent the standard for a particular taxon and which serves as the standard for the original name and description of the species.

Home range

The area that an animal uses in the course of its daily activities. Not necessarily defended.

Homeobox genes

Pattern genes that establish the body plan and position of organs in response to gradients of regulatory molecules.

Homeostasis

The process by which an organism maintains constant internal conditions in the face of a varying external environment.

Homeothermy

Ability to maintain constant body temperature in the face of fluctuating environmental temperature; warm-blooded.

Hominid

Primate group that includes humans and all fossil forms leading to man only.

Hominoid

Primate group that includes common ancestors of humans and apes.

Homologous structures

Body parts in different organisms that have similar bones and similar arrangements of muscles, blood vessels, and nerves and undergo similar embryological development, but do not necessarily serve the same function; e.g., the þipper of a whale and the forelimb of a horse.

Homologues

A pair of chromosomes in which one member of the pair is obtained from the organism's maternal parent and the other from the paternal parent; found in diploid cells. Also commonly referred to as homologous chromosomes.

Homology

Two structures are considered homologous when they are inherited from a common ancestor which possessed the structure. This may be difficult to determine when the structure has been modified through descent.

Homosporous

Producing only one size or kind of spore.

Homozygous

Having identical alleles for a given gene.

Hormones

The chemicals produced by glands in the body and circulate in the bloodstream. Hormones control the actions of certain cells or organs.

Host

Bird whose nest receives eggs laid by brood parasites. The hosts then provide parental care to the unrelated young that hatch from the parasitic egg, often to the detriment of their own young.

Hosts and Vectors

Most routine manipulations in gene cloning use Eschericha coli (E.coli) as the host organism. Plasmids and bacteriophages may be used as cloning vectors in E.coli.

Hotspot

A localized, somewhat persistent (tens of millions of years), and relatively fixed zone of mantle melting, inferred from surface volcanic activity. Evidence of a hotspot's existence is left behind as tectonic plates move across it, for example, the Hawaiian Islands.

Housing

A mechanical structure that surrounds and supports the membrane or filter element. The housing normally has feed, retentate, and permeate ports that direct the flow of process fluids into and out of the filter assembly.

Human chorionic gonadotropin (HCG)

A peptide hormone secreted by the chorion that prolongs the life of the corpus luteum and prevents the breakdown of the uterine lining.

Human genome project

Federally funded project to determine the DNA base sequence of every gene in the human genome.

Human immunodeficiency virus (HIV)

The retrovirus that attacks T-cells in the human immune system, destroying the body's defenses and allowing the development of AIDS.

Huntington disease

A progressive and fatal disorder of the nervous system that develops between the ages of 30 and 50 years; caused by an expansion of a trinucleotide repeat and inherited as a dominant trait.

Hyaline

Glass like, transparent like glass. Also hyalin. Some structures of fungi are hyaline.

Hydrogen bond

A weak bond between two atoms (one of which is hydrogen) with partial but opposite electrical charges.

Hydrophilic

Water-loving. Term applied to polar molecules that can form a hydrogen bond with water.

Hydrophobic

Filters that do not wet out easily with water but typically do wet out easily with nonpolar solvents such as alcohol. Once wetted, many aqueous solutions can be processed in a hydrophobic filter.

Hydrophytic leaves

The leaves of plants that grow in water or under conditions of abundant moisture.

Hydrosphere

The part of the physical environment that consists of all the liquid and solid water at or near the Earth's surface.

Hydrostatic skeleton

Fluid-filled closed chambers that give support and shape to the body in organisms such as jellyfish and earthworms. No to be confused with the water-vascular system of echinoderms.

Hydrothermal vent

A place on the seafloor, generally associated with spreading centres, where warm to super-hot, mineral-rich water is released; may support a diverse community of organisms.

Hyoid apparatus
A collective term for the bones of the tongue and associated connective tissues, found in the upper throat.

Hypersaline
Extremely salty, having much more salt than normal seawater.

Hypertension
High blood pressure; blood pressure consistently above 140/90.

Hypertonic
A solution having a high concentration of solute.

Hypha
One filament of a fungus, a hollow tube in which the nuclei move freely; not separate cells as in plants. The mass of hyphae (pl) is the mycelium; the fungus body.

Hyphae
The multinucleate or multicellular blaments that make up the mycelium (body) of a fungus.

Hypocotyl
Part of the embryo in a seed. It is the space between the radicle and theplumule. It develops into a stem.

Hypogeous
Related with seed. In germination, when the cotyledons remain below ground level.

Hypogynous
Related with flower. The ovary is placed above the rest of the floral segments.

Hypostracum
The innermost layer of a snail's shell, closest to the snail's body.

Hypothalamus
A region in the brain beneath the thalamus; consists of many aggregations of nerve cells and controls a variety of autonomic functions aimed at maintaining homeostasis.

Hypothesis
An idea that can be experimentally tested.

Hypotonic
A solution having a low concentration of solute.

I

Iapetus ocean
A relatively small ocean that existed between the continents of Laurentia, Baltica, and Avalonia from the Late Precambrian to the Devonian.

Ice age
Interval of geologic time between 2 million and 10,000 years ago during which the northern hemisphere experienced several episodes of continental glacial advance and retreat along with a climatic cooling. The icing over of Antarctica was also completed during this time.

Ichnology
The study of trace fossils.

Igneous rock
Any rock solidified from molten or partly molten material.

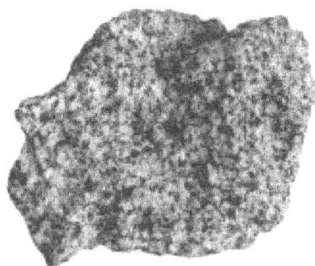

Ileum
The third and last section of the small intestine.

Imago
The fourth, or adult, stage in the life of certain insects, such as the butterfly or moth.

Immature
A young bird no longer under parental care but not yet old enough to breed; a bird that is not yet fully adult.

Immovable joint
A joint in which the bones interlock and are held together by fibres or bony processes that prevent the joint from moving; e.g., the bones of the cranium.

Immune system
One of the eleven major body organ systems in vertebrates; defends the internal environment against invading microorganisms and viruses and provides defense against the growth of cancer cells.

Immunoglobulins
The live classes of protein to which antibodies belong (IgD, IgM, IgG, IgA, IgE).

Implantation
The process in which the blastocyst embeds in the endometrium.

Impressions
Prints or marks made when an organism's body has been compressed.

Impressions are different from compressions because no thin organic material is left behind.

Imprinting
The tendency of young animals to follow the first moving thing they see. In the wild, this is usually the mother, but in captivity, where the mother may not be the first thing they see, they might follow a human being or any moving object.

In vitro
An experiment performed in a test tube, Petri dish or other lab apparatus with parts of a living organism, such as testing a drug with tissue samples. From Latin, meaning "in glass."

In vivo
An experiment performed using a living organism. From Latin, meaning "in live."

Incomplete dominance
A type of inheritance in which the heterozygote has a phenotype intermediate to those of the homozygous parents.

Incomplete flower
Condition in which one or more "typical" flower parts are absent. Example: grass flowers such as corn tassels which are male.

Incubate
hold bird eggs, culture of organisms, or chemical reaction at a desired temperature.

Incubation
In birds and reptiles, the maintaining of a constant temperature during the development of the embryo. Birds incubate their eggs by sitting on them (also called brooding), while other animals, like crocodiles, bury their eggs in organic matter. If eggs are not incubated, the embryos within those eggs generally die. Some dinosaurs may have incubated their eggs by burial in sediment, in organic matter, or by brooding like birds.

Incubation patch
A defeathered area on the lower abdomen in which the skin has thickened and become rich with blood vessels.

Incus
One of the three bones comprising the middle ear of mammals.

Indehiscent
Types of dry fruits. They are those fruits that do not open when becoming ripe, leaving their seeds inside them. We have several types of this kind of fruits but the most important are the following: achenes, nuts, caryopsis and samaras.

Inflammation
A reaction to the invasion of microorganisms through the skin or through the epithelial layers of the respiratory, digestive, or urinary system; characterized by four signs: redness, swelling, heat, and pain.

Inflammatory response
The body's reaction to invading infectious microorganisms; includes an increase in blood þow to the affected area, the release of chemicals that draw white blood cells, an increased þow of plasma, and the arrival of monocytes to clean up the debris.

Inflorescence
(Related with flower) Flowers do not appear solitary in a stem. They are

generally arranged in a fixed pattern we call inflorescence. Flowers included in the inflorescence are called florets.

Influent
Affluent, or fluid entering a filter or filter system; opposite of effluent.

Informatics
The study of the application of computer and statistical techniques to the management of information.

Ingestion
The intake of water or food particles by "swallowing" them, taking them into the body cavity or into a vacuole.

Ingestive feeders
Animals that ingest food through mouth.

Ingroup
In a cladistic analysis, the set of taxa which are hypothesized to be more closely related to each other than any are to the out group.

Inheritance of acquired characteristics
Lamarck's view that features acquired during an organism's lifetime would be passed on to succeeding generations, leading to inheritable change in species over time.

Inhibition
The suppression of a colonizing population by another that is already established, especially during successional sequences.

Inhibitor
A molecule that "inhibits," or blocks, the biological action of another molecule.

Initiation
The first step in translation; occurs when a messenger RNA molecule, a

ribosomal subunit, and a transfer RNA molecule carrying the Þrst amino acid bind together to form a complex; begins at the start codon on mRNA.

Initiation codon (AUG)
Three-base sequence on the messenger RNA that codes for the amino acid methionine; the start command for protein synthesis.

Inlet air
Air drawn or injected into a system, typically into a fermentor or reactor. Inlet air generally requires a hydrophobic filter element to ensure sterility.

Inlet pressure
The pressure of a fluid at the feed port of a separations device.

Inorganic
Not containing carbon. Not from living things, e.g., minerals, water, oxygen, etc.

Insectivore
Used as a term of classification, this word denotes an insect-eating mammal of the Order Insectovira (such as the shrew). The word is more generally used of any insectivorous creature (such as the bat), a creature that eats mainly insects.

Insertion
A type of mutation in which a new DNA base is inserted into an existing sequence of DNA bases. This shifts the reference frame in protein synthesis, resulting (sometimes) in altered amino acid sequences.

Instinct
Inborn or innate behaviour.

Insulin
A hormone secreted by the pancreas that stimulates the uptake of glucose

by body cells. Insulin works antagonistically with glucagon to control blood sugar levels.

Integration
The process of combining incoming information; one of the functions of the nervous system.

Integrin
Adhesive protein of the extra cellular matrix in animals.

Integrity testing
The evaluation of the completeness of sealing on the filter medium, between affluent and effluent, and of the homogeneity of filter membrane pore size. Reveals internal leakage and/or oversize pores or torn membrane. Test protocols to evaluate integrity include: bubble point, diffusive flow, and water intrusion.

Integument
Something that covers or encloses, e.g., the skin.

Integumentary system
The skin and its derivatives (hair, nails, feathers, horns, antlers, and glands), which in multicellular animals protect against invading foreign microorganisms and prevent the loss or exchange of internal fluids.

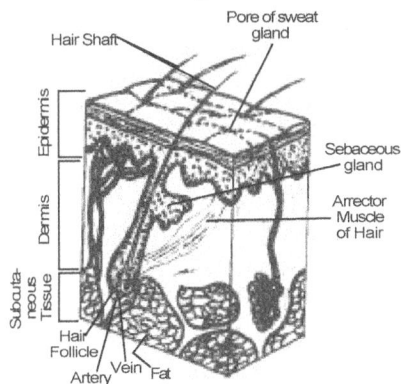

Interbedded
Describes beds (layers) of rock lying between or alternating with beds of a different kind of rock.

Interferons
Proteins released by cells in response to viral infection; activate the synthesis and secretion of antiviral proteins.

Intergrading
The merging of characteristics of two populations where their ranges come into contact.

Internal compass
The hypothesized mechanism that allows organisms to orient themselves so as to proceed in the proper direction during long-distance movements such as migration.

Internal environment
In multicellular organisms, the aqueous environment that is outside the cells but inside the body.

Interneurons
Neurons that process signals from one or more sensory neurons and relay signals to motor neurons. Aka connector neurons.

Internode
The region of a stem between two nodes, when there is no branching of the vascular tissue.

Interphase
The period between cell divisions when growth and replacement occur in preparation for the next division; consists of gap 1 (G1), synthesis (S), and gap 2 (G2).

Interstitial
Being situated within a particular organ or tissue.

Interstitial fluid
Fluid surrounding the cells in body tissues; provides a path through which nutrients, gases, and wastes can travel between the capillaries and the cells.

Interstitial skin
Skin between a snake's scales.

Intertidal
The coastal zone measuring from the lowest to the highest tide mark. The intertidal zone is subject to alternating periods of flooding and drying.

Intestine
The portion of the digestive tract between the stomach and anus; it is the region where most of the nutrients and absorbed.

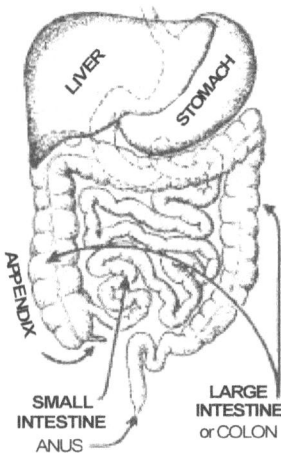

Intracellular digestion
A form of digestion in which food is taken into cells by phagocytosis; found in sponges and most protozoa and coelenterates.

Intracellular parasites
Viruses that enter a host cell and take over the host's cellular machinery to produce new viral particles.

Intracellular route
Path taken by water through the cells of the root between the epidermis and the xylem, moving through plasmodesmata.

Introduced species
A species that humans have placed into an ecosystem or community (either accidentally or intentionally) in which it does not naturally occur.

Intron
In eukaryotes, bases of a gene transcribed but later excised from the mRNA prior to exporting from the nucleus and subsequent translation of the message into a polypeptide.

Invasion
Sudden large movement of individuals into an area where they are generally uncommon, often on an unpredictable basis.

Inversion
A reversal in the order of genes on a chromosome segment.

Invertebrate
Animal without a backbone. Invertebrates make up over 90 percent of all animal species.

Ion
An atom that has lost or gained electrons from its outer shell and therefore has a positive or negative charge, respectively; symbolized by a superscript plus or minus sign and sometimes a number, e.g., H^+, Na^{+1}, Cl^{-2}.

Ionic bond
An ionic bond is a type of chemical bond formed through an electrostatic attraction between two oppositely charged ions. Ionic bonds are formed between a cation, which is usually a

metal, and an anion, which is usually a nonmetal. Pure ionic bonding cannot exist: all ionic compounds have some degree of covalent bonding. Thus, an ionic bond is considered a bond where the ionic character is greater than the covalent character. The larger the difference in electronegativity between the two atoms involved in the bond, the more ionic (polar) the bond is. Bonds with partially ionic and partially covalent character are called polar covalent bonds. Ionic bonding is a form of noncovalent bonding.

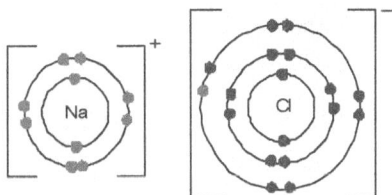

Ipm

IPM Integrated Pest Management-best coordinated used of biocontrol, time of spray.

Iris

(The iris family - iridaceae) it comprises about 1800 species of bulbous or rhizomatous plants which mainly grow in Africa, America and Mediterranean region. Because of their importance in floriculture, many of their members can be seen as cultivated species throughout the world.

Irruption

Sudden large movement of individuals into an area where they are generally uncommon, often on an unpredictable basis.

Island arc

A curved chain of islands that rise from the sea floor, usually near a continent. The convex side usually faces the open ocean, while the concave side usually faces the continent, e.g., the Aleutian Islands in Alaska; volcanic arc- syn.

Isoelectric point

The pH at which a protein carries no electric charge.

Isolating mechanism

An obstacle to interbreeding, either extrinsic, such as a geographical barrier, or intrinsic, such as structural or behavioural incompatibility.

Isomers

A pair of chemical compounds composed of the same atomic subunits, and with the same molecular weight, but with different chemical or physical properties, and a different arrangement of component atoms in space.

Isotonic

Term applied to two solutions with equal solute concentrations.

Isotope

A form of a chemical element that contains the same number of protons but a different number of neutrons than other forms of the element. Isotopes are often used to trace atoms or molecules in a metabolic pathway. In NMR, only one isotope of each element contains the correct magnetic properties to be useful.

Isotopic analysis

The study of the geochemistry of stable isotopes in naturally occurring sediments and biological structures. Stable isotopes are atomic variations of elements that are stable over long periods of time, meaning they do not radioactively decay. Several elements, like oxygen and carbon, have several stable forms. Oxygen, for example, occurs in nature as ^{16}O and ^{18}O — these two forms are isotopes. They have different numbers of neutrons (^{16}O has two more neutrons than ^{18}O), and is therefore heavier. Because the two isotopes have different masses, chemical and physical reactions like bonding, evaporation, and precipitation occur at different frequencies. The ratio of stable isotopes is preserved in chemical compounds like water, ice, and calcium carbonate and provides information on the environmental conditions at the time the compound formed. For example, the ratio of $^{18}O/^{16}O$ in an ice sample is linked to the water temperature of ancient oceans, which in turn reflects ancient climates.

J

Jaw
Often loosely applied to any movable, toothed structures at or near the mouth of an animal, such as the scolecodonts of annelids. In vertebrates, the jaw is derived from the first gill arch.

Jejunum
The second portion of the small intestine. Also, a popular month for weddings!

Jointed
When stiff body parts are connected by a soft flexible region, the body is said to be jointed.

Jurassic period
Middle period of the Mesozoic Era, between 185-135 million years ago. Characterized by the (possible) origin of angiosperms and the continued split of the worldwide supercontinent of Pangaea.

K

Karst

A type of topography formed by dissolution of rocks like limestone and gypsum that is characterized by sinkholes, caves, and subterranean passages.

Karyogamy

A process of fusion of the nuclei of two cells; the second step in syngamy.

Karyotype

The chromosomal characteristics of a cell; also, a representation of the chromosomes aligned in pairs.

Kelp forest

Marine ecosystem dominated by large kelps. These forests are restricted to cold and temperate waters, and are most common along the western coasts of continents.

Keratin

An sturdy, insoluble protein that is present in the feathers of birds, the scales of reptiles, and the hooves, hair, and nails of mammals.

Keratinocytes

The basic cell type of the epidermis; produced by basal cells in the inner layer of the epidermis.

Kettle lakes

Lakes formed as water fills a hole formerly occupied by a block of stranded ice.

Kidney stones

Crystallized deposits of excess wastes such as uric acid, calcium, and magnesium that may form in the kidney.

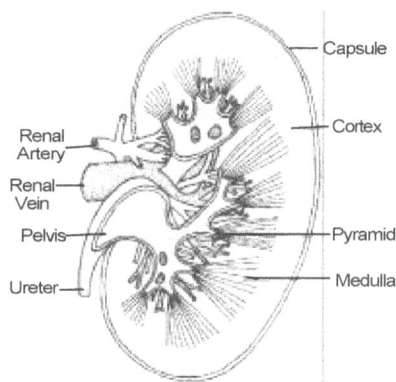

Kilocalorie

The energy needed to heat 1000 grams of water from 14.5 to 15.5 degrees C.

Kilodalton

A unit of mass equal to 1,000 daltons. A dalton is a unit used to measure the mass of atoms and molecules. One dalton equals the atomic weight of a hydrogen atom (1.66×10^{-24} grams).

Kinetochores

Structures at the centromeres of the chromosomes to which the Þbers of the mitotic spindle connect.

Kingdoms

Five broad taxonomic categories (Monera, Protista, Plantae, Fungi, Animalia) into which organisms are grouped, based on common characteristics.

Kleptoparasitism

A form of parasitism in which parasite steals items such as food or nest materials from other host individuals.

Klinefelter syndrome

In humans, a genetically determined condition in which the individual has two X and one Y chromosome. Affected individuals are male and typically tall and infertile.

Kreb's cycle

Biochemical cycle in cellular aerobic metabolism where acetyl CoA is

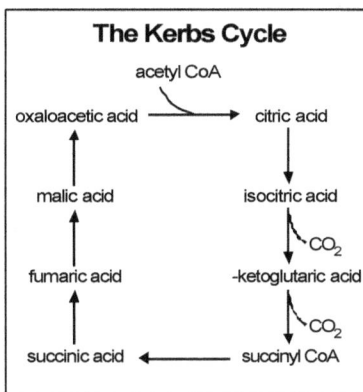

The Kerbs Cycle

acetyl CoA

oxaloacetic acid → citric acid

malic acid   isocitric acid

CO_2

fumaric acid   -ketoglutaric acid

CO_2

succinic acid ← succinyl CoA

combined with oxaloacetate to form citric acid; the resulting citric acid is converted into a number of other chemicals, eventually reforming oxaloacetate; NADH, some ATP, and $FADH_2$ are produced and carbon dioxide is released.

L

Labia majora
The outer folds of skin that cover and protect the genital region in women.

Labia minora
Thin membranous folds of skin outside the vaginal opening.

Lactose intolerance
A genetic trait characterized by the absence of the enzyme lactase, which breaks down lactose, the main sugar in milk and other dairy products.

Lamina
Any broad and flattened region of a plant or alga, which allows for increased photosynthetic surface area.

Laminarin
A beta-glucan polysaccharide produced by many chromists through photosynthesis.

Lanceolate
Type of leaf. Spear-shaped. Gradually extending at the base and lessening to the apex.

Langerhans' cells
Epidermal cells that participate in the inflammatory response by engulfing microorganisms and releasing chemicals that mobilize immune system cells.

Large intestine
Consists of the cecum, appendix, colon, and rectum; absorbs some nutrients, but mainly prepares feces for elimination.

Larva
Among invertebrates, an immature stage in the life cycle which usually is much smaller than, and morphologically different from, the adult. In insects with metamorphosis, the larva must become a pupa before reaching adulthood.

Larynx
A hollow structure at the beginning of the trachea. The vocal cords extend across the opening of the larynx.

Lateral roots
Roots extending away from the main (or taproot) root.

Latitudinal diversity gradient
The decrease in species richness that occurs as one moves away from the equator.

Latitudinal gradient
As latitude increases, a gradient of cooler, drier conditions occurs.

Laurasia
A supercontinent that existed from the Jurassic to Early Tertiary after splitting from Pangea; composed of Laurentia, Baltica, Avalonia, (modern North America, Scandinavia, Greenland, Western and Central Europe); eventually fragmented into Eurasia

and North America in the Tertiary with the opening of the North Atlantic Ocean.

Laurentia
A separate continental plate that existed from the Late Precambrian to Silurian, consisting of the major part of North America, northwest Ireland, Scotland, Greenland, and pieces of Norway and Russia.

Lava
Any molten material that is extrusive or volcanic, or the rock that forms from a molten extrusive.

Law of the minimum
Holds that population growth is limited by the resource in shortest supply.

L-dopa
A chemical related to dopamine that is used in the treatment of Parkinson's disease.

Leaf
An organ found in most vascular plants; it consists of a flat lamina (blade) and a petiole (stalk). Many flowering plants have additionally a pair of small stipules near the base of the petiole.

Leaf primordia
Young leaves, recently formed by the shoot apical meristem, located at the tip of a shoot.

Leaf trace
The strand of vascular tissue which connects the leaf veins to the central vascular system of the stem.

Leaf veins
Vascular tissue in leaves, arranged in a net-like network (reticulate vennation) in dicots, and running parallel (parallel vennation) to each other in monocots.

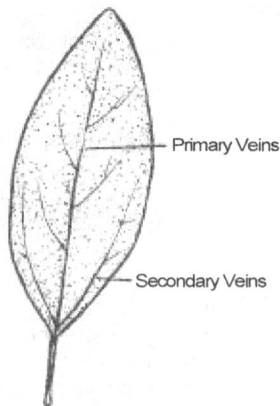

Primary Veins

Secondary Veins

Leaflet
(Part of a leaf) Each one of the fragments, similar to a leaf, a compound leaf is made of.

Leaves
The site of photosynthesis; one of the three major organs in plants.

Leukocytes
White blood cells; primarily engaged in fighting infection.

Librigenae
The "free cheeks"; separate, detachable portions of the trilobite cephalon.

Lichens
Autotrophic organisms composed of a fungus (sac or club fungus) and a photosynthetic unicellular organism (e.g., a cyanobacterium or alga) in a symbiotic relationship; are resistant to extremes of cold and drought and can grow in marginal areas such as Arctic tundra.

Life history
The age at sexual maturity, age at death, and age at other events in an individual's lifetime that inþuence reproductive traits.

Ligaments
Dense parallel bundles of connective tissue that strengthen joints and hold the bones in place.

Light reactions
The photosynthetic process in which solar energy is harvested and transferred into the chemical bonds of ATP; can occur only in light.

Ligneous
Type of stem ligneous stems have developed rigid, stiffened structures, what we normally know as "wood".

Lignin
A polymer in the secondary cell wall of woody plant cells that helps to strengthen and stiffen the wall; related term lignified.

Ligule
Related with flower. Each one of the exterior flowers of a head , similar to a tongue.

Limestone
A carbonate sedimentary rock composed of more than 50 percent of the mineral calcium carbonate ($CaCO_3$).

Limnology
The study of river system ecology and life.

Limy
Describes sediments, soils, or rocks that contain a significant amount of lime (calcium oxide, CaO).

Lineage
Any continuous line of descent; any series of organisms connected by reproduction by parent of offspring.

Linear
Type of leaf. Strip-shaped leaf. Several times longer than wide. Not pointed at the apex like in the acicular type.

Linkage
The condition in which the inheritance of a specific chromosome is coupled with that of a given gene. The genes stay together during meiosis and end up in the same gamete.

Lip
Part of the corolla. Each one of the lobes dividing the petals.

Lipases
Enzymes secreted by the pancreas that are active in the digestion of fats.

Lipids
One of the four classes of organic macromolecules. Lipids function in the long-term storage of biochemical energy, insulation, structure and control. Examples of lipids include the fats, waxes, oils and steroids (e.g. testosterone, cholesterol).

Lithosphere
The solid outer layer of the Earth; includes both the land area and the land beneath the oceans and other water bodies.

Litter
Leaf litter, or forest litter, is the detritus of fallen leaves and bark which accumulate in forests.

Littoral
A shallow-water habitat found immediately along the coasts or edges of lakes and oceans.

Live-bearing
Of an animal that gives birth to nonates, rather than lays eggs.

Loafing platform
A nest-like structure built by coots and waterfowl where young can rest out of the water.

Lobe-finned
Fish with muscular fins containing large jointed bones that attach to the body; one of the two main types of bony fish.

Lobulate
(Type of leaf) lobulate leaves have lobules. divisions that do not arrive the centre of half blade.

Loess
A widespread, loose deposit consisting mainly of silt; most loess deposits formed during the Pleistocene as an accumulation of wind-blown dust carried from deserts, alluvial plains, or glacial deposits.

Logistic growth model
A model of population growth in which the population initially grows at an exponential rate until it is limited by some factor; then, the population enters a slower growth phase and eventually stabilizes.

Long-day plants
Plants that flower in the summer when nights are short and days are long; e.g., spinach and wheat.

Loop of Henle
A U-shaped loop between the proximal and distal tubules in the kidney.

Lophophore
Complex ring of hollow tentacles used as a feeding organ. The tentacles are covered by cilia, which generate a current to bring food particles into the mouth. The structure is only found in the brachiopods, phoronids, and bryozoans.

Lores
The area between the eyes and the base of the bill.

Lorica
A vase-shaped or cup-shaped outer covering. Found in many protists, including some flagellates, ciliates, chrysophytes, and choanoflagellates, as well as in some animal cells.

Lowland
Large area of relatively low relief, usually applied to coastal regions that do not rise high above sea level.

Luciferase
Enzyme which activates luciferin to produce bioluminescence.

Luciferin
Compound whose activated form emits light.

Lumen
The inner, open space of a hollow fibre.

Lungfish
A type of lobe-finned fish that breathe by a modified swim bladder (or lung) as well as by gills.

Lungs
Sac-like structures of varying complexity where blood and air

exchange oxygen and carbon dioxide; connected to the outside by a series of tubes and a small opening. In humans, the lungs are situated in the thoracic cavity and consist of the internal airways, the alveoli, the pulmonary circulatory vessels, and elastic connective tissues.

Luteal phase
The second half of the ovarian cycle when the corpus luteum is formed; occurs after ovulation.

Luteinizing hormone (LH)
A hormone secreted by the anterior pituitary gland that stimulates the secretion of testosterone in men and estrogen in women.

Lymph
Interstitial fluid in the lymphatic system.

Lymph hearts
Contractile enlargements of vessels that pump lymph back into the veins; found in fish, amphibians, and reptiles.

Lymphatic circulation
A secondary circulatory system that collects buids from between the cells and returns it to the main circulatory system; the circulation of the lymphatic system, which is part of the immune system.

Lymphatic system
The tissues and organs, including the bone marrow, spleen, thymus, and lymph nodes, that produce and store cells that fight infection.

Lymphocytes
White blood cells that arise in the bone marrow and mediate the immune response; include T cells and B cells.

Lyon hypothesis
Idea proposed by Mary Lyon that mammalian females inactivate one or the other X-chromosome during early embryogenesis. This deactivated chromosome forms the Barr body.

Lysosomes
Membrane-enclosed organelles containing digestive enzymes. The lysosomes fuse with food vacuoles and enzymes contained within the lysosome chemically breakdown and/or digest the food vacuole's contents.

M

Macroevolution

The combination of events associated with the origin, diversification, extinction, and interactions of organisms which produced the species that currently inhabit the Earth. Large scale evolutionary change such as the evolution of new species (or even higher taxa) and extinction of species.

Macromolecules

Large molecules made up of many small organic molecules that are often referred to as monomers; e.g., carbohydrates, lipids, proteins, and nucleic acids. Macromolecules are polymers of monomers.

Macronucleus

In ciliates, the large nucleus that carries up to several hundred copies of the genome and controls metabolism and asexual reproduction.

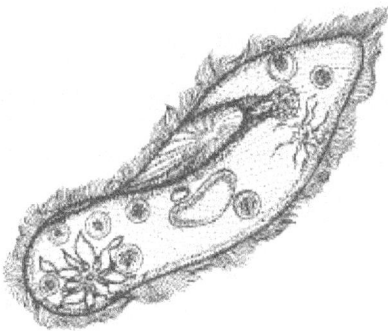

Macronutrients

1. Elements needed by plants in relatively large (primary) or smaller (secondary) quantities.
2. Foods needed by animals daily or on a fairly regular basis.

Macrophages

A type of white blood cell derived from monocytes that engulf invading antigenic molecules, viruses, and microorganisms and then display fragments of the antigen to activate helper T cells; ultimately stimulating the production of antibodies against the antigen.

Macroscopic

Objects or organisms that are large enough to be seen with the naked eye.

Macrovoid

A generally undesirable open space in the substructure of a membrane filter that is appreciably larger than the average pore size. Macrovoids can lead to pinhole defects resulting in unwanted passage that directly impacts final product yield. Macrovoids can also impact the overall membrane strength and thus the device's ability to maintain integrity under pressure.

Mafic

Term used to describe the amount of dark-coloured iron and magnesium minerals in an igneous rock.

Magma

Molten rock generated within the Earth; forms intrusive (solidifies below the surface) and extrusive (solidifies above the surface) igneous rocks.

Magnoliid

Any member of the basal assemblage of flowering plants.

Male

In organisms with separate sexes, the one which produces sperm.

Malleus

One of the bones comprising the middle ear of mammals.

Mallow

The mallow family -malvaceae. comprises about 1000 species of plants. They are mainly herbs or little shrubs. Some of them are very important in gardening, such as genera malva or hibiscus. Many are important as medicinal flowers.

Malpighian tubules

The excretory organs of insects; a set of long tubules that open into the gut.

Mammalia

Mammals, as a group of animals, belong to the Class Mammalia. The Class Mammalia, in turn, belongs to the larger group known as the vertebrates (animals with backbones; also called the Phylum Chordata).

Mammal-like reptiles

Group of Permian-Triassic reptiles having some possible mammalian features, notably a more prominent dentary (tooth-bearing) bone and reduction of the incus and malleus (which are part of the reptilian jaw along with the dentary). The mammal-like reptiles are thought to have been the reptile group from which the mammals later evolved.

Mammilla

In eggshell, the cone-like structure at the base of the shell unit where the shell unit attaches to the inner organic membrane.

Mandible

The lower portion of a bird's bill, also referred to as the lower mandible.

Mannoxylic

Wood in which there is a great deal of parenchyma tissue among the xylem is called mannoxylic. Cycads and pteridosperms have mannoxylic wood.

Mantle

In mollusks, a membranous or muscular structure that surrounds the visceral mass and secretes a shell if one is present.

Mare

A female horse, more than four years old.

Margin or edge

(Part of the leaf) the margin is the rim or final limit of the blade

Marine

pertains to sea or ocean, saltwater. Marine bacteria are found in oceans.

Marine biome

The aquatic biome consisting of waters containing 3.5% salt on average; includes the oceans and covers more than 70% of the Earth's surface; divided into benthic and pelagic zones.

Marine terrace

A platform of marine deposits (typically sand, silt, gravel) sloping gently seaward. Such a platform may be exposed along the coast, forming cliffs, due to uplift and/or the lowering of sea level, e.g., marine terraces of coastal Southern California.

Marl

A loose, crumbly deposit consisting of clay and calcium carbonate and formed in marine or freshwater conditions.

Marsh

Tract of low wetlands often home of reeds or sedges; may be salt or fresh water.

Marsupials

Pouched mammals. The young develop internally, but are born while in an embryonic state and remain in a pouch on the mother's abdomen until development is complete; this group includes kangaroos, koalas, and opossums. One of the three reproductive "strategies" of living mammals g-laying and placental bcing the other two), marsupials finish development in a pouch or under hairy coverings attached to the mother.

Mass extinction

A time during which extinction rates are generally accelerated so that more than 50% of all species then living become extinct; results in a marked decrease in the diversity of organisms. Mass extinctions are thought to have occurred numerous times in Earth history, often from a variety of reasons: impacts, tectonism, changes in primary productivity of the seas, etc.

Mast

Nuts, large fruits, and other plant material that accumulates on the forest floor.

Mast cells

Cells that synthesize and release histamine, as during an allergic response; found most often in connective tissue surrounding blood vessels.

Mastigoneme

Small hair-like filaments found on the "hairy" flagellum of the Chromista.

Matter

Anything that has mass and occupies space.

Matter cycling

The flow of matter through various organisms and the physical environment of an ecosystem.

Maxilla

The upper part of a bird's bill, also referred to as the upper mandible.

Maximum differential pressure

Value of the greatest differential pressure a filter can withstand without collapse or failure.

Maximum operating pressure

Value of the greatest allowable pressure in a system, generally lower than the maximum pressure of any of the components, as a safety factor.

Maximum sustainable yield (MSY)

The maximum number of a food or game population that can be harvested without harming the population's ability to grow back.

Media exchange

A filtration step used to exchange one type of media for an alternative type of media during an aseptic cell culture separation.

Medical device

A diagnostic or therapeutic article that does not work by chemical action.

Medium

A mixture used for growing organism. Milk is a good medium for Lactobacilli.

Medulla

1. A term referring to the central portion of certain organs; e.g., the medulla oblongata of the brain and the adrenal medulla, which synthesizes epinephrine and norepinephrine.
2. In more common usage, the area in the brain that regulates breathing, heartbeat, blood pressure and similar activities.

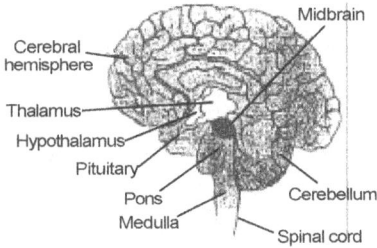

Medulla oblongata

The region of the brain that, with the pons, makes up the hindbrain; controls heart rate, constriction and dilation of blood vessels, respiration, and digestion.

Medusa

A stage in the life cycle of a coelenterate in which it is free-swimming.

Megahertz

A unit of measurement equal to 1,000,000 hertz. A hertz is defined as one event or cycle per second and is used to measure the frequency of radio waves and other forms of electromagnetic radiation. The strength of NMR magnets is often reported in megahertz, with most NMR magnets ranging from 500 to 900 megahertz.

Megakarocytes

Cells found in the bone marrow that produce platelets.

Megaspore

Four haploid cells produced by meiosis in the ovule of a power. Usually, three of these cells degenerate, with the remaining cell becoming the female gametophyte phase of the plant's life cycle. Large (palynologists consider the megaspores to generally be above 200 micrometers in diameter) spores that develop into the megagametophyte, which in turn produces eggs.

Megaspore mother cell

Cells that undergo meiosis to produce megaspores.

Meguma

A terrane or microcontinent that formed in the Cambrian as part of the continental shelf of Gondwana, rifted apart in the Ordovician, and collided with the Laurentia in the Devonian; it forms the southern part of mainland Nova Scotia (Meguma Zone), separated from the Avalon Zone by a large fault that runs from Cobequid Bay to Chedabucto Bay.

Meiosis

A two-stage type of cell division in sexually reproducing organisms. In meiosis, a diploid cell divides to produce four haploid cells, each with half the original chromosome content. For this reason, meiosis is often called a "reduction division". In organisms with a diploid life cycles, the products of meiosis are usually called gametes. In organisms with an alternation of generations, the products of meiosis are caled spores.

Meissner's corpuscles
Sensory receptors concentrated in the epidermis of the fingers and lips that make these areas very sensitive to touch.

Melange
A body of rocks consisting of large blocks (mappable size) of different rocks jumbled together with little continuity of contacts.

Melanin
A pigment that gives the skin colour and protects the underlying layers against damage by ultraviolet light; produced by melanocytes in the inner layer of the epidermis.

Melanism
An increase in the average amount of black or nearly black pigmentation in an organism or group of organisms, resulting from the presence of melanin.

Melanocytes
The cells in the inner layer of the epidermis that produce melanin.

Membrane
A thin layer of a highly engineered material with controlled pore size used to separate particulates, biological matter, and molecules from a solution.

Membrane recovery
The degree to which the original performance of a membrane can be restored by cleaning.

Membrane-attack complex (MAC)
A large cylindrical multiprotein complex formed by the complement system; kills invading microorganisms by embedding in their plasma membrane, creating a pore through which þuid þows, ultimately causing the cell to burst.

Mendelian trait
A trait that is regulated by a single locus and shows a simple Mendelian inheritance pattern.

Menstrual cycle
The recurring secretion of hormones and associated uterine tissue changes; typically 28 days in length.

Menstruation
The process in which the uterine endometrium breaks down and sheds cells, resulting in bleeding; occurs approximately once a month. The first day marks the beginning of the menstrual and ovarian cycles.

Meristem
Group of undifferentiated cells from which new tissues are produced. Most plants have apical meristems which give rise to the primary tissues of plants, and some have secondary meristems which add wood or bark.

Meristematic tissue
Embryonic tissue located at the tips of stems and roots and occasionally along their entire length; can divide to produce new cells; one of the four main tissue systems in plants.

Merophytes
Group of cells which have all been produced from the same initial cell. Leaves and stems in particular are often built from specific patterns of merophytes.

Mesentary
Epithelial cells supporting the digestive organs.

Mesocarp
(Part of the fruit) It is the middle covering of the pericarp. In a peach, for example, what we ordinary call the "flesh".

Mesoderm

The middle layer of cells in embryonic development; gives rise to muscles, bones, and structures associated with reproduction. The middle embryonic tissue layer. Cells and structures arising from the mesoderm include the bone, blood, muscle, skin, and reproductive organs.

Mesoglea

A gel-like matrix that occurs between the outer and inner epithelial layers in cnidarians.

Mesogloea

Jellylike material between the outer ectoderm and the inner endoderm of cnidarians. May be very thin or may form a thick layer (as in many jellyfish).

Mesokaryotic

Nuclear condition unique to the dinoflagellates in which the chromosomes remain permanently condensed.

Mesophyll

Layer of leaf tissue between the epidermis layers; literally meaning "middle of the leaf".

Mesophytic leaves

The leaves of plants that grow under moderately humid conditions with abundant soil and water.

Mesozoic era

The period of geologic time beginning 245 million years ago and ending 65 million years ago; the age of the dinosaurs and cycads, the Mesozoic falls between the Paleozoic and Cenozoic Eras and includes the Triassic, Jurassic, and Cretaceous Periods.

Messenger RNA (MRNA)

"Blueprint" for protein synthesis that is transcribed from one strand of the DNA (gene) and which is translated at the ribosome into a polypeptide sequence.

Metabolic pathway

A series of individual chemical reactions in a living system that combine to perform one or more important functions. The product of one reaction in a pathway serves as the substrate for the following reaction.

Metabolism

The chemical processes within an organic body that supply the energy necessary for life. The rate of metabolic processes is sometimes used as a way to differentiate organisms. For example, mammals generally have a higher metabolism than reptiles and can thus sustain higher levels of activity for longer periods of time.

Metamorphic rock

Any rock derived from other rocks by chemical, mineralogical and structural changes resulting from pressure, temperature or shearing stress.

Metamorphism

The process of altering the chemical or mineralogical composition of a rock through different amounts of heat and pressure below the surface of the Earth.

Metamorphosis

A process of developmental change whereby a larva reaches adulthood only after a drastic change in morphology; occurs in most amphibians and insects, for some insects, this change may include another stage (pupa) before the adult stage.

Metaphase

The stage of eukaryotic cell division (mitosis or meiosis) in which the chromosomes line up at the equator of the cell.

Metastasis
The spread of cancer from one part of the body to another. Cells in the metastatic (secondary) tumour are like those in the original (primary) tumour.

Methanogens
A group of archaebacteria that produce methane as a by product of their metabolism.

Methionine
The amino acid coded for by the initiation codon; all polypeptides begin with methionine, although post-translational reactions may remove it.

Micelles
Structures formed when bile salts surround digested fats in order to enable the water-insoluble fats to be absorbed by the epithelial cells lining the small intestine.

Microbiology
Microbiology is the study of microbes, all small organisms which require using a microscope to see. Microbiology includes bacteriology, protozoology, mycology (fungi), zymology (yeasts).

Microevolution
A small-scale evolutionary event such as the formation of a species from a preexisting one or the divergence of reproductively isolated populations into new species.

Microfilaments
Rods composed of actin that are found in the cytoskeleton and are involved in cell division and movement.

Microfiltration
The process of removing particles from a liquid by passing it through a porous membrane under pressure. Microfiltration usually refers to removing submicron-size particles.

Microfossil
A very small fossil, best studied with the aid of a microscope, e.g. foraminifera, radiolarians, and small vertebrate fossils such as teeth.

Microgametophyte
Stage of the plant life cycle that develops from or within a microspore. The microgametophyte produces sperm in specialized structures known as antheridia.

Microhabitat
The elements of a habitat that are used by an individual during its daily activities. Refers to a subset of conditions within a wider scope of habitat characteristics.

Micron (micrometer, im)
One one-millionth of one metre. The average human eye can discern particles down to ~40 im.

Micronucleus
In the protistan group known as the ciliates, the small nucleus containing a single copy of the genome that is used for sexual reproduction.

Micronutrients
Elements that are required by plants in very small quantities, but are toxic in large quantities: iron, manganese, molybdenum, copper, boron, zinc, and chloride.

Microphyll
A kind of leaf, specifically one which has a single, unbranched vein in it. Microphylls are only found in the lycophytes.

Microporous membrane

A thin, porous film or hollow fibre having pores ranging from 0.1 to 10 im. Cross flow microfilters typically range from 0.1 to 1 im.

Micropyle

(Part of the seed) It is a litle pore on the seed coat , through whom, apart from entering the sperm, the seed absorbs water to begin germination.

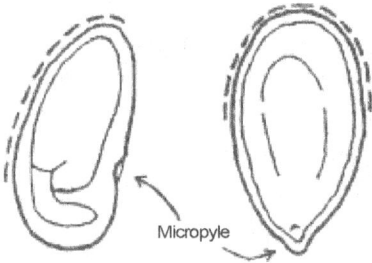

Micropyle

Microscopic

Objects or organisms that are too small to be seen with the naked eye.

Microsporangia

Structures of the sporophyte in which microspores are produced by meiosis. In flowering plants the microsporangia are known as anther sacs.

Microspore

Four haploid cells produced by the meiotic division in the pollen sacs of þowers or microsporangia of gymnosperms. Microspores undergo mitotic division and become encased in a thick protective wall to form pollen grains. Small, size usually less than 200 micrometers, spores produced by meiosis. Microspores either germinate into the male gametophyte or have the male gametophyte develop inside the microspore wall.

Microspore mother cell

Cells in the microsporangium that undergo meiosis to produce microspores. In flowering plants the microspore is known as the pollen grain, and contains a three-celled male.

Microstructure

In eggshell, the shape, size, orientation, and distribution of components of the shell.

Microtubules

Type of filament in eukaryotic cells composed of units of the protein tubulin. Among other functions, it is the primary structural component of the eukaryotic flagellum.

Microvilli

Thin fingerlike protrusions from the surface of a cell, often used to increase absorptive capacity or to trap food particles. The "collar" of choanoflagellates is actually composed of closely spaced microvilli.

Midbrain

A network of neurons that connects with the forebrain and relays sensory signals to other integrating centres.

Middle lamella

A layer composed of pectin that cements two adjoining plant cells together.

Mid-oceanic ridges

Elongated rises on the ocean floor where basalt periodically erupts, forming new oceanic crust; similar to continental rift zones.

Midrib

The central vein of a leaf.

Migration

Movement of organisms either permanently (as in the migration of humans to the Americas) or temporarily (migratory birds such as Canadian geese).

Migratory overshooting

A phenomenon in which migratory animals move along the correct route but travel beyond the normal distance and thus over-shoot their destination.

Mimic

To copy the sound, colour, odor, or other characteristic of an object or organism.

Mineralization

The process of replacing any organism's original material with a mineral.

Mineralocorticoids

A group of steroid hormones produced by the adrenal cortex that are important in maintaining electrolyte balance.

Minerals

Trace elements required for normal metabolism, as components of cells and tissues, and in nerve conduction and muscle contraction.

Minimum process volume

The least amount of fluid able to be handled effectively by a filtration system.

Minimum viable population (MVP)

The smallest population size that can avoid extinction due to breeding problems or random environmental buctuations.

Mirror-image orientation

A migratory phenomenon in which individuals seem to reverse the east-west orientation of their migration route.

Mites

Microscopic 8-legged roundish hairy arthopods eat dead organic matter, living plants, living animals.

Mitochondria

Self-replicating membrane-bound cytoplasmic organelles in most eukaryotic cells that complete the breakdown of glucose, producing NADH and ATP (singular term: mitochondrion). The powerhouse of the cell. Organelles within eukaryotes that generate (by chemiosmosis) most of the ATP the cell needs to function and stay alive.

Mitochondrial dna study

A study of the origins and relationships among species and other taxa that examines the mitocondrial DNA of the organisms to establish genetic similarities and differences and in turn establish phylogenetic relationships based on genetic evidence.

Mitochondrion

Complex organelle found in most eukaryotes; believed to be descended from free-living bacteria that established a symbiotic relationship with a primitive eukaryote. Mitochondria are the site of most of the energy production in most eukaryotes; they require oxygen to function.

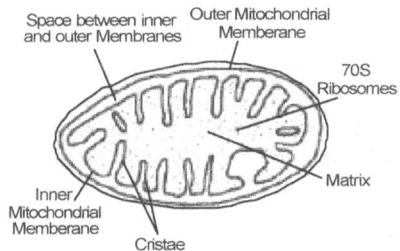

Space between inner and outer Membranes — Outer Mitochondrial Memberane — 70S Ribosomes — Matrix — Inner Mitochondrial Memberane — Cristae

Mitosis

The division of the cell's nucleus and nuclear material of a cell; consists of four stages: prophase, metaphase, anaphase, and telophase. Cell xeroxing. Mitosis occurs only in eukaryotes. The DNA of the cell is replicated during interphase of the cell cycle and then segregated during the four phases of mitosis.

Mitotic spindle

A network of microtubules formed during prophase. Some microtubules attach to the centromeres of the chromosomes and help draw the chromosomes apart during anaphase.

Mobbing

A form of behaviour in some birds in which a group of birds harass a predator or other intruding animal in order to force that animal to leave the area.

Mold

Type of fossil preservation where the original material of the fossil has decayed but has left an impression in the surrounding sediments. Molds are often filled with a different material, producing strikingly beautiful fossils.

Mole

Avogadro's number (6.02 X 10^{23} atoms) of a substance.

Molecular biology

the branch of biology concerned with the structure and development of biological systems in terms of the biochemistry of their molecular components. Molecular biology overlaps a wide variety of other disciplines in use of molecular techniques e.g. PCR, RFLP analysis, etc.

Molecular weight

Mass of one molecule of a nonionic substance in atomic mass units.

Molecular weight cutoff,

The size designation in Daltons (Da) for ultrafiltration membranes. Typically measured as the molecular weight of a globular protein that is 90% retained by the membrane. No industry standard exists; hence the MWCO ratings of different manufacturers are not always comparable.

Molecule

The smallest unit of matter that retains all of the physical and chemical properties of that substance. It consists of one or more identical atoms or a group of different atoms bonded together.

Molt

To shed hair, feathers, shell, or skin such that it can then be renewed and replaced with a new coat, plumage, shell, or skin.

Molt migration

An annual migration pattern in birds in which individuals move from the breeding ground to a temporary location where they molt and then migrate again to a wintering range. Occurs in ducks and some passerines.

Monera

Prokaryotic kingdom that includes (in the most widely accepted classification system) archaebacteria, eubacteria, and cyanobacteria. Members of this kingdom were among the first forms of life over 3.5 billion years ago.

Monocots

One of the two major types of þowering plants; characterized by having a single cotyledon, þoral organs arranged in threesd or multiples of three, and parallel-veined leaves; include grasses, cattails, lilies, and palm trees. One of the two major groups in the Angiosperms, monocots are characterized by having a single seed leaf (cotyledon), flower parts in 3's or multiples of 3, monoaperturate pollen (although some dicots also have this feature), parallel veins in their leaves, and scattered vascular bundles in their stems.

Monocotyledon or monocot

(Type of plant according to the cotyledons) Plants with one cotyledon. In this group we find so important plants as cereals, palms, lilies, tulips or orchids.

Monoculture

The growth of only one species in a given area; such as a cornfield or other agricultural field.

Monocytes

White blood cells that clean up dead viruses, bacteria, and fungi and dispose of dead cells and debris at the end of the inþammatory response.

Monogamy

A pair relationship in which a single male and a single female establish an exclusive bond during a reproductive cycle.

Monohybrid cross

In genetics, a cross that involves only one characteristic.

Monomer

An organic chemical unit linked to other units (usually by a covalent bond formed by the removal of water) to produce a larger molecule (macromolecule) known as a polymer.

Monophyletic

Term applied to a group of organisms which includes the most recent common ancestor of all of its members and all of the descendants of that most recent common ancestor. A monophyletic group is called a clade.

Monophyletic group

A group of organisms descended from a common ancestor. For example: your immediate family may be considered such a group, being descended from a common ancestral group (grandparents, etc.).

Monosaccharides

Simple carbohydrates, usually with a five- or six-carbon skeleton; e.g., glucose and fructose. A carbohydrate composed of a single sugar unit, such as glucose, ribose, deoxyribose, etc.

Monotreme

A mammal that lays eggs rather than giving live birth. Though laying eggs is a primitive reptilian trait, monotremes share many morphological, physiological, and reproductive characteristics with other mammals, making them true mammals. Extant monotremes include the duck-billed platypus and echidna.

Monsoon

A seasonal weather pattern where winds, and often rain, come consistently from one direction for many months. It is caused by the temperature differences between land and ocean, and in general, a larger landmass makes a greater difference, which makes a more extreme monsoon.

Monsoonal

Describes a climate pattern with a wind system that changes direction with the seasons; this pattern is dominant over the Arabian Sea and Southeast Asia.

Moraine

A mound or ridge of sediment deposited by a glacier; lateral moraine- n. deposited to the side of a glacier; terminal moraine- n. deposited to the front of a glacier; ground moraine- n. deposited on the land surface.

Morph
A distinct type or variant of an individual in which it differs in its physical attributes from other types or variants.

Morphological convergence
The evolution of basically dissimilar structures to serve a common function. For example: the wings of birds and insects.

Morphology
The form and structure of anything, usually applied to the shapes, parts, and arrangement of features in living and fossil organisms.

Morphotype
An individual or set of organisms within a population distinguished by having a distinct physical structure.

Morula
The solid-ball stage of the pre-emplantation embryo.

Mosaic evolution
A pattern of evolution where all features of an organism do not evolve at the same rate. Some characteristics are retained from the ancestral condition while others are more recently evolved.

Motile
Able to move oneself about, capable of self-locomotion.

Motor (efferent) pathways
The portion of the peripheral nervous system that carries signals from the central nervous system to the muscles and glands.

Motor neurons
Neurons that receive signals from interneurons and transfer the signals to effector cells that produce a response. Nerve cells connected to a muscle or gland. Sometimes also known as effector neurons.

Motor output
A response to the stimuli received by the nervous system. A signal is transmitted to organs that can convert the signals into action, such as movement or a change in heart rate.

Motor units
Consist of a motor neuron with a group of muscle fibres; form the units into which skeletal muscles are organized; enable muscles to contract on a graded basis.

Mouth
Front opening of the digestive tract, into which food is taken for digestion. In flatworms, the mouth is the only opening into the digestive cavity, and is located on the "belly" of the worm.

Mouthparts
Appendages located close to the mouth of some animals that function in the manipulating of food.

MTOC
(Microtubule Organizing Centre) MTOCs are bundles of protein tubes which may be found at the base of a eukaryotic flagellum. In animals, they also function in creating the arrays of microtubules that pull the chromosomes apart during mitosis.

Mucus
A thick, lubricating fluid produced by the mucous membranes that line the respiratory, digestive, urinary, and reproductive tracts; serves as a barrier against infection and, in the digestive

tract, moistens food, making it easier to swallow.

Multicellular
Organisms composed of multiple cells and exhibiting some division of labor and specialization of cell structure and function.

Multi-dimensional NMR
A technique used to solve complex NMR problems.

Multinucleate
Cells having more than one nucleus per cell.

Multi-wavelength anomalous diffraction (MAD)
A technique used in X-ray crystallography that accelerates the determination of protein structures. It uses X-rays of different wavelengths, relieving crystallographers from having to make several different metal-containing crystals.

Muscle
Bundle of contractile cells which allow animals to move. Muscles must act against a skeleton to effect movement.

Muscle fibres
Long, multinucleated cells found in skeletal muscles; made up of myofibrils. One of the four major groups of vertebrate cell/tissue types. Muscle cells contract/relax, allowing movement of and/or within the animal.

Muscular system
One of eleven major body organ systems in animals; allows movement and locomotion, powers the circulatory, digestive, and respiratory systems, and plays a role in regulating temperature.

Muskeg
A habitat type common in the northern boreal forest that comprises poorly drained wetlands and scattered trees.

Mutation
Any heritable change in the nucleotide sequence of DNA; can involve substitutions, insertions, or deletions of one or more nucleotides.

Mutation rate
The average occurrence of mutations in a species per a given unit of time.

Mutualism
A form of symbiosis in which both species benefit. A type of symbiosis where both organisms benefit. The classic example is lichens, which is a symbiosis between an alga and a fungus. The alga provides food and the fungus provides water and nutrients.

Mycelium
The mass of interwoven filaments of hyphae in a fungus.

Mycorrhiza
Occurs when a fungus (basidiomycete or zygomycete) weaves around or into a plant's roots and forms a symbiotic relationship. Fungal hyphae absorb minerals from the soil and pass them on to the plant roots while the fungus obtains carbohydrates from the plant (pl.: mycorrhizae).

Myelin sheath
Layers of specialized glial cells, called Schwann cells, that coat the axons of many neurons.

Myofibrils
Striated contractile microfilaments in skeletal muscle cells.

Myosin

Thick protein filaments in the centre sections of sarcomeres.

Myotome

Segment of the body formed by a region of muscle. The myotomes are an important feature for recognizing early chordates.

Mysticetes

A group of cetaceans that includes the filter-feeding whales such as Right whales, the gray whale and rorquals.

N

Nanometer
A unit of measure; one millionth (10^{-9}) of a metre.

Nares
Nostrils; the openings in the nose through which air enters.

Nastic movement
A plant's response to a stimulus in which the direction of the response is independent of the direction of the stimulus. Non-directional plant movements.

Natural selection
The process of differential survival and reproduction of Þtter genotypes; can be stabilizing, directional, or disruptive. Better adapted individuals are more likely to survive to reproductive age and thus leave more offspring and make a larger contribution to the gene pool than do less Þt individuals. The differential survival and reproductive successes of individuals in a variable population that powers the evolutionary process. When all individuals survive and reproduce (except for chance occurrences) natural selection works at a lower rate, if at all.

Nearctic
Relating to the biogeographic subregion that includes Greenland and North America north of tropical Mexico.

Nectaries
Nectar-secreting organs in þowering plants that serve as insect feeding stations and thus attract insects, which then assist in the transfer of pollen.

Negative feedback
The stopping of the synthesis of an enzyme by the accumulation of the products of the enzyme-mediated reaction.

Negative feedback control
Occurs when information produced by the feedback reverses the direction of the response; regulates the secretion of most hormones.

Negative feedback loop
A biochemical pathway where the products of the reaction inhibit production of the enzyme that controlled their formation.

Nektonic organisms
"Swimmers"; one of the two main types of organisms in the pelagic zone of the marine biome.

Nematocyst
A specialized stinging cell in coelenterates; contains a hair like structure that can be ejected.

Neonate
Newborn snake or lizard when it is the product of a live birth.

Neotropics

The biogeographic region that includes southern Mexico and Central America, the Caribbean, and South America.

Nephridium

An excretory organ consisting of an open bulb and a tubule leading to the exterior; found in many invertebrates, such as segmented worms.

Nephron

A tubular structure that is the filtering unit of the kidney; consists of a glomerulus and renal tubule.

Neritic

Relating to the portion of the ocean composed of the shallow waters over the continental shelf.

Nerve cord

Primary bundle of nerves in chordates, which connects the brain to the major muscles and organs of the body.

Nerve net

An interconnected mesh of neurons that sends signals in all directions; found in radially symmetrical marine invertebrates, such as jellyfish and sea anemones, that have no head region or brain.

Nerve(s)

Bundles of neuronal processes enclosed in connective tissue that carry signals to and from the central nervous system.

Nervous system

One of eleven major body organ systems in animals; coordinates and controls actions of internal organs and body systems, receives and processes sensory information from the external environment, and coordinates short-term reactions to these stimuli.

Nest parasitism

Reproduction by laying eggs in the nests of other birds, leaving the nest owners to provide prenatal care. May be interspecific (eggs laid in the nests of other species) or intraspecific (eggs laid in nests of the same species).

Net primary productivity (NPP)

The rate at which producer (usually plants) biomass is created in a community.

Net secondary productivity (NSP)

The rate at which consumer and decomposer biomass is produced in a community.

Neural tube

A tube of ectoderm in the embryo that will form the spinal cord.

Neurobiology

The branch of biology concerned with the structure and function of cells of the nervous system.

Neuromuscular junction

The point where a motor neuron attaches to a muscle cell.

Neurons

Highly specialized cells that generate and transmit bioelectric impulses from one part of the body to another; the functional unit of the nervous system. A cell of the nerve tissue having a cell body input zone of dendrites and an output zone of an axon (of varying length). The electrochemical nerve impulse/ message is transmitted by neurons.

Neurotoxin

Chemical that paralyzes nerves. Neurotoxins are produced by a variety of organisms, most notably some of the heterotrophic dinoflagellates.

Neurotransmitters

Chemicals released from the tip of an axon into the synaptic cleft when a nerve impulse arrives; may stimulate or inhibit the next neuron. The chemical that crosses the synaptic cleft and causes the transmission of the nerve message in an adjacent neuron or the stimulation of an effector cell (muscle or gland).

Neutron

An uncharged subatomic particle in the nucleus of an atom. The large (mass approximately equal to 1 atomic mass unit), electrically neutral particle that may occur in the atomic nucleus.

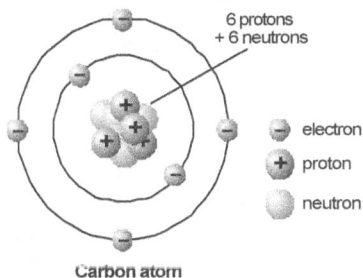

6 protons
+ 6 neutrons

electron
proton
neutron

Carbon atom

Niche

The portion of the environment that a species occupies, defined in terms of the conditions under which an organism can survive, and the presence of other competing organisms.

Niche overlap

The extent to which two species require similar resources; speciþes the strength of the competition between the two species.

Nicotine adenine dinucleotide phosphate (NADP⁺)

A substance to which electrons are transferred from photosystem I during

photosynthesis; the addition of the electrons reduces NADP, which acquires a hydrogen ion to form NADPH, which is a storage form of energy that can be transferred to the Calvin Cycle for the production of carbohydrate.

Nidicolous

Reared for a time in a nest.

Nidifugous

Leaving the nest soon after hatching. Nidifugous young are always precocial.

Nitrogen cycle

The nitrogen cycle is the process by which nitrogen is converted between its various chemical forms. This transformation can be carried out by both biological and non-biological processes.

Nitrogen Cycle

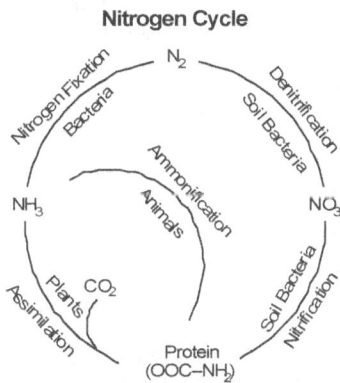

Nitrogen fixation

The conversion of gaseous nitrogen into a form usable by plants. Ususally by bacteria.

NMR

Nuclear magnetic resonance.

NMR-active atom

An atom that has the correct magnetic properties to be useful for NMR. For some atoms, the NMR-active form is a rare isotope, such as ^{13}C or ^{15}N.

Nocturnal

Active only at night.

Node

(Part of the stem) Nodes are some bulginess in the stems. Leaves grow at their level.

Node of Ranvier

A gap between two of the Schwann cells that make up an axon's myelin sheath; serves as a point for generating a nerve impulse.

Nomadism

Movement in which a population shifts from site to site between seasons in a relatively unpredictable manner.

Nominal filter rating

A rating that indicates the percentage of particles of a specific size or molecules of a specific molecular weight that will be removed by a filter. No industry standard exists; hence the ratings from manufacturer to manufacturer are not always comparable.

Nominal molecular weight cutoff, (NMWC)

In ultrafiltration, the molecular weight size of a protein or other solute (in Daltons) that will be retained to 90% by the membrane.

Non coding dna

DNA in eukaryotic cells that does not code for protein. At the gene level these can be large intron sequences of unknown function. Much of this DNA consists of multiple repeats, sometimes thousands or hundreds of thousands of copies, of a few relatively short sequence elements.

Nondisjunction

The failure of chromosomes to separate properly during cell division. The unequal segregation of chromosomes during meiosis. This forms cells with either too many (possibly one or more single or sets of chromosomes too many) or too few chromosomes. Thought to be a common cause for Down Syndrome, where sufferers often have an extra copy of chromosome 21.

Non-steroidal anti-inflammatory drugs

A class of medicines used to treat pain and inflammation. Examples include aspirin and ibuprofen. They work by blocking the action of the COX-2 enzyme. Because they also block the COX-1 enzyme, they can cause side effects such as stomach ulcers.

Nonvascular plants

Plants lacking lignified vascular tissue (xylem), vascularized leaves, and having a free-living, photosynthetic gametophyte stage that dominates the life cycle. Common examples are the mosses and liverworts.

Non-woven

In filter material, fibres in a random array, as opposed to woven, where a more or less regular, interlaced network of fibres is created, as in cloth.

Norepinephrine

A hormone produced in the adrenal medulla and secreted under stress; contributes to the "Þght or Þight" response.

Normal flow filtration

Also called dead-ended filtration. In normal flow filtration, liquid flows perpendicular to the filter media and all of the feed passes through.

Normalized water permeability, (NWP)

The water flux temperature corrected to a standardized temperature.

Notochord

In chordates, a cellular rod that runs the length of the body and provides dorsal support. Also, a structure of mesoderm in the embryo that will become the vertebrae of the spinal column. The stiff rod-like structure that all members of the Phylum Chordata develop at some stage during their life.

Nsaids

Non-steroidal anti-inflammatory drugs such as aspirin or ibuprofen.

Nuclear area

In prokaryotic cells, a region containing the cell's genetic information. Unlike the nucleus in eukaryotic cells, it is not surrounded by a membrane.

Nuclear magnetic resonance (NMR) spectroscopy

A technique used to determine the detailed, three-dimensional structure of molecules and, more broadly, to study the physical, chemical, and biological properties of matter. It uses a strong magnet that interacts with the natural magnetic properties in atomic nuclei.

Nuclear membrane

The double membrane which surrounds the eukaryotic nucleus. It has many pores in its surface which regulate the flow of large compounds into and out of the nucleus.

Nuclear Overhauser effect spectroscopy (NOESY)

An NMR technique used to help determine protein structures. It reveals how close different protons (hydrogen nuclei) are to each other in space.

Nuclear pores

Openings in the membrane of a cell's nuclear envelope that allow the exchange of materials between the nucleus and the cytoplasm.

Nucleic acid

class of biochemical compounds which includes DNA and RNA. They are among the largest molecules known.

Nucleoid

Region in prokaryotes where the DNA is concentrated. Unlike a nucleus, it is not bound by a membrane.

Nucleolus

A round or oval body in the nucleus of a eukaryotic cell; consists of DNA and RNA and produces ribosomal RNA (pl.: nucleoli).

Nucleosomes

Spherical bodies formed by coils of chromatin. The nucleosomes in turn are coiled to form the þbers that make up the chromosomes.

Nucleotide sequences

The genetic code encrypted in the sequence of bases along a nucleic acid.

Nucleotides

The subunits of nucleic acids; composed of a phosphate, a sugar, and a nitrogen-containing base. The fundamental structural unit of the nucleic acid group of organic macromolecules. Some nucleotides are involved in information storage (as nucleotides in DNA), protein synthesis (as nucleotides in RNA), and energy transfers (as single nucleotide ATP, GTP, and double nucleotide NADH and NADPH).

Nucleus

Membrane-bound organelle which contains the DNA in the form of chromosomes. It is the site of DNA replication, and the site of RNA synthesis.

Nucleus (atom)

An atom's core; contains protons and one or more neutrons (except hydrogen, which has no neutrons).

Nucleus (cell)

The largest, most prominent organelle in eukaryotic cells; a round or oval body that is surrounded by the nuclear envelope and contains the genetic information necessary for control of cell structure and function.

Nucleus (*pl.* Nuclei)

1. The membrane-bounded centre of a cell, which contains genetic material.
2. The centre of an atom, made up of protons and neutrons.

Nut

(Type of indehescent dry fruit) Nuts are fruits with a stiffened pericarp, covered with a cupule at the base.

Nutrient

Any dement or simple compound necessary for the health and survival of an organism. This includes air and water, as well as food.

Nutrient cycling

All the processes by which nutrients are transferred from one organism to another. For instance, the carbon cycle includes uptake of carbon dioxide by plants, ingestion by animals, and respiration and decay of the animal.

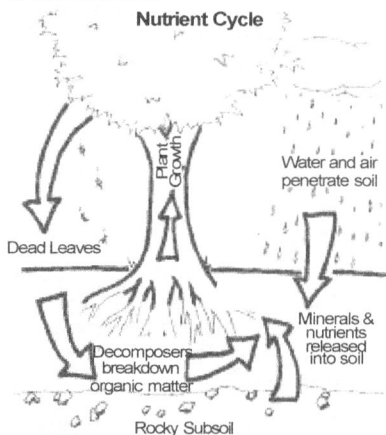

Nutrient Cycle

Nyctinasty

A nastic movement in a plant that is caused by light and dark.

Nymph

In aquatic insects, the larval stage.

O

Occipital lobe
The lobe of the cerebral cortex located at the rear of the head; is responsible for receiving and processing visual information.

Oceanic crust
The Earth's crust which is formed at mid-oceanic ridges, typically 5 to 10 kilometres thick with a density of 3.0 grams per centimetre cubed.

Oceanic trench
Deep steep-sided depression in the ocean floor caused by the subduction of oceanic crust beneath either other oceanic crust or continental crust.

Off-gassing
Generation of gases during fermentation and/or reaction processes.

Oils
Triglycerides that are liquid at room temperature.

Oleander
(Type of shrub) Perennial shrub of the Apocynaceae Family with lanceolate leaves and very big flowers, red or white. It leaves in the dry streams of Mediterranean climate, being very used in gardening to decorate garden hedges. Poisonous plant.

Oleophobic
Membranes that repel nonpolar fluids, such as oil and lubricants.

Omnivore
Literally, an organism that will eat anything. Refers to animals who do not restrict their diet to just plants or other animals.

Oncogene
A unit of DNA that normally directs cell growth, but which can also promote or allow the uncontrolled growth of cancer if damaged (mutated) by an environmental exposure to carcinogens.

One gene one polypeptide hypothesis
A revision of the one gene, one enzyme hypothesis. Some proteins are composed of different polypeptide chains encoded by separate genes, so the hypothesis now holds that mutation in a gene encoding a specifc polypeptide can alter the ability of the encoded protein to function and thus produce an altered phenotype.

One gene, one enzyme hypothesis
Holds that a single gene controls the production, specificity, and activity of each enzyme in a metabolic pathway. Thus, mutation of such a gene changes the ability of the cell to carry out a particular reaction and disrupts the entire pathway.

Ontogeny
The growth of an organism through all its developmental stages (embryonic stage through death).

Oocyte
A cell that will/is undergo/ing development into a female gamete.

Oogenesis
The production of ova. The development of a diploid cell into a haploid ovum or egg cell.

Open community
A community in which the populations have different density peaks and range boundaries and are distributed more or less randomly.

Opposable
The capability of being placed against the remaining digits of a hand or foot; e.g., the ability of the thumb to touch the tips of the fingers on that hand.

Opposite
Two leaves per node, facing opposite sides of the stem

Opsins
Molecules in cone cells that bind to pigments, creating a complex that is sensitive to light of a given wavelength.

Orbital ring
A fleshy ring around the eye; contrastingly coloured in some species.

Orchid
(The Orchid family - Orchidaceae) is the most numerous family of the flower plants . It stands for more than 25000 species worldwide. There are many kinds, some living over other plants, specially trees ephifytes- ; other are lianas or just terrestrial. Some species are saprophytes without chlorophyll feeding themselves from the humus they are living on.

Orders
Taxonomic subcategories of classes.

Ordovician extinction
Paleozoic-aged mass extinction possibly related to glaciation in the southern-hemisphere supercontinent Gondwana.

Ordovician period
Geologic period of the Paleozoic Era after the Cambrian Period between 500 and 435 million years ago. Major advances during this period include the bony fish and possibly land plants (during the late Ordovician).

Organ
Collection of tissues which performs a particular function or set of functions in an animal or plant's body. The heart, brain, and skin are three organs found in most animals. The leaf, stem, and root are three organs found in most plants. Organs are composed of tissues, and may be organized into larger organ systems.

Organ system
Collection of organs which have related roles in an organism's functioning. The nervous system, vascular system, and muscle system are all organ systems.

Organelle
A membrane-bound structure in a eukaryotic cell that partitions the cell into regions which carry out different cellular functions, e.g., mitochondria, endoplasmic reticulum, lysosomes.

Organic
Pertaining to compounds containing carbon. Also refers to living things or the materials made by living things.

Organism
An individual, composed of organ systems (if multicellular). Multiple organisms make up a population.

Organs

Differentiated structures consisting of tissues and performing some specific function in an organism. Structures made of two or more tissues which function as an integrated unit. e.g. the heart, kidneys.

Orgasm

Rhythmic muscular contractions of the genitals (sex organs) combined with waves of intense pleasurable sensations; in males, results in the ejaculation of semen.

Orogeny

The tectonic processes of folding, faulting, and uplifting of the earth's crust that result in the formation of mountains.

Oscines

One of two major subdivisions of the order Passeriformes. Oscines have a more complex syrinx and distinctive DNA patterns and middle ear bone shapes, and they generally must learn their most complex vocalizations.

Osculum

The main opening through which filtered water is discharged.

Osmoconformers

Marine organisms that have no system of osmoregulation and must change the composition of their body þuids as the composition of the water changes; include invertebrates such as jellyfish, scallops, and crabs.

Osmoregulation

The regulation of the movement of water by osmosis into and out of cells; the maintenance of water balance within the body.

Osmoregulators

Marine vertebrates whose body þuids have about one-third the solute concentration of seawater; must therefore undergo osmoregulation.

Osmosis

Diffusion of water molecules across a membrane in response to differences in solute concentration. Water moves from areas of high-water/low-solute concentration to areas of low-water/high-solute concentration. Diffusion of water across a semi-permeable barrier such as a cell membrane, from high water potential (concentration) to lower water potential (concentration).

Osmotic pressure

Pressure generated by water moving by osmosis into or out of a cell.

Ossification

The process of bone formation. Special cells called osteoblasts secrete minerals that combine with a network of collagen fibres, forming the hard bone matrix.

Osteichthyes

The class of fishes characterized by a swim bladder, bony skeletal systems, and an operculum.

Osteoarthritis

A degenerative condition associated with the wearing away of the protective cap of cartilage at the ends of bones. Bone growths or spurs develop, restricting movement and causing pain.

Osteoblasts

Bone-forming cells.

Osteoclasts

Cells that remove material to form the central cavity in a long bone.

Osteocytes

Bone cells that lay down new bone; found in the concentric layers of compact bone. Bone cell, a type of connective tissue.

Osteoporosis
A disorder in which the mineral portion of bone is lost, making the bone weak and brittle; occurs most commonly in postmenopausal women.

Ostracum
The middle, shell building layer, of a snail's shell. Consists of prism-shaped calcium carbonate crystals and organic (proteid) molecules.

Out of Africa hypothesis
Holds that modern human populations (Homo sapiens) are all derived from a single speciation event that took place in a restricted region in Africa.

Outcrop
Any place where bedrock is visible on the surface of the Earth. The exposing of bedrock at the Earth's surface.

Outgroup
In a cladistic analysis, any taxon used to help resolve the polarity of characters, and which is hypothesized to be less closely related to each of the taxa under consideration than any are to each other.

Oval
Egg shape that is rounded at the largest end and tapered at the oterh end. Often used to describe the typical egg shape.

Ovaries
1) In animals, the female gonads, which produce eggs (ova) and female sex hormones.
2) In þowers, part of the female reproductive structure in the carpel; contain the ovules, where egg development occurs. The lower part of the carpel that contains the ovules within which the female

gametophyte develops.

Ovary
In flowering plants, the part of the flower which encloses the ovules. When the ovary matures, it becomes the fruit.

Ovate
Egg-shaped leaf. Wider at the base than the apex.

Overkill
The shooting, trapping, or poisoning of certain populations, usually for sport or economic reasons.

Oviducts
Tubes that connect the ovaries and the uterus; transport sperm to the ova, transport the fertilized ova to the uterus, and serve as the site of fertilization; also called the fallopian tubes or uterine tubes.

Ovulation
The process by which an egg (the female gamete) is released from the ovary. In animals other than mammals, with the exception of monotremes, this results in the laying of an egg outside of the body. When female mammals ovulate, the egg, if fertilized, is retained within the uterus.

Ovule
In seed plants, a protective structure in which the female gametophyte develops, fertilization occurs, and seeds develop; contained within the ovary. Structures inside the ovary of the flower within which the female gametophyte develops after megasporogenesis has produced a megaspore inside each ovule.

Ovum
The female gamete, egg.

Oxidation

The loss of electrons from the outer shell of an atom; often accompanied by the transfer of a proton and thus involves the loss of a hydrogen ion. The loss of electrons or hydrogens in a chemical reaction.

Oxytocin

A peptide hormone secreted by the posterior pituitary that stimulates the contraction of the uterus during childbirth.

Ozone

Ozone (O_3), or trioxygen, is a triatomic molecule, consisting of three oxygen atoms. It is an allotrope of oxygen that is much less stable than the diatomic allotrope (O_2). Ozone in the lower atmosphere is an air pollutant with harmful effects on the respiratory systems of animals and will burn sensitive plants; however, the ozone layer in the upper atmosphere is beneficial, preventing potentially damaging electromagnetic radiation from reaching the Earth's surface.

P

Pacinian corpuscles
Sensory receptors located deep in the epidermis that detect pressure and vibration.

Palearctic
The biogeographic region that includes Europe, North Africa (north of the Sahara), northern Arabia.

Paleobiology
A field of science that uses biological studies of living organisms to answer questions about the evolution and physiology of extinct organisms.

Paleoherb
Any member of a group of basal flowering herbs which may be the closest relatives of the monocots. They include the water lilies, Piperales, and Aristolochiales.

Paleontology
The study of ancient life by collection and analysis of fossils.

Paleosol
Soil horizon from the geologic past.

Paleo-tethys ocean
A large ocean that originated between eastern Gondwana, Siberia, Kazakhstan, and Baltica in the Ordovician and finally closed in the Jurassic; replaced by the Tethys Ocean as eastern Pangea was assembled.

Paleozoic era
The period of time beginning 570 million years ago ending 245 million years ago; falls between the Proterozoic and Mesozoic Eras and is divided into the Cambrian, Ordovician, Silurian, Devonian, Carboniferous, and Permian Periods.

Palindrome
A sequence that reads the same in either direction; in genetics, refers to an enzyme recognition sequence that reads the same on both strands of DNA.

Palisade
Layer of mesophyll cells in leaves that are closely placed together under the epidermal layer of the leaf. Palisade parenchyma: Columnar cells located just below the upper epidermis in leaves the cells where most of the light absorbtion in photosynthesis occurs.

Palmate
The nerves of a leaf diverge from the main point such as the fingers do in the palm of the hand.

Palynology
The study of palynomorphs and other acid-resistant microfossils usually produced by plants, protists, and fungi.

Palynomorph
Palynomorph is the geological term used to describe a particle of a size

between five and 500 micrometres, found in rock deposits (sedimentary rocks) and composed of organic material such as chitin, pseudochitin and sporopollenin. The word is derived from Greek, meaning "strewn or sprinkled forms." Palynology is the study of palynomorph fossils and can be considered a subdiscipline of micropaleontology or paleobotany. Expressed more simply, palynology is the study of organic microfossils.

Pancreas
A gland in the abdominal cavity that secretes digestive enzymes into the small intestine and also secretes the hormones insulin and glucagon into the blood, where they regulate blood glucose levels. A digestive organ that produces trypsin, chymotrypsin and other enzymes as a pancreatic juice, but which also has endocrine functions in the production of the hormones somatostatin, insulin, and glucagon.

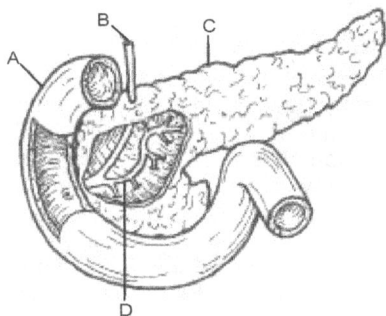

A. Duodenum, B. Bile duct,
C. Pancreas, D. Pancreatic duct

Pancreatic islets
Clusters of endocrine cells in the pancreas that secrete insulin and glucagon; also known as islets of Langerhans.

Pangaea
The name proposed by German meteorologist Alfred Wegener for a supercontinent that existed at the end of the Paleozoic Era and consisted of all the Earth's landmasses.

Pangea
A supercontinent that existed from the the end of the Permian to the Jurassic, assembled from large continents like Euramerica, Gondwana, and Siberia, as well as smaller landmasses like the Cathaysian and Cimmerian terranes; Greek for "all lands."

Panicle
(Type of compound inflorescences) A panicle is formed by several racemes gathered together.

Pannotia
A supercontinent that existed in the Late Precambrian and gave rise to the continents of Gondwana, Laurentia, Siberia, and Baltica in the Cambrian.

Panthalassic ocean
A vast ocean that existed from the Late Precambrian to the Jurassic, circling the globe and connecting to smaller oceans that developed throughout the Phanerozoic; also known as the Panthalassa.

Pantropical
Occurring throughout the tropical regions of the world.

Papilla(e)
Cellular outgrowths. These look like little bumps or fingers on the surface of cells.

Parallel evolution
The development of similar characteristics in organisms that are not closely related (not part of a monophyletic group) due to adaptation to similar environments and/or strategies of life.

Parallel-veined
The veins of a leaf run at the same distance to each other, like in canes.

Paraphyletic
Term applied to a group of organisms which includes the most recent common ancestor of all of its members, but not all of the descendants of that most recent common ancestor.

Parapodia
A sort of "false foot" formed by extension of the body cavity. Polychaetes and some insect larvae have parapodia in addition to their legs, and these provide extra help in locomotion.

Parasite
(Type of roots) They are stuck on another plant , sucking the nutrients from it. The mistletoe is a clear example of this type.

Parasite
An organism that lives on or within a host (another organism); it obtains nutrients from the host without benefiting or killing (although it may damage) the host; parasitic- adj.; parasitism- n. a type of symbiotic relationship in which one organism benefits and the other does not.

Parasitism
A form of symbiosis in which the population of one species benefits at the expense of the population of another species; similar to predation, but differs in that parasites act more slowly than predators and do not always kill the host. A type of symbiosis in which one organism benefits at the expense of the other, for example the influenza virus is a parasite on its human host. Viruses, are obligate intracellular parasites.

Parasympathetic system
The subdivision of the autonomic nervous system that reverses the effects of the sympathetic nervous system. Part of the autonomic nervous system that controls heartbeat, respiration and other vital functions.

Parataxonomy
The grouping of organisms based on common morphology; does not imply evolutionary relationships. For example, fossil eggs can be assigned to parataxons without any knowledge of which specific organism produced them.

Parenchyma
One of the three major cell types in plants. Parenchyma cells have thin, usually multisided walls, are unspecialized but carry on photosynthesis and cellular respiration and can store food; form the bulk of the plant body; found in the fleshy tissue of fruits and seeds, photosynthetic cells of leaves, and the vascular system.

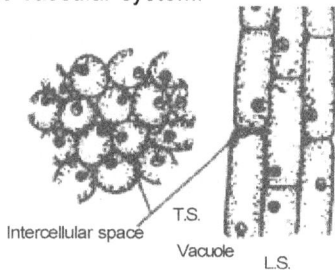

Intercellular space
T.S.
Vacuole
L.S.

Parenchyma

Generalized plant cells whose numerous functions include photosynthesis, storage, bulk of herbaceous stem tissues, lateral transport in woody stems. Parenchyma are variously shaped but are characterized by thin walls and remain alive at functional maturity.

Parietal lobe
The lobe of the cerebral cortex that lies at the top of the brain; processes information about touch, taste, pressure, pain, and heat and cold.

Parsimony
Refers to a rule used to choose among possible cladograms, which states that the cladogram implying the least number of changes in character states is the best.

Partial molt
The replacement of feathers in only some of the body's feather tracts.

Particle size distribution
The dispersion of particle sizes (number or weight fraction) in a fluid.

Passerine
A member of the order Passerini-formes, often referred to as a songbird.

Passive transport
Diffusion across a plasma membrane in which the cell expends no energy.

Patagium
A membrane of double-sided skin that forms the wing material in bats.

Pathogenic
Organism which causes a disease within another organism.

Pathology
1. The study of disease and abnormalities.

2. The manifestation of a disease, injury, or abnormality, as in bone or eggshell for example. adj. pathological

PCBS
Polychlorinated biphenyls, a class of chemicals used as lubricants and insulation materials and in printing ink.

PCR
The Polymerase Chain Reaction is used to amplify a sequence of DNA using a pair of oligonucleotide primers each complementary to one end of the DNA target sequence. These are extended towards each other by a thermostable DNA Polymerase in a reaction cycle of 3 steps: denaturation, primer annealing and polymerisation.

Pea
(The pea family - leguminosae - papilionaceae) It has about 12000 species of plants growing mainly in the temperate regions. The most common species are herbs, but some of them are shrubs and trees, too.

Peat
A deposit of partly decayed plant remains in a very wet environment; marsh or swamp deposit of plant remains containing more than 50 percent carbon.

Pectin
A substance in the middle lamella that cements adjoining plant cells together.

Pectinate
Having tooth-like projections similar to the teeth of a comb.

Pectoral girdle
In humans, the bony arch by which the arms are attached to the rest of

147

the skeleton; composed of the clavicle and scapula.

Pedigree analysis

A type of genetic analysis in which a trait is traced through several generations of a family to determine how the trait is inherited. The information is displayed in a pedigree chart using standard symbols.

Pedipalps

The second pair of appendages of cheliceromorphs. In many arachnids, such as spiders, the pedipalps are enlarged in the male and used for copulation.

Peduncle

(Part of the leaf) Stalk that joins the receptacle to the stem.

Pedicell

Peduncle

Peep

General name for several small sandpiper species in the genus Calidris.

Pelagic

Pelagic organisms swim through the ocean, and may rise to the surface, or sink to the bottom. They are not confined to live on the bottom as benthic organisms do.

Pelagic zone

One of the two basic subdivisions of the marine biome; consists of the water above the sea floor and its organisms.

Pellet

A mass of indigestible material including fur, feathers, and bones regurgitated by hawks, owls, herons, and other predatory birds.

Pelvic girdle

In humans, the bony arch by which the legs are attached to the rest of the skeleton; composed of the two hipbones.

Pelvis

The pelvis is an anatomical structure found in humans (see human pelvis) or in animals. It contains a large compound bone structure at the base of the spine, which is connected with the legs or rear limbs. This bony structure is called the pelvis skeleton or bony pelvis, and consists of os coxa, sacrum and coccyx.

Lliac crest
Llium
Sacroiliac joint
Sacrum
Ischial spine
Pubis
Obturator foramen
Ischium
Coccyx
Acetabulum
Symphysis pubis

Penicillin

The first of the so-called wonder drugs; discovered by Sir Alexander Fleming.

Pentaradial symmetry

A type of radial symmetry, characteristic of echinoderms, in which body parts are arranged along five rays of symmetry.

Pepo

(Type of fruit) Pepos are fruits that come from an inferior ovary with the outer part of the pericarp stiffened. For instance, melons or pumpkins.

Pepsin

An enzyme produced from pepsinogen that initiates protein digestion by breaking down protein into large peptide fragments. An enzyme, produced by the stomach, that chemically breaks down peptide bonds in polypeptides and proteins.

Pepsinogen

An inactive form of pepsin; synthesized and stored in cells lining the gastric pits of the stomach.

Peptic ulcer

A peptic ulcer, also known as PUD or peptic ulcer disease, is the most common ulcer of an area of the gastrointestinal tract that is usually acidic and thus extremely painful. It is defined as mucosal erosions equal to or greater than 0.5 cm. As many as 70–90% of such ulcers are associated with Helicobacter pylori, a spiral-shaped bacterium that lives in the acidic environment of the stomach; however, only 40% of those cases go to a doctor. Ulcers can also be caused or worsened by drugs such as aspirin, Plavix (clopidogrel), ibuprofen, and other NSAIDs.

Peptide

A molecule consisting of 2 to approximately 20 amino acids connected by peptide bonds; a short segment of a larger protein or a completely functional molecule unto itself.

Peptide bond

A peptide bond (amide bond) is a covalent chemical bond formed between two molecules when the carboxyl group of one molecule reacts with the amino group of the other molecule, causing the release of a molecule of water (H_2O), hence the process is a dehydration synthesis reaction (also known as a condensation reaction), and usually occurs between amino acids. The resulting C(O)NH bond is called a peptide bond, and the resulting molecule is an amide. The four-atom functional group -C(=O)NH- is called a peptide link. Polypeptides and proteins are chains of amino acids held together by peptide bonds, as is the backbone of PNA.

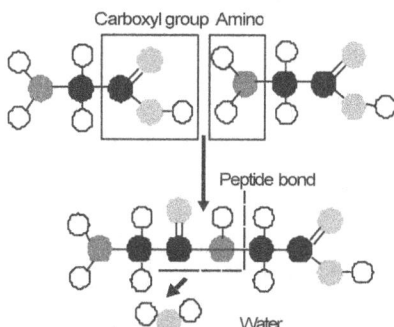

Peptidoglycan

Carbohydrate polymer cross-linked by proteins. It is found in the cell wall of Gram positive bacteria, where it stains with the dye crystal-violet.

Perennial

A perennial plant or simply perennial (Latin per, "through", annus, "year") is a plant that lives for more than two years. The term is often used to differentiate a plant from shorter lived annuals and biennials. The term is sometimes misused by commercial gardeners or horticulturalists to describe only herbaceous perennials. More correctly, woody plants like shrubs and trees are also perennials.

Perianth

The sepals and petals of a flower are together called the perianth; literally "around the anthers".

Pericarp
(Part of the fruit) It is all that surrounds the seed. It is divided in three parts

Perichondrium
A layer of connective tissue that forms around the cartilage during bone formation. Cells in the perichondrium lay down a peripheral layer that develops into compact bone.

Peridinin
Carotenoid pigment found in dinoflagellates.

Period
The fundamental unit in the hierarchy of time units; a part of geologic time during which a particular sequence of rocks designated as a system was deposited. Units of geological time that are the major subdivisions of Eras.

Periosteum
A fibrous membrane that covers bones and serves as the site of attachment for skeletal muscles; contains nerves, blood vessels, and lymphatic vessels.

Periostracum
The outermost layer of a snail's shell. Consists of conchin (a mixture of organic compounds), gives the shell color.

Peripheral nervous system
The division of the nervous system that connects the central nervous system to other parts of the body. Components of the nervous system that transmit messages to the central nervous system.

Periphyton
Dense strands of algal growth that cover the water surface between the emergent aquatic plants. Spirogyra is commonly responsible for this growth.

Peristalsis
Involuntary contractions of the smooth muscles in the walls of the esophagus, stomach, and intestines that propel food along the digestive tract. Waves of muscle contraction in the esophagus that propel food from the oral cavity to the stomach.

Peristome
A set of cells or cell parts which surround the opening of a moss sporangium. In many mosses, they are sensitive to humidity, and will alter their shape to aid in spore dispersal.

Permeate
Also called filtrate. The portion of a process fluid that passes through a membrane.

Permian period
The last geologic time period of the Paleozoic Era, noted for the greatest mass extinction in earth history, when nearly 96% of species died out.

Permineralization
Fossilization process that occurs when minerals, carried by ground water, enter and harden in the pores of an organism's structures.

Peroxisomes
Membrane-bound vesicles in eukaryotic cells that contain oxidative enzymes.

Pesticides
Chemicals that are applied to agricultural crops or domesticated plants and which kill or inhibit growth of insects.

Petals
Usually brightly colored elements of a flower that may produce fragrant oils; nonreproductive structures that attract

pollinators. Sterile leaf-like (white, colorless, but usually colored) structures in flowers that serve to attract pollinators.

Petiolated
(Type of leaf) we call petiolated those leaves that have a petiole.

Petiole
The generally non-leafy part of the leaf that attaches the leaf blade to the stem; celery and rhubarb are examples of a leaf petiole that we use as food. The stalk connecting the leaf blade to the stem.

Petrifaction
Petrifaction, petrification or silicification is the process by which organic material is converted into stone by impregnation with silica. It is a rare form of fossilization. Petrified wood is the most well known result of this process, but all organisms from bacteria to vertebrates can be petrified.

PGA (phosphoglycerate)
A three-carbon molecule formed when carbon dioxide is added to ribulose biphosphate (RuBP) during the dark reaction of photosynthesis (Calvin, or Calvin-Benson Cycle). PGA is converted to PGAL, using ATP and NADPH.

PGAL (phosphoglyceraldehyde)
A substance formed from PGA during the dark reaction of photosynthesis. Some PGAL leaves the cycle and can be converted to glucose, while other PGAL molecules are used to reform ribulose biphosphate (RuBP) to continue the dark reaction.

Ph
The negative logarithm of the H^+ ion concentration. The pH is a measure of the acidity or basic character of a solution. Since it measures a fraction, the larger the pH number, the less H ions are present in a solution.

Phagocytes
White blood cells that can engulf (by phagocytosis) and destroy microorganisms including viruses and bacteria; cells in this category include neutrophils and monocytes.

Phagocytosis
A form of endocytosis in which white blood cells surround and engulf invading bacteria or viruses.

Phanerozoic
The geologic eon that includes the interval of time from approximately 543 million years ago to the present, comprising the Paleozoic, Mesozoic, and Cenozoic eras.

Pharyngeal slits
Characteristic of chordates, pharyngeal slits are openings through which water is taken into the pharynx, or throat. In primitive chordates the pharyngeal slits are used to strain water and filter out food particles; in fishes they are modified for respiration. Most terrestrial vertebrates have pharyngeal slits only in the embryonic stage.

Pharynx
The passageway between the mouth and the esophagus and trachea. Food passes from the pharynx to the esophagus, and air passes from the pharynx to the trachea.

Phenotype
Observable characteristics of an organism produced by the organism's genotype interacting with the environment.

Pheromones

Chemical signals that travel between organisms rather than between cells within an organism; serve as a form of communication between animals.

Phloem

Tissue in the vascular system of plants that moves dissolved sugars and other products of photosynthesis from the leaves to other regions of the plant. Phloem tissue consists of cells called sieve tubes and companion cells. Cells of the vascular system in plants that transport food from leaves to other areas of the plant.

Phosphate

An ion consisting of a phosphorus atom and four oxygen atoms. Among other things, it is used in the constuction of nucleic acids.

Phosphate group

A chemical group found in DNA and RNA, and often attached to proteins and other biological molecules. It is composed of one phosphorous atom bound to four oxygen atoms.

Phospholipids

Asymmetrical lipid molecules with a hydrophilic head and a hydrophobic tail. Lipids with a phosphate group in place of one of the three fatty acid chains. Phospholipids are the building blocks of cellular membranes. Phospholipids have hydrophilic heads (glycerol and phosphate) and hydrophobic tails (the non-polar fatty acids).

Phosphorylation

The chemical attachment of phosphorous to a molecule, usually associated with the storage of energy in the covalent bond that is also formed. Example: attachment of the third phosphate group to ADP in the formation of the higher energy form, ATP. Photophosphorylation is a type of phosphorylation associated with the formation of ATP in the photosynthesis process.

Photic zone

Region of the ocean through which light penetrates; and the place where photosynthetic marine organisms live.

Photoperiodism

The ability of certain plants to sense the relative amounts of light and dark in a 24-hour period; controls the onset of þowering in many plants.

Photosynthesis

The process by which plant cells use solar energy to produce ATP. The conversion of unusable sunlight energy into usable chemical energy, associated with the actions of chlorophyll.

Photosystems

Clusters of several hundred molecules of chlorophyll in a thylakoid in which photosynthesis takes place. Eukaryotes have two types of photosystems: I and II. The series of green photoreceptive pigments involved in the light reactions, which occur in the thylakoids of the chloroplast (in eukaryotes). Energy from light is passed to the electrons as they move through the photosystem pigments.

Phototrophs

Organisms that use sunlight to synthesize organic nutrients as their energy source; e.g., cyanobacteria, algae, and plants.

Phototropism

The reaction of plants to light in which the plants bend toward the light. Plant response to light by unequal growth caused by concentration of the plant hormone Indole Acetic Acid (IAA, an auxin) on the darker side of the plant shoot.

Phragmoplast

The phragmoplast is a plant cell specific structure that forms during late cytokinesis. It serves as a scaffold for cell plate assembly and subsequent formation of a new cell wall separating the two daughter cells. The phragmoplast is a complex assembly of microtubules (MTs), microfilaments (MFs), and endoplasmic reticulum (ER) elements, that assemble in two opposing sets perpendicular to the plane of the future cell plate during anaphase and telophase. It is initially barrel-shaped and forms from the mitotic spindle between the two daughter nuclei while nuclear envelopes reassemble around them. The cell plate initially forms as a disc between the two halves of the phragmoplast structure.

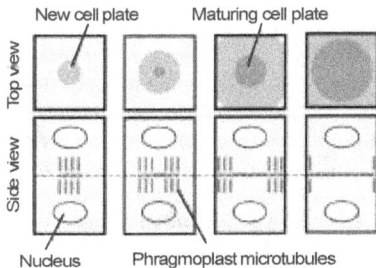

New cell plate   Maturing cell plate

Top view   Side view

Nucleus   Phragmoplast microtubules

Phycocyanin

Phycocyanin is a pigment from the light-harvesting phycobiliprotein family, along with allophycocyanin and phycoerythrin. It is an accessory pigment to chlorophyll. All phycobiliproteins are water-soluble and therefore cannot exist within the membrane as do carotenoids, but aggregate forming clusters that adhere to the membrane called phycobilisomes. Phycocyanin is a characteristic light blue colour, absorbing orange and red light, particularly near 620 nm (depending on which specific type it is), and emits fluorescence at about 650 nm (also depending on which type it is).

Phycoerythrin

Phycoerythrin is a red protein from the light-harvesting phycobiliprotein family, present in cyanobacteria, red algae and cryptomonads. Phycoerythrin is an accessory pigment to the main chlorophyll pigments responsible for photosynthesis. The light energy is captured by phycoerythrin and is then passed on to the reaction centre chlorophyll pair, most of the time via the phycobiliproteins phycocyanin and allophycocyanin.

Phylloclade

(Type of stem) They appear because the real leaves are very small , therefore non functional. A clear example is the butcher's broom .

Phylogenetic

In biology, phylogenetics is the study of evolutionary relatedness among groups of organisms (e.g. species, populations), which is discovered through molecular sequencing data and morphological data matrices. The term phylogenetics derives from the Greek terms phyle and phylon, denoting "tribe" and "race"; and the term genetikos, denoting "relative to birth", from genesis "origin" and"birth".

Phylogeny

The evolutionary relationships among organisms; the patterns of lineage branching produced by the true evolutionary history of the organisms being considered.

Phylum

At the most basic level, a phylum can be defined in two ways: as a group of organisms with a certain degree of morphological or developmental similarity (the phenetic definition), or a group of organisms with a certain degree of evolutionary relatedness (the phylogenetic definition). Attempting to define a level of the Linnean hierarchy without referring to (evolutionary) relatedness is an unsatisfactory approach, but the phenetic definition is more useful when addressing questions of a morphological nature—such as how successful different body plans were.

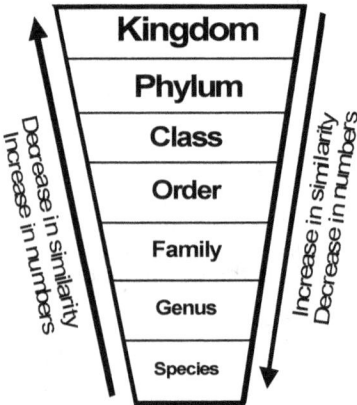

Phytochrome

A pigment in plant leaves that detects day length and generates a response; partly responsible for photoperiodism.

Phytomelanin

A papery "sooty" black layer over the seed of plants in the Asparagales, which includes agaves, aloes, onions and hyacinths. It is an important character for defining the group.

Phytoplankton

A floating layer of photosynthetic organisms, including algae, that are an important source of atmospheric oxygen and form the base of the aquatic food chain.

Pigment

Any colorful compound, used by living things to absorb or block sunlight, and in sexual displays.

Pillow lava

Lava extruded beneath water characterised by pillow-type shapes.

Pilus

Projection from surface of a bacterial cell (F+) that can donate genetic material to another (F-).

Pineal eye

Third eye in the forehead of tuataras and many lizards that can register light intensity and may help to regulate body temperature.

Pineal gland

A small gland located between the cerebral hemispheres of the brain that secretes melatonin.

Pinnate

(Type of leaf) There is a main nerve in the leaf, called midrib, from which the other nerves derive, remembering a plume.

Pinnately compound

Leaves which are divided up like a feather are said to be pinnately compound.

Pioneer community

The initial community of colonizing species.

Pistil

Female reproductive structures in flowers, consisting of the stigma, style, and ovary. Also known as a carpel in some books.

Pith
To severely damage the brain of a frog, also any central region of parenchyma tissue within a plant stem.

Pits
Thin regions of the cell wall in xylem conducting cells. Their structure is an important characteristic for recognizing different kinds of wood.

Pituitary gland
A small gland located at the base of the brain; consists of an anterior and a posterior lobe and produces numerous hormones. The master gland of the endocrine system, the pituitary releases hormones that have specific targets as well as those that stimulate other glands to secrete hormones. Part of the pituitary is nerve tissue, the rest is glandular epithelium.

Placenta
In mammals, a tissue formed within the uterus through which nutrients are passed from the mother to the embryo (and later the fetus) and its wastes are removed. It is analogous to the protective membranes in the egg of other amniotes. placental n. A mammal that gives live birth to well-developed young that have prolonged embryonic development within the mother's uterus. Marsupial mammals also have a placenta, but the embryo spends less time developing in the uterus before birth. Placentals include animals as diverse as humans, elephants, dogs, and mice.

Placental
A mammal that gives live birth to well-developed young that have prolonged embryonic development within the mother's uterus. Marsupial mammals also have a placenta, but the embryo spends less time developing in the uterus before birth. Placentals include animals as diverse as humans, elephants, dogs, and mice.

Placental mammals
One of three groups of mammals that carry their young in the mother's body for long periods during which the fetus is nourished by the placenta. Humans are placental mammals.

Planaria
Small free-living þatworms (Phylum Platyhelminthes) with bilateral symmetry and cephalization. The freshwater type is often used as an experimental organism.

Plankton
Plankton are microscopic organisms that drift on the oceans' currents. They include organisms such as diatoms, dinoflagillates, krill, and copepods as well as the microscopic larva of crustaceans, sea urchins, and fish.

Planktonic organisms
"Floaters"; one of the two main types of organisms in the pelagic zone of thc marine biome.

Plantae
The plant kingdom; nonmobile, autotrophic, multicellular eukaryotes. Kingdom of the plants, autotrophic eukaryotes with cellulose in their cell walls and starch as a carbohydrate storage product, with chlorophylls a and b as photosynthesis pigments.

Plasma
The liquid portion of the blood. Along with the extracellular þuid, it makes up the internal environment of multicellular organisms.

Plasma cells
Cells produced from B cells that synthesize and release antibodies.

Plasma membrane
Outer membrane of a cell, sometimes called the cell membrane. The term plasma membrane is used more frequently when discussing prokaryotes.

Plasmids
Self-replicating, circular DNA molecules found in bacterial cells; often used as vectors in recombinant DNA technology. Small circles of double-stranded DNA found in some bacteria. Plasmids can carry from four to 20 genes. Plasmids are a commonly used vector in recombinant DNA studies.

Plasmodesmata
Junctions in plants that penetrate cell walls and plasma membranes, allowing direct communication between the cytoplasm of adjacent cells (sing.: plasmodesma).

Plasmogamy
A process of fusion of the cytoplasm of two cells; the first step in syngamy.

Plasmolysis
Osmotic condition in which a cell loses water to its outside environment.

Plastids
Membrane-bound organelles in plant cells that function in storage (of food or pigments) or food production. Term for any double membrane-bound organelle. Chloroplasts contain the chemicals for photosynthesis, amyloplasts (also known as leukoplasts) store starch, chromoplasts contain colorful pigments such as in the petals of a flower or epidermis of a fruit.

Plastron
The shell or shield on the ventral surface (belly) of tortoises and turtles.

Plate
Rigid parts of the Earth's crust and part of the Earth's upper mantle that move and adjoin each other along zones of seismic activity. The theory that the crust and part of the mantle are divided into plates that interact with each other causing seismic and tecotnic activity is called plate tectonics.

Plate tectonics
The movement of the plates that make up the surface of the Earth. The revolutionary paradigm in geology that the earth's crust is composed of rigid segments (plates) in constant (although considered slow in a human-scale time frame) motion (tectonics) relative to each other.

Platelets
In vertebrates, cell fragments that bud off from the megakaryocytes in the bone marrow; carry chemicals needed for blood clotting. Cell fragment functioning in blood clotting.

Platyspermic
Having seeds which are flattened and disc-like. Contrast with radiospermic.

Pleating
Folding flat sheet filter media to increase the surface area that can be fitted into a given separations device generally used in dead-ended filtration.

Pleiotropic
A term describing a genotype with multiple phenotypic effects. For example: sickle-cell anemia produces a multitude of consequences in those it affects, such as heart disease, jidney problem, etc.

Pleistocene
The first geologic epoch of the Quaternary Period of the Cenozoic

Era that ended 10,000 years ago with the retreat of the last glaciers.

Plesiomorphy

A primitive character state for the taxa under consideration.

Pleura

A thin sheet of epithelium that covers the inside of the thoracic cavity and the outer surface of the lungs.

Pleurae

In trilobites and other arthropods, pleurae are elongated flat outgrowths from each body segment, that overlie and protect the appendages.

Pleural cavity

The space between the sheets of pleura (one covering the inside of the thoracic cavity, the other covering the outside of the lungs).

Plicate

Folded like a paper fan, as in the leaves of palms, cyclanthoids, and some orchids.

Plum

(Fruit) It is a drupe with a fleshy mesocarp and a stone-like stiffened endocarp.

Plumule

(Part of the embryo in a seed) It is like a leaf in its early development.

Pluton

A pluton in geology is a body of intrusive igneous rock (called a plutonic rock) that crystallized from magma slowly cooling below the surface of the Earth. Plutons include batholiths, dikes, sills, laccoliths, lopoliths, and other igneous bodies. In practice, "pluton" usually refers to a distinctive mass of igneous rock, typically several kilometers in dimension, without a tabular shape like those of dikes and sills. Batholiths commonly are aggregations of plutons.

Plutonic

Applies to igneous rocks formed beneath the surface of the Earth; typically with large crystals due to the slowness of cooling.

Pod

(Type of dehiscent fruit) Pods derive from a single carpel, too. Differently to follicles, they open both sides.

Polar covalent bond

A covalent bond in which atoms share electrons in an unequal fashion. The resulting molecule has regions with positive and negative charges. The presence of polar covalent bonds allows other polar molecules to surround molecule: example: glucose sugar in water.

Polarity of characters

The states of characters used in a cladistic analysis, either original or derived. Original characters are those acquired by an ancestor deeper in the phylogeny than the most recent common ancestor of the taxa under consideration. Derived characters are those acquired by the most recent common ancestor of the taxa under consideration.

Pollen

Pollen is a fine to coarse powder containing the microgametophytes of seed plants, which produce the male gametes (sperm cells). Pollen grains have a hard coat that protects the sperm cells during the process of their movement from the stamens to the pistil of flowering plants or from the male cone to the female cone of coniferous plants. When pollen lands on a compatible pistil or female cone (i.e., when pollination has occurred), it germinates and produces a pollen tube that transfers the sperm to the ovule (or female gametophyte).

Pollen grains
The containers for male gametophytes of seed plants produced in a microsporangium by meiosis. Microspores produced by seed plants that contain the male gametophyte.

Pollen tube
Structure produced by the tube nucleus in the pollen grain through which the sperm nucleus (or nuclei in angiosperms) proceed to travel through to reach the egg.

Pollination
Process of transferring the pollen from its place of production to the place where the egg cell is produced. This may be accomplished by the use of wind, water, insects, birds, bats, or other means. Pollination is usually followed by fertilization, in which sperm are released from the pollen grain to unite with the egg cell.

Pollinator
Animal which carries pollen from one seed plant to another, unwittingly aiding the plant in its reproduction. Common pollinators include insects, especially bees, butterflies, and moths, birds, and bats.

Pollinia
A mass of fused pollen produced by many orchids.

Polyandry
The mating of one female with more than one male during the course of a mating season.

Polydrupe
(Type of fruit) Polydrupes are aggregate fruits that combine several drupes at the same time, like in the case of blackberries.

Polygenic inheritance
Occurs when a trait is controlled by several gene pairs; usually results in continuous variation.

Polygyny
The mating of one male with more than one female during the course of a mating season.

Polymer
Organic molecule composed of smaller units known as monomers. A large molecule composed of smaller subunits, for example starch is a polymer of glucose, proteins are polymers of amino acids.

Polymerase chain reaction
A method of amplifying or copying DNA fragments that is faster than cloning. The fragments are combined with DNA polymerase, nucleotides, and other components to form a mixture in which the DNA is cyclically amplified.

Polynucleotides
Long chains of nucleotides formed by chemical links between the sugar and phosphate groups.

Polyp
The sessile form of life history in cnidarians; e.g., the freshwater hydra.

Polypetalous
(Type of flower) In a flower if the petals are not joined.

Polyphyletic
Term applied to a group of organisms which does not include the most

recent common ancestor of those organisms; the ancestor does not possess the character shared by members of the group.

Polyploidy
Abnormal variation in the number of chromosome sets. The condition when a cell or organism has more than the customary two sets of chromosomes. This is an especially effective speciation mechanism in plants since the extra chromosomes will establish reproductive isolation with the parental population(s), an essential for speciation.

Polysaccharides
Long chains of monosaccharide units bonded together; e.g., glycogen, starch, and cellulose.

Polysepalous or Separated
(Type of flowers) if the sepals are clearly separated each other.

Pome
(Type of fruit) Pomes are fruits with soft mesocarp and a coriaceous endocarp. They become from an inferior ovary, like apples or pears.

Pons
The region that, with the medulla oblongata, makes up the hindbrain, which controls heart rate, constriction and dilation of blood vessels, respiration, and digestion.

Poppy
(The Poppy family - Papaveraceae) It comprises about 200 species of plants mainly spread in temperate countries. Most of them are herbs with big colorful flowers. They are very important because all of them contain alkaloids therefore they are cultivated as drugs or medicinal plants.

Population
A group of individuals of the same species living in the same area at the same time and sharing a common gene pool. A group of potentially interbreeding organisms in a geographic area.

Population dynamics
The study of the factors that affect the growth, stability, and decline of populations, as well as the interactions of those factors.

Pore size distribution
The range of pore sizes in a membrane. The tighter the pore size distribution, the better control one has over the filtration process.

Pores
The open spaces in a filter membrane; also, a small, interconnecting passage through the membrane. The removal rating of a membrane is dependent on the (irregular) path and size of the membrane's pores.

Porosity
A measurement of the open space in a membrane. The higher the membrane porosity, the more pores there are, hence, a higher flow rate is anticipated.

Portal system
In the circulatory system of animals, a portal venous system occurs when a capillary bed pools into another capillary bed through veins, without first going through the heart. Both capillary beds and the blood vessels that connect them are considered part of the portal venous system. They are relatively uncommon as the majority of capillary beds drain into veins which then drain into the heart, not into another capillary bed. Portal venous systems are considered

venous because the blood vessels that join the two capillary beds are either veins or venules.

Positive feedback

Biochemical control where the accumulation of the product stimulates production of an enzyme responsible for that product's production.

Positive feedback control

Occurs when information produced by the feedback increases and accelerates the response.

Potato

Potato family (Nightshade family) - Solanaceae - comprises about 2500 species of plants spread all over the world but mainly in tropical America. They are herbs, trees and shrubs. Many of these species are very important for mankind because of their value as food Potaoes, tomatoes, peppers, etc.,), because of their alkaloid properties and as garden plants.

Precambrian

Informal term describing 7/8 of geologic time from the beginning of the earth to the beginning of the Cambrian Period of the Paleozoic Era. During this time the atmosphere and oceans formed, life originated (or possibly "colonized" Earth), eukaryotes and simple animals evolved and by the end of the precambrian they began to accumulate hard preservable parts, the common occurrence of which marks the beginning of the Cambrian.

Precipitation

The part of the hydrologic cycle in which the water vapor in the atmosphere falls to Earth as rain or snow.

Pre-coat

In a filter system, a material introduced to coat the surface, forming a build-up or cake that enhances filtration.

Precocial

Describes young that are mobile and fairly self-sufficient at birth. Precocial young are generally well-developed (and large) at birth, born with their eyes open, and able to walk. Chickens and grebes are examples of precocial birds; sheep and guinea pigs are examples of precocial mammals.

Predation

Predation describes a biological interaction where a predator (an organism that is hunting) feeds on its prey (the organism that is attacked). Predators may or may not kill their prey prior to feeding on them, but the act of predation always results in the death of its prey and the eventual absorption of the prey's tissue through consumption. Other categories of consumption are herbivory (eating parts of plants) and detritivory, the consumption of dead organic material (detritus). All these consumption categories fall under the rubric of consumer-resource systems. It can often be difficult to separate various types of feeding behaviors.

Predator

Organism which hunts and eats other organisms. This includes both carnivores, which eat animals, and herbivores, which eat plants.

Predatory release

Occurs when a predator species is removed from a prey species such as by great reduction in the predator's population size or by the migration of the prey species to an area without major predators. The removal of the predator releases the prey from one of the factors limiting its population size.

Preen gland

"The source of the oil that a preening bird rubs on its feathers to maintain them in good condition; located on the lower back near the rump." The gland is found near the base of the tail and is shaped into two symmetric parts. The oil of each part of the gland is secreted through the surface of the skin through a grease nipple-like nub.

Prefilter

A device installed before—upstream from—the main filtration process, generally to remove large solids that might prematurely clog the primary filter.

Prefiltration

The act of using a prefilter to remove large particles prior to final filtration.

Prehensile movement

The ability to seize or grasp.

Prenatal testing

Testing to detect the presence of a genetic disorder in an embryo or fetus; commonly done by amniocentesis or chorionic villi sampling.

Pressure drop

The difference in pressure between two points.

Pressure, absolute

Gauge pressure plus 1 barg (14.7 psig)

Pressure, atmospheric

Pressure at any point in an atmosphere attributable solely to the weight of the atmospheric gases at that point. Expressed as 1 barg, approximately 75 cm of mercury (14.7 lbs/in2) at sea level.

Presymptomatic screening

Testing to detect genetic disorders that only become apparent later in life. The tests are done before the condition actually appears, such as with Huntington disease.

Prey

Organism hunted and eaten by a predator.

Prey switching

The tendency of predators to switch to a more readily available prey when one prey species becomes rare; allows the Þrst prey population to rebound and helps prevent its extinction.

Prickle

(Part of the plant) Thorn or pointed structured developed by plants.

Primary body

Those parts of a plant produced by the shoot and root apical meristems.

Primary cell wall

The cell wall outside the plasma membrane that surrounds plant cells; composed of the polysaccharide cellulose.

Primary compounds

Chemicals made by plants and needed for the plant's own metabolism.

Primary growth

Cells produced by an apical meristem. The growth a plant by the actions of apical meristems on the shoot and root apices in producing plant primary tisues.

Primary macronutrients

Elements that plants require in relatively large quantities: nitrogen, phosphorus, and potassium.

Primary meristems

The apical meristems on the shoot and root apices in plants that produce plant primary tissues.

Primary root
The first root formed by a plant.

Primary structure
The sequence of amino acids in a protein.

Primates
The taxonomic order of mammals that includes prosimians (lemurs and tarsiers), monkeys, apes, and humans; characteristics include large brain, stereoscopic vision, and grasping hand.

Primitive
It refers to a character or feature in a group of organisms that is inherited from a common ancestor. Teeth are a primitive characteristic of birds since birds inherited them from their dinosaur ancestors.

Primrose
(Primrose family - primulaceae-) It comprises about 1000 species of plants living in temperate countries. They are mainly herbs. Some genera such as primula or cyclamen are very interesting for gardening.

Principle of independent assortment
Mendel's second law; holds that during gamete formation, alleles in one gene pair segregate into gametes independently of the alleles of other gene pairs. As a result, if enough gametes are produced, the collective group of gametes will contain all combinations of alleles possible for that organism.

Principle of segregation
Mendel's first law; holds that each pair of factors of heredity separate during gamete formation so that each gamete receives one member of a pair.

Prions
Infectious agents composed only of one or more protein molecules without any accompanying genetic information.

Proboscis
Elongated organ, usually associated with the mouth. The proboscis is an important feeding appendage in echiurans.

Producers
The first level in a food pyramid; consist of organisms that generate the food used by all other organisms in the ecosystem; usually consist of plants making food by photosynthesis.

Progesterone
One of the two female reproductive hormones secreted by the ovaries.

Programmable logic controller, (PLC)
A device for industrial control. Types of operations common to PLC's are polling or checking sensors and activating/deactivating valves and switches, compared against programmed presets or default levels.

Prokaryote
Type of cell that lacks a membrane-bound nucleus and has no membrane organelles; a bacterium. Prokaryotes are more primitive than eukaryotes. Cells lacking membrane-bound organelles and having a single circular chromosome, and ribosomes surrounded by a cell membrane. Prokaryotes were the first forms of life on earth, evolving over 3.5 billion years ago.

Prokaryotic
Literally "before the nucleus", the term applies to all bacteria and archaea. Prokaryotic cells have no internal

membranes or cytoskeleton. Their DNA is circular, not linear.

Prolactin
A hormone produced by the anterior pituitary; secreted at the end of pregnancy when it activates milk production by the mammary glands.

Promiscuity
A form of polygyny or polyandry in which a member of one sex mates with more than one member of the other sex but the relationship is ephemeral and dissolves after mating as opposed to sustaining through time via the formation of a social bond.

Promoter
A promoter is a region of DNA that facilitates the transcription of a particular gene. Promoters are located near the genes they regulate, on the same strand and typically upstream (towards the 5' region of the sense strand).

Prophase
1) The first stage of mitosis during which chromosomes condense, the nuclear envelope disappears, and the centrioles divide and migrate to opposite ends of the cell.
2) The first stage of mitosis and meiosis (although in meiosis this phase is denoted with either a roman numeral I or II) where the chromatin condenses to form chromosomes, nucleolus dissolves, nuclear envelope dissolves, and the spindle begins to form.

Prostaglandins
A hormone-like group of molecules involved in a variety of functions in the body, including inflammation, blood flow in the kidney, protection of the stomach lining, blood clotting, and relaxation or contraction of muscles in the lungs, uterus, and blood vessels. The formation of prostaglandins is blocked by NSAIDs.

Prostate gland
A gland that is located near and empties into the urethra; produces a secretion that enhances sperm viability. Gland involved in the reproductive system in males, the prostate secretes a sperm activating chemical into the semen during the arousal/ejaculation response.

Protein
A large, complex molecule composed of amino acids. Wide variety of functions e.g. enzymes catalysing biochemical reactions, membrane receptors in cell signalling, transport and storage, antibody proteins, nutritional proteins, contractile muscle fibers (actin and myosin) etc.

Protein passage
The channel of protein into the permeate stream. This could be the result of using too "open" a membrane pore structure; a mechanical failure in the cartridge; or degradation of the membrane over time due to chemical incompatibility.

Proteinaceous
Describes any structure which is composed of protein.

Proteinoids
Polymers of amino acids formed spontaneously from inorganic molecules; have enzyme-like properties and can catalyze chemical reactions.

Proteins
Polymers made up of amino acids that perform a wide variety of cellular functions. One of the classes of organic macromolecules that function

as structural and control elements in living systems. Proteins are polymers of amino acids linked together by peptide bonds.

Proteomics
The identification and analysis of the total protein complement expressed by any given cell type under defined conditions.

Prothallus
In ferns, a small heart-shaped bisexual gametophyte.

Protista
The taxonomic Kingdom from which the other three eukaryotic kingdoms (Fungi, Animalia and Plantae) are thought to have evolved. The earliest eukaryotes were single-celled organisms that would today be placed in this admittedly not monophyletic group. The endosymbiosis theory suggests that eukaryotes may have evolved independently several times.

Protists
Single-celled organisms; a type of eukaryote.

Proton
A subatomic particle in the nucleus of an atom that carries a positive charge. The positively charged (+1) subatomic particle located in the atomic nucleus and having a mass slightly less than that of a neutron. Elements differ by the number of protons in their atoms.

Protoplasm
All the contents of a cell, including the nucleus.

Protostele
When a plant's vascular tissue develops in a solid central bundle, it is said to have a protostele. See also siphonostele and eustele.

Protostomes
Animals in which the Þrst opening that appears in the embryo becomes the mouth; e.g., mollusks, annelids, and arthropods.

Protozoa
Single-celled protists grouped by their method of locomotion. This group includes Paramecium, Amoeba, and many other commonly observed protists.

Proximal tubule
The winding section of the renal tubule where most reabsorption of water, sodium, amino acids, and sugar takes place.

Pseudocoelom
In nematodes, a closed fluid-containing cavity that acts as a hydrostatic skeleton to maintain body shape, circulate nutrients, and hold the major body organs.

Pseudocoelomates
Animals that have a body cavity that is in direct contact with the outer muscular layer of the body and does not arise by splitting of the mesoderm; e.g., roundworms.

Pseudoelaters
Moisture-sensitive cells produced in the sporangium of hornworts.

Pseudoextinction
The apparent disappearance of a taxon. In cases of pseudoextinction, this disappearance is not due to the death of all members, but the evolution of novel features in one or more lineages, so that the new clades are not recognized as belonging to the paraphyletic ancestral group, whose members have ceased to exist. The Dinosauria, if defined so as to exclude the birds, is an example

of a group that has undergone pseudoextinction.

Pseudopodia

Fingerlike extensions from an amoeboid cell; literally "false feet".

Psig

(English system) Pounds per square inch, a unit of pressure. 1 psig = 6.78 kPa = 70.05 grams per square centimeter.

Pteridophyte

Plant in which the sporophyte generation is the larger phase and in which the gametophyte lives an existence independent of its parent sporophyte. Pteridophytes are almost all vascular plants, and include the lycophytes, trimerophytes, sphenophytes, and ferns.

Pteridosperm

An extinct group of seed plants which bore fern-like leaves.

Pulmonary artery

The artery that carries blood from the right ventricle of the vertebrate heart to the lungs. Artery carrying oxygen-poor blood from the heart to the lungs.

Pulmonary circuit

The loop of the circulatory system that carries blood to and from the lungs.

Pulmonary vein

The vein that carries oxygenated blood from the lungs to the left atrium of the heart. Veins carrying oxygenated blood from the lungs to the heart.

Pulmonate

Terrestrial snails belong to a group within the Order Stylommatophora called the 'pulmonates'.

Punctuated equilibrium

A model that holds that the evolutionary process is characterized by long periods with little or no change interspersed with short periods of rapid speciation.

Pupa

In metamorphozing insects, a stage between the larva and adult during which the organism undergoes major developmental changes.

Pupal case (skin, shell), cocoon

Silky puparium of moths and many other insects; also silky egg case of spiders.

Purine

One of the groups of nitrogenous bases that are part of a nucleotide. Purines are adenine and guanine, and are double-ring structures.

Pycnoxylic

Wood in which there is little or no parenchyma tissue among the xylem is called pycnoxylic. Conifers and flowering plants have pycnoxylic wood.

Pygidium

In trilobites, the posterior division of the body, formed by fusion of the telson with one or more posterior pleurae.

Pyloric sphincter

The ring of muscle at the junction of the stomach and small intestine that regulates the movement of food into the small intestine.

Pyrimidine

One of the groups of nitrogenous bases that are part of a nucleotide. Pyrimidines are single ringed, and consist of the bases thymine (in DNA), uracil (replacing thymine in RNA), and cytosine.

Pyrogen

A substance that produces a fever within a warm-blooded animal when injected into the bloodstream. Filtration materials of construction that come in contact with injectable liquids must meet pyrogenicity standards and be nonpyrogenic.

Pyrogenicity

The tendency of a substance to raise body temperature in a warm-blooded animal when injected into the bloodstream. Filtration materials intended for the processing of injectable liquids must meet pyrogenicity standards and classified as non-pyrogenic. The Limulus Amoebocyte Lysate (LAL) test is a standard test for pyrogenicity.

Q

Qa

Qualitative analysis is the process of determining which elements or compounds are present. Quantitative analysis is determination of how much of one substance is present.

Quantum models of speciation

Models of evolution that hold that speciation sometimes occurs rapidly as well as over long periods, as the classical theory proposed.

Quaternary period

The most recent geologic period of the Cenozoic Era, the Quaternary began 2 million years ago with the growth of northern hemisphere continental glaciers and the ice age.

Quaternary structure

In some proteins, a fourth structural level created by interactions with other proteins. Aspect of protein structure determined by the number and arrangement of polypeptides in a large protein such as hemoglobin.

R

Race

A subdivision of a species that is capable of interbreeding with other members of the species.

Raceme

(Type of inflorescence). In a raceme the florets are attached along a floral peduncle with stems similar in length. Young florets appear above the old ones.

Radially symmetrical

In animals, refers to organisms with their body parts arranged around a central axis. Such animals tend to be circular or cylindrical in shape.

Radiation

"The evolution of several closely related species from a single ancestor, especially when the species evolve morphological differences that allow the coexistence or spread of the species to occupy many different habitats or ecological roles."

Radicle

(Part of the embryo in a seed) is the part of the embryo which emerges first. Once outside it develops into a taproot producing root hairs and secondary roots.

Radioactive decay

The spontaneous decay of an atom to an atom of a different element by emission of a particle from its nucleus (alpha and beta decay) or by electron capture.

Radio-carbon dating

Method for determining the age of an organic substance by measuring the amount of the carbon isotope, carbon-14, remaining in the substance; useful for determining ages in the range of 500 to 70,000 years.

Radioisotope

Term applied to a radioactive isotope, such as carbon-14 or uranium 238. Radioisotope nuclei are unstable and spontaneously breakdown and emit one of a number of types of radiation.

Radiometric time

Type of absolute time determined by the relative porportions of radioisotopes to stable daughter isotopes.

Radiospermic

Having seeds which are round or ovoid.

Radula

A rough, raspy tongue used to grate food, characteristic of most mollusks.

Rain shadow

The dry region on the leeward side of a mountain range, where rainfall is noticeably less than on the windward side. For example, the White Mountains in east central California are in the rain shadow of the Sierra Nevada.

Range

The geographic area or spatial distribution in which a species is normally found.

Rank

In traditional taxonomy, taxa are ranked according to their level of inclusiveness. Thus a genus contains one or more species, a family includes one or more genera, and so on.

Rare

"Present in a given location but unlikely to be seen without considerable effort, usually because the species is found in small numbers or because (for nonresident species) it is present in only some years."

Rattle

Loosely interlocking remnants of shed skin, present on a rattlesnake's tail, that are vibrated to make a rattling sound to deter predators.

Ray-finned

Taxonomic group of fish, such as trout, tuna, salmon, and bass, that have thin, bony supports holding the ᵭns away from the body and an internal swim bladder that changes the buoyancy of the body; one of the two main types of bony ᵭshes.

Rbcl

A gene which is located in the chloroplast of photosynthetic organisms. It codes for the large subunit of the protein rubisco, and its sequence has been useful in plant phylogenies.

Reabsorption

The return to the blood of most of the water, sodium, amino acids, and sugar that were removed during filtration; occurs mainly in the proximal tubule of the nephron.

Rebound

To spring back after a weight has been removed.

Receptacle

It is the lower structure which supports the flower. Besides protecting floral pieces, it takes care of the ovules.

Receptor

Protein on or protruding from the cell surface to which select chemicals can bind. The opiate receptor in brain cells allows both the natural chemical as well as foreign (opiate) chemicals to bind.

Receptor protein

Specific proteins found on the cell surface to which hormones or other molecules bind, triggering a specific reaction within the cell. Receptor proteins are responsible for initiating reactions as diverse as nerve impulses, changes in cell metabolism, and hormone release.

Recessive

Refers to an allele of a gene that is expressed when the dominant allele is not present. An allele expressed only in homozygous form, when the dominant allele is absent.

Recombinant DNA molecules

New combinations of DNA fragments formed by cutting DNA segments from two sources with restriction enzyme and then joining the fragments together with DNA ligase. Interspecies transfer of genes usually through a vector such as a virus or plasmid.

Recombinant DNA technology

A series of techniques in which DNA fragments are linked to self-replicating forms of DNA to create recombinant DNA molecules. These molecules in turn are replicated in a host cell to create clones of the inserted segments.

Recombination

A way in which meiosis produces new combinations of genetic information. During synapsis, chromatids may exchange parts with other chromatids, leading to a physical exchange of chromosome parts; thus, genes from both parents may be combined on the same chromosome, creating a new combination.

Recovery

Percentage of the target substance that can be collected in the retentate or permeate solution after processing.

Rectrices

Rectrices (from the Latin for "helmsman"), which help the bird to brake and steer in flight, lie in a single horizontal row on the rear margin of the anatomical tail. Only the central pair are attached (via ligaments) to the tail bones; the remaining rectrices are embedded into the rectricial bulbs, complex structures of fat and muscle that surround those bones. Rectrices are always paired, with a vast majority of species having six pairs. They are absent in grebes and some ratites, and greatly reduced in size in penguins.

Red algae

Common name for the algae placed in the division Rhodophyta.

Red bed

Sedimentary layers composed primarily of sandstone, siltstone, and shale, that are predominantly red in color due to the presence of iron oxides; often used in reference to the Permian or Triassic sediments of the western U.S.

Red blood cell

Component of the blood that transports oxygen with the hemoglobin molecule.

Red tides

Phenomenon associated with population explosions (blooms) of certain types of dinoflagellates; red structures inside the dinoflagellates cause the water to have a reddish color.

Redox; reduction

Gain electrons; oxidation lose electrons. Occur at the same time. redox When an iron nail rusts, the iron is oxidized and oxygen is reduced. Oxidation is a loss of electrons and reduction is a gain of electrons. Here the iron gave electrons to the oxygen. In other examples, oxygen may not be involved. redox energy transfers are the basis of all life on earth. We will devote an entire page to redox later.

Reduction

The gain of an electron or a hydrogen atom. The gain of electrons or hydrogens in a chemical reaction.

Reductional division

The first division in meiosis; results in each daughter cell receiving one member of each pair of chromosomes.

Reef

A large ridge or mound-like structure within a body of water that is built by calcareous organisms such as corals, red algae, and bivalves; barrier reef- n. A reef growing offshore from a land mass and separated by a lagoon or estuary, e.g, the Great Barrier Reef of Australia; patch reef- A discontinuous reef growing in small areas, separated by bare areas of sand or debris, often part of a larger reef complex.

Reflex

A response to a stimulus that occurs without conscious effort; one of the simplest forms of behavior.

Reflex arc

Pathway of neurons, effector(s) and sensory receptors that participate in a reflex.

Region of division

The area of cell division in the tip of a plant root.

Region of elongation

The area in the tip of a plant root where cells grow by elongating, thereby increasing the length of the root.

Region of maturation (differentiation)

The area where primary tissues and root hairs develop in the tip of a plant root.

Regression

A drop in sea level that causes an area of the land to be uncovered by seawater.

Rejection

Amount, in percent, of a particle or molecule that does not pass through (that is, is retained by) a membrane. Equivalent to retention.

Relatedness

Two clades are more closely related when they share a more recent common ancestor between them than they do with any other clade.

Relative time

Type of geologic time (absolute time being the other) that places events in a sequence relative to each other.

Remiges

Remiges (from the Latin for "oarsman") are located on the posterior side of the wing. Ligaments attach the long calami, or quills, firmly to the wing bones, and a thick, strong band of tendinous tissue—known as the postpatagium—helps to hold and support the remiges in place. Corresponding remiges on individual birds are symmetrical between the two wings, matching to a large extent in size and shape (except in the case of mutation or damage), though not necessarily in pattern. They are given different names depending on their position along the wing.

Renal tubule

The renal tubule is the portion of the nephron containing the tubular fluid filtered through the glomerulus. After passing through the renal tubule, the filtrate continues to the collecting duct system, which is not part of the nephron.

Reniform

Type of leaf. Kidney-shaped leaf.

Renin

Renin also known as an angiotensinogenase, is an enzyme that participates in the body's renin-angiotensin system (RAS) -- also known as the Renin-Angiotensin-Aldosterone Axis -- that mediates extracellular volume (i.e., that of the blood plasma, lymph and interstitial fluid), and arterial vasoconstriction. Thus, it regulates the body's mean arterial blood pressure.

Repeat sequences

The length of a nucleotide sequence that is repeated in a tandem cluster.

Replacement

Fossilization process in which the original material in an organism is broken down and replaced by different minerals.

Replication

Process by which DNA is duplicated prior to cell division.

Reproduction

The manufacture of offspring as part of an organism's life cycle. This is not the same as dispersal. Reproduction may be sexual, involving the fusion of gametes, or asexual.

Reproductive isolating mechanism

Biological or behavioral characteristics that reduce or prevent interbreeding with other populations; e.g., the production of sterile hybrids. Establishment of reproductive isolation is considered essential for development of a new species.

Reproductive system

One of eleven major body organ systems in animals; is responsible for reproduction and thus the survival of the species.

Reptiles

Reptiles (Reptilia) are members of a group of air-breathing, ectothermic (cold-blooded) vertebrates which are characterized by laying shelled eggs (except for some vipers and constrictor snakes that give live birth), and having skin covered in scales and/or scutes. They are tetrapods, either having four limbs or being descended from four-limbed ancestors. Modern reptiles inhabit every continent with the exception of Antarctica. Reptiles originated around 320-310 million years ago during the Carboniferous period, having evolved from advanced reptile-like amphibians that became increasingly adapted to life on dry land.

Reptilia

The class of vertebrates whose members have dry skin with scales and reproduce by amniotic eggs. This class includes snakes, lizards, and alligators.

Resident

A nonmigratory species that completes its annual cycle within a fixed area.

Resistance

Viruses can also develop resistance to antiviral drugs.

Resolution

In relation to microscopes, the ability to view adjacent objects as distinct structures.

Resource partitioning

The division of resources such that a few dominant species exploit most of the available resources while other species divide the remainder; helps explain why a few species are abundant in a community while others are represented by only a few individuals.

Respiration

1) Breathing as part of gas exchange; or
2) Cellular metabolism.

Respirator

A safety device worn over the nose and mouth to remove noxious substances from air. The respirator must contain the proper filter for the hazard present.

Respiratory surface

A thin, moist, epithelial surface that oxygen can cross to move into the body and carbon dioxide can cross to move out of the body.

Respiratory system

The respiratory system is the anatomical system of an organism that introduces respiratory gases to the interior and performs gas exchange. In humans and other mammals, the anatomical features of the respiratory system include airways, lungs, and the respiratory muscles. Molecules of oxygen and carbon dioxide are passively exchanged, by diffusion, between the gaseous external environment and the blood. This exchange process occurs in the alveolar region of the lungs. Other animals, such as insects, have respiratory systems with very simple anatomical features, and in amphibians even the skin plays a vital role in gas exchange. Plants also have respiratory systems but the directionality of gas exchange can be opposite to that in animals. The respiratory system in plants also includes anatomical features such as holes on the undersides of leaves known as stomata.

Resting potential

The difference in electrical charge across the plasma membrane of a neuron.

Restriction enzymes

A series of enzymes that attach to DNA molecules at speciÞc nucleotide sequences and cut both strands of DNA at those sites. A bacterial enzyme that cuts DNA at a specific recognition sequence. This is a bacterial defense against viral DNA and plasmid DNA and is now used as an important tool in biotechnology.

Restriction fragment length polymorphism (RFLP)

A heritable difference in DNA fragment length and fragment number; passed from generation to generation in a codominant way.

Retentate

The portion of the feed solution that does not pass through a cross flow membrane filter.

Retention

The ability of a separations device to retain an entity of a given size.

Reticulate

Interconnecting, like a network.

Reticulated

Arranged in a network pattern.

Reticulation

Joining of separate lineages on a phylogenetic tree, generally through hybridization or through lateral gene transfer. Fairly common in certain land plant clades; reticulation is thought to be rare among metazoans.

Reticulopodia

Long thread-like pseudopodia that branch apart and rejoin, forming a fine network. They are characteristic of forams.

Retina

The vertebrate retina (from Latin re-te, meaning "net") is a light-sensitive tissue lining the inner surface of the eye. The optics of the eye create an image of the visual world on the retina, which serves much the same function as the film in a camera. Light striking the retina initiates a cascade of chemical and electrical events that ultimately trigger nerve impulses. These are sent to various visual centers of the brain through the fibers of the optic nerve.

Retroviruses

Viruses that contain a single strand of RNA as their genetic material and reproduce by copying the RNA into a complementary DNA strand using the enzyme reverse transcriptase. The single-stranded DNA is then copied, and the resulting double-stranded DNA is inserted into a chromosome of the host cell.

Reverse migration

A phenomenon in which migrating individuals orient in the direction opposite the normal one for the species at that season.

Reverse osmosis

Type of cross flow filtration used for removal of very small solutes (<1,000 Daltons) and salts. It uses a semipermeable membrane under high pressure to separate water from ionic materials. High pressure is necessary to overcome the natural osmotic pressure created by the concentration gradient across the membrane.

Reverse transcriptase

An enzyme found in retroviruses that copies the virus' genetic material from single-stranded RNA into double-stranded DNA.

Reverse transcription

Process of transcribing a single-stranded DNA from a single-stranded RNA (the reverse of transcription); used by retroviruses as well as in biotechnology.

Rheumatoid arthritis

A crippling form of arthritis that begins with inflammation and thickening of the synovial membrane, followed by bone degeneration and disfigurement.

Rhizoid

A cellular outgrowth of a plant that usually aids in anchoring to the surface and increasing surface area to acquire water or nutrients; found in mosses, liverworts, and hornworts.

Rhizome

(Type of plant according to the stem) Rhizomes are stems that grow horizontally under the surface of the ground. From them roots are born, moving downwards into the ground and other herbaceous stems follow the opposite way searching the air. So, apart from storing food, they are a way of plant propagation. Canes would be a good example of them.

Rhodopsin

A visual pigment contained in the rods of the retina in the eye..

Rhyolite

Rhyolite is an igneous, volcanic (extrusive) rock, of felsic (silica-rich) composition (typically > 69% SiO_2 — see the TAS classification). It may have any texture from glassy to aphanitic to porphyritic. The mineral assemblage is usually quartz, alkali feldspar and plagioclase (in a ratio > 1:2 — see the QAPF diagram). Biotite and hornblende are common accessory minerals.

Ribonucleic acid (RNA)

Nucleic acid containing ribose sugar and the base Uracil; RNA functions in protein synthesis. The single starnded molecule transcribed from one strand of the DNA. There are three types of RNA, each is involved in protein synthesis. RNA is made up nucleotides containing the sugar ribose, a phosphate group, and one of four nitrogenous bases (adenine, uracil, cytosine or guanine).

Ribose

Sugar found in nucleotides of RNA and in ATP.

Ribosomal RNA

One of the three types of RNA; rRNA is a structural component in ribosomes.

Ribosomal subunits
Two units that combine with mRNA to form the ribosomal-mRNA complex at which protein synthesis occurs.

Ribosomes
Small organelles made of rRNA and protein in the cytoplasm of prokaryotic and eukaryotic cells; aid in the production of proteins on the rough endoplasmic reticulum and ribosome complexes. The site of protein synthesis. The ribosome is composed of two subunits that attach to the mRNA at the beginning of protein synthesis and detach when the polypeptide has been translated.

Rictal bristles
Stiff, hair-like modified contour feathers that occur in a row and project from each side of the corners of the mouth.

Rift
A long, narrow crack in the entire thickness of the Earth's crust, which is bounded by normal faults on either side and forms as the crust is pulled apart; v. To split the Earth's crust; rift zone- The area on continents where a trough bounded by normal faults is forming; the site of crustal extension, similar to that which occurs at mid-oceanic ridges; rift basin or rift valley-n. The long, and fairly wide trough that has formed as a section of the Earth's crust has dropped down along faults, e.g., African Rift Valley in East Africa.

Riparian
Having to do with the edges of streams or rivers.

River dolphins
A group of dolphins that live in the major rivers of the world, including the Amazon in Brazil, the Ganges in India, the Yangtze in China, and the Irrawady in Myanmar, to name a few.

RNA (ribonucleic acid)
A long, usually single-stranded chain of nucleotides that has structural, genetic, and enzymatic roles. There are three major types of RNA, which are all involved in making proteins: messenger RNA (mRNA), transfer RNA (tRNA), and ribosomal RNA (rRNA). RNA is composed of the sugar ribose, phosphate groups, and the bases adenine, uracil, guanine, and cytosine. Certain viruses contain RNA, instead of DNA, as their genetic material.

RNA polymerase
During transcription, an enzyme that attaches to the promoter region of the DNA template, joins nucleotides to form the synthesized strand of RNA and detaches from the template when it reaches the terminator region.

RNA sequencing
A set of four RNases that cleave 3' to specific nucleotides are used to produce a ladder of fragments from end-labelled RNA. Polyacrylamide gel electrophoresis analysis allows the sequence to be read

RNA transcript
Term applied to RNA transcribed in the nucleus.

Roche moutonee
A rock formation created by a glacier. The front and sides of the rock are rounded where ice moved over it, and the back is angular, where freezing and thawing broke off pieces; the name comes from the French for "fleecy rock," also called a sheepback.

Rock cycle
The process through which one type of rock (igneous, sedimentary, or

metamorphic) is converted into another.

Rockrose

The Rockrose family - Cistaceae-comprises about 150 species of mainly Mediterranean plants. They are almost always bushes.

Rodinia

A supercontinent that existed during the Late Precambrian before the supercontinent Pannotia; the oldest supercontinent for which we have a good record; Russian for "homeland."

Rods

Light receptors in primates' eyes that provide vision in dim light.

Root

Part of the plant which usually grows below the ground. The root is an important part of the plant.

Root cap

Part of the root. It is a kind of protection the root ends with. It is designed to drill the soil and it is able to guide the root growth by perceiving gravity.

Root hairs

Part of the root. They are minute filaments roots are covered with. They absorb water and nutrients from the soil.

Root system

Plant organ systems that anchors the plant in place, stores excess sugars, and absorbs water and mineral nutrients. That part of the plant below ground level.

Root-leaf-vascular system axis

Refers to the arrangement in vascular plants in which the roots anchor the plant and absorb water and nutrients, the leaves carry out photosynthesis, and the vascular system connects the roots and leaves, carrying water and nutrients to the leaves and carrying sugars and other products of photosynthesis from the leaves to other regions of the plant.

Rootlet

(Part of the root) The arise from the primary root. (Taproot) They are not as thick as the primary one, growing sidewards.

Rosette

A series of whorls of leaves or leaf-like structure produced at the base of the stem, just above the ground.

Rostral scale

The rostral scale, or rostral, in snakes and other scaled reptiles is the median plate on the tip of the snout that borders the mouth opening. It corresponds to the mental scale in the lower jaw. The term pertains to the rostrum, or nose. In snakes, the shape and size of this scale is one of many characteristics used to differentiate species from one another.

Rostrum

An anatomical structure that projects from the head of an animal, such as a snout.

Rosulate

Type of leaf forming a rosette, like a ring around the stem .

Rough

Related to leaves and stems. Not smooth. somewhat unpleasant to touch.

Rounded

The shortest version of an elliptical egg shape; spherical.

Rubisco

Protein which fixes carbon in photosynthetic organisms. It binds molecules of carbon dioxide to a five-carbon molcule. Rubisco is the most common protein on earth.

Rubp

Ribulose biphosphate; the 5-carbon chemical that combines with carbon dioxide at the beginning of the Calvin Cycle.

S

S phase
That period of interphase when new DNA is synthesized as part of replication of the chromatin.

Salinity
A measure of the salt concentration of water. Higher salinity means more dissolved salts.

Salivary amylase
An enzyme secreted by the salivary glands that begins the breakdown of complex sugars and starches.

Salivary glands
The salivary glands in mammals are exocrine glands, glands with ducts, that produce saliva. They also secrete amylase, an enzyme that breaks down starch into maltose. In other organisms such as insects, salivary glands are often used to produce biologically important proteins like silk or glues, and fly salivary glands contain polytene chromosomes that have been useful in genetic research.

Salt lick
A natural or artificial deposit of exposed salt that animals lick for nutrients.

Samara
Type of indehescent dry fruit. A samara is a winged achene

Sandstone
Sedimentary rock composed of sand-sized clasts.

Sanitization
A cleaning process that destroys most living microorganisms.

Saprophyte
Organism which feeds on dead and decaying organisms, allowing the nutrients to be recycled into the ecosystem. Fungi and bacteria are two groups with many important saprophytes.

Sapwood
Layers of secondary xylem that are still functional in older woody plants; visible as the outer lighter areas in the cross section of a tree trunk.

Sarcomeres
The functional units of skeletal muscle; consist of ƀlaments of myosin and actin.

Saturated fat
A fat with single covalent bonds between the carbons of its fatty acids.

Saw-scaling
Action of a snake curving its body in concentric curves and rasping its keeled scales together to make a sawing sound as a warning.

Saxitoxin
Neurotoxin found in a variety of dinoflagellates. If ingested, it may cause respiratory failure and cardiac arrest.

Scale

Soft, usually overlapping body covering in snakes, lizards, and amphisbaenians.

Scanning electron microscope (SEM)

A special kind of microscope that scans samples with a high-energy beam of electrons to produce a high-resolution, detailed, three-dimensional image. An SEM can magnify a sample up to 250 times that of the best light microscopes.

Scape

The first segment in an insect's anteannae, nearest its head.

Scavenger

An organism that feeds upon dead and dying organisms.

Schwann cells

Schwann cells or neurolemmocytes are the principal glia of the peripheral nervous system (PNS). Glial cells function to support neurons and in the PNS, also include satellite cells, olfactory ensheathing cells, enteric glia and glia that reside at sensory nerve endings, such as the Pacinian corpuscle. Myelinating Schwann cells wrap around axons of motor and sensory neurons to form the myelin sheath.

Scientific method

Systematic apporach of observation, hypothesis formation, hypothesis testing and hypothesis evaluation that forms the basis for modern science.

Sclereids

Plant cells with thick secondary walls that provide the gritty textures in pears.

Sclerenchyma

One of the three major cell types in plants; have thickened, rigid, secondary walls that are hardened with lignin; provide support for the plant. Sclerenchyma cells include Þbers and sclereids. Plant tissue type consisting of elongated cells with thickened secondary walls for support of the plant.

Sclerophyllous

Type of leaf. Showing hard, rough texture, covered with waxen substances, generally easy broken when folded.

Scrape nest

A rudimentary ground nest site, usually with no lining, that a bird forms by creating a shallow depression in the ground.

Screen or membrane filter

Filter that works by size exclusion (sieving) via a regular porous matrix.

Scrotum

In mammals, a pouch of skin located outside the body cavity into which the testes descend; provides proper temperature for the testes.

Scrub

Type of vegetation. Vegetation composed of bushes, shrubs and small trees.

Scute

A scute or scutum (Latin scutum, plural: scuta "shield") is a bony external plate or scale, as on the shell of a turtle, the skin of crocodilians, the feet of some birds or the anterior portion of the mesonotum in insects. Scutes are similar to scales and serve the same function. Unlike the scales of fish and snakes, which are formed from the epidermis, scutes are formed in the lower vascular layer of the skin and the epidermal element is only the top surface.

Sea-floor spreading

The process of adding to the Earth's crust at mid-ocean ridges as magma wells up and forces previously formed crust apart.

Season

period of time related with a kind of climate and the subsequent vegetation.

Seaweed

Any large photosynthetic protist, including rhodophytes and kelps. Seaweeds are not true plants, but like plants they can make their own food.

Second law of thermodynamics (entropy)

The energy available after a chemical reaction is less than that at the beginning of a reaction; energy conversions are not 100% efficient.

Second messenger

The mechanism by which nonsteroid hormones work on target cells. A hormone binds to receptors on the cell's plasma membrane activating a molecule & emdash; the second messenger & emdash; that activates other intracellular molecules that elicit a response. The second messenger can be cyclic AMP, cyclic GMP, inositol triphosphate, diacrylglycerol, or calcium.

Secondary

One of the shorter flight feathers of the wing, attached along the ulna in the inner wing.

Secondary (lateral) meristems

Plant meristems that produce secondary growth from a cambium. Secondary cell wall

In woody plants, a second wall inside the primary cell wall; contains alternating layers of cellulose and lignin.

Secondary compounds

Plant products that are not important in metabolism but serve other purposes, such as attracting animals for pollination or killing parasites.

Secondary extinction

The death of one population due to the extinction of another, often a food species.

Secondary growth

Cells in a plant that are produced by a cambium. Increase in girth of a plant due to the action of lateral meristems such as the vascular cambium. The main cell produced in secondary growth is secondary xylem, better known as wood.

Secondary immunity

Resistance to an antigen the second time it appears. Because of the presence of B and T memory cells produced during the first exposure to the antigen, the second response is faster and more massive and lasts longer than the primary immune response.

Secondary macronutrients

Elements that plants require in relatively small quantities: calcium, magnesium, and sulfur.

Secondary phloem

Phloem produced by the vascular cambium in a woody plant stem or root.

Secondary structure

The structure of a protein created by the formation of hydrogen bonds between different amino acids; can be a pleated sheet, alpha helix, or random coil. Shape of a protein caused by attraction between R-groups of amino acids.

Secondary xylem

Xylem produced by the vascular cambium in a woody plant stem or root; wood.

Secretin

A hormone produced in the duodenum that stimulates alkaline secretions by the pancreas and inhibits gastric emptying.

Secretion

The release of a substance in response to the presence of food or specific neural or hormonal stimulation.

Sedentary

Living in a fixed location, as with most plants, tunicates, sponges, etc. Contrast with motile.

Sedges

Grass-like plants, many in the genus Carex, that are often found in wetlands.

Sediment

Loose aggregate of solids derived from preexisting rocks, or solids precipitated from solution by inorganic chemical processes or extracted from solution by organisms.

Sedimentary rock

Sedimentary rocks are types of rock that are formed by the deposition of material at the Earth's surface and within bodies of water. Sedimentation is the collective name for processes that cause mineral and/or organic particles (detritus) to settle and accumulate or minerals to precipitate from a solution. Particles that form a sedimentary rock by accumulating are called sediment. Before being deposited, sediment was formed by weathering and erosion in a source area, and then transported to the place of deposition by water, wind, mass movement or glaciers which are called agents of denudation.

Seed

Structure produced by some plants in which the next generation sporophyte is surrounded by gametophyte nutritive tissues. An immature sporophyte in an arrested state of development, surrounded by a protective seed coat.

Seed coat

Part of the seed. It is the outer layer of the seed. It protects the seed from aggressions included those of the hervivores.

Seedling

Related with germination of the seed. It is the young plant born from the seed.

Segmentation

In many animals, the body is divided into repeated subunits called segments, such as those in centipedes, insects, and annelids. Segmentation is the state of having or developing a body plan in this way.

Segments

Repeating units in the body parts of some animals.

Segregation

Separation of replicated chromosomes to opposite sides of the cell. Distribution of alleles on chromosomes into gametes during meiosis.

Selection

Process which favors one feature of organisms in a population over another feature found in the population. This occurs through differential reproduction—those with the favored feature produce more offspring than those with the other feature, such that they become a greater percentage of the population in the next generation.

Selective breeding
The selection of individuals with desirable traits for use in breeding. Over many generations, the practice leads to the development of strains with the desired characteristics.

Selectively permeable
Term describing a barrier that allows some chemicals to pass but not others. The cell membrane is such a barrier.

Semen
Semen is an organic fluid, also known as seminal fluid, that may contain spermatozoa. It is secreted by the gonads (sexual glands) and other sexual organs of male or hermaphroditic animals and can fertilize female ova. In humans, seminal fluid contains several components besides spermatozoa: proteolytic and other enzymes as well as fructose are elements of seminal fluid which promote the survival of spermatozoa and provide a medium through which they can move or "swim".

Semiconservative replication
Process of DNA replication in which the DNA helix is unwound and each strand serves as a template for the synthesis of a new complementary strand, which is linked to the old strand. Thus, one old strand is retained in each new molecule.

Semilunar valve
A valve between each ventricle of the heart and the artery connected to that ventricle. These are located at the base of both the pulmonary trunk (pulmonary artery) and the aorta, the two arteries taking blood out of the ventricles. These valves permit blood to be forced into the arteries, but prevent backflow of blood from the arteries into the ventricles. These valves do not have chordae tendineae, and are more similar to valves in veins than atrioventricular valves.

Seminal vesicles
Glands that contribute fructose to sperm. The fructose serves as an energy source. The structures that add fructose and hormones to semen.

Seminiferous tubules
Tubules on the interior of the testes where sperm are produced.

Semiplumes
Feathers that lie beneath the count our feathers and that, like down, lack interlocking barbules and barbicels.

Semi-precocial
Describes young that have characteristics of precocial young at hatch.

Sensor
In a closed system, the element that detects change and signals the effector to initiate a response.

Sensory (afferent) pathways
The portion of the peripheral nervous system that carries information from the organs and tissues of the body to the central nervous system.

Sensory cortex
A region of the brain associated with the parietal lobe.

Sensory input
Stimuli that the nervous system receives from the external or internal environment; includes pressure,

taste, sound, light, and blood pH.

Sensory neurons

Neurons that carry signals from receptors and transmit information about the environment to processing centers in the brain and spinal cord. Neurons carrying messages from sensory receptors to the spinal cord. Sometimes referred to as an afferent neuron.

Sepal

Modified leaves that protect a flower's inner petals and reproductive structures. Small, leaf-like structures in flowers that enclose and protect the developing flower. These are often green, but in many monocots they are the same color as the petals (in which case the term tepal is applied since sepals and petals look so much alike).

Separated or polysepalous

(Type of flowers) if the sepals are clearly separated each other.

Separation

Dividing a liquid or gas feed stream into separate components.

Septum

Partition which divides up a larger region into smaller ones, such as in the central body cavity of some anthozoa.

Serrate

(Type of leaf) serrate leaves have little bent teeth like those of a saw.

Sessile or stalkless

Leaves which do not possess a petiole The leaf expands itself directly from the blade.

Severe combined immunodeficiency (SCID)

A genetic disorder in which afflicted individuals have no functional immune system and are prone to infections.

Both the cell-mediated immune response and the antibody-mediated response are absent.

Sex chromosomes

The chromosomes that determine the sex of an organism. In humans, females have two X chromosomes, and males have one X chromosome and one Y chromosome. Chromosome that determines the gender (sex) of the individual. Human males have a large X and a smaller Y sex chromosomes, while human females have two X sex chromosomes.

Sex hormones

A group of steroid hormones produced by the adrenal cortex. Hormones that are produced in the gonads and promoted development and maintainence of the secondary sex characteristics and structures, prepare the female for pregnancy, and aid in development of gametes. Males produce testosterone, while females produce estrogen and progesterone.

Sex linkage

The condition in which the inheritance of a sex chromosome is coupled with that of a given gene; e.g., red-green color blindness and hemophilia in humans. Traits located on the X-chromosome.

Sexual reproduction

A type of reproduction in which two parents give rise to offspring that have unique combinations of genes inherited through the gametes of the two parents. Sexual reproduction involves meiosis and syngamy.

Sexual selection

A type of natural selection affecting traits that influence an individual's ability to attain or choose a mate, rather than traits that influence an individual's ability to survive.

Shaft

A feather's stiff central structure, to which the vanes are attached.

Shear rate

A ratio of velocity and distance expressed in units of sec-1. The shear rate for a hollow fiber cartridge is based on the flow rate through the fiber lumen and can be calculated as follows:

$$y = (4*q)/pi*R3$$

Where:

y = shear rate, sec-1
q = flow rate through the fiber lumen cm^3/sec
R = fiber radius, cm

Sheathed

(Type of leaf) Covered with a kind of sheath. This is applied to certain types of leaves having the base covered like this, as wheat.

Shell

Protective outer covering of a turtle or tortoise, comprising a carapace and a plastron.

Shoot

The plant stem; provides support for the leaves and flowers; one of the three major plant organs; also referred to as the shoot system.

Shorebirds

Sandpipers, plovers, and their close relatives of similar size and ecology, often associated with coastal and inland wetlands.

Short-day plants

Plants that flower during early spring or fall when nights are relatively long and days are short; e.g., poinsettia and dandelions.

Shrub

(Type of plant according to the stem) Shrubs are those plants with ligneous stems, from one to five meters tall. In this case, branching begins at soil level.

Siberia

A separate continental plate that existed from the Latest Precambrian to the Carboniferous, composed of a large part of central Russia, namely Siberia.

Siblicide

The death of young caused by fighting with siblings. Often occurs in larger birds (eagles, herons) in years when there is not enough food to feed all chicks.

Sickle cell anemia

Human autosomal recessive disease that causes production of abnormal red blood cells that collapse (or sickle) and cause circulatory problems.

Side chain

The part of an amino acid that confers its identity. Side chains range from a single hydrogen atom (for glycine) to a group of 15 or more atoms.

Siderite

Also called ironstone, that is a concretion of iron carbonate.

Sieve cells

Conducting cells in the phloem of vascular plants.

Sieve elements

Tubular, thin-walled cells that form a system of tubes extending from the roots to the leaves in the phloem of plants; lose their nuclei and organelles at maturity, but retain a functional plasma membrane.

Sieve plates

Pores in the end walls of sieve elements that connect the sieve elements together. The end walls of sieve tube cells that are perforated (sieves).

Sieve tube element

Sieve tubes are mainly to transport sugars and nutrients up and down the plant. In plant anatomy, sieve vascular tissue tube elements, also called sieve tube members, are a type of elongated sclerenchyma cells in phloem tissue. The ends of these cells are connected with other sieve elements, and together they constitute the sieve tube. The main function of the sieve tube is transport of carbohydrates in the plant (e.g., from the leaves to the fruits and roots). Unlike vessel elements, which are elongated cells that transport water and minerals in the xylem/wood that are dead when mature, and represent another kind of vascular tissue in the plant, sieve elements are living cells. They are thick and circular and can be different colours. Sieve tubes are not known as 'Real Cells' as they lack a substantial amount of cytoplasm.

Sieving

Removal of particulates from a feed stream as a result of entrapment within the depth of the membrane pore structure.

Signal transduction

The process by which chemical, electrical, or biological signals are transmitted into and within a cell.

Silica

Amorphous silicon dioxide (glass). It is a structural component in many organisms, such as diatoms and horsetails.

Silicification

Process whereby silica replaces the original material of a substance. For example, silicified wood.

Silique

Type of dehiscent dry fruit. Siliques come from joined carpels than open when grow up. It is the characteristic fruit of the Cruciferae family.

Sill

A sheet-like igneous intrusion that parallels the plane of the surrounding rock.

Silurian period

The geological time period of the Paleozoic Era following the Ordovician, between 435 and 395 million years ago, when plants colonized the land.

Simple

Type of leaf. A simple leaf shows an undivided blade or in case it has, they do not arrive the midrib.

Simple leaf

A leaf in which the blade does not form leaflets.

Sink

A body or process that acts as a storage device or disposal mechanism; e.g., plants and the oceans act as sinks absorbing atmospheric carbon dioxide. Also, a location in a plant where sugar is being consumed, either in metabolism or by conversion to starch.

Sink population

A breeding group that does not produce enough offspring to maintain itself in coming years without immigrants from other populations.

Sinkhole

A natural depression in the surface of the land caused by the collapse of the roof of a cavern or subterranean passage, generally occurring in limestone regions.

Sinoatrial (SA) node

A region of modified muscle cells in the right atrium that sends timed impulses to the heart's other muscle cells, causing them to contract; the heart's pacemaker.

Sinuate

Sinuate leaves have smooth edges, like waves.

Siphon

Opening in molluscs or in urochordates which draws water into the body cavity. In many molluscs, the siphon may be used to expel water forcibly, providing a means of propulsion.

Siphonostele

When a plant's vascular tissue develops as a central cylinder, it is said to have a siphonostele.

Sister chromatids

Chromatids joined by a common centromere and carrying identical genetic information (unless crossing-over has occurred).

Sister group

The two clades resulting from the splitting of a single lineage.

Size exclusion

Mechanism for removing particulates from a feed stream based strictly on the size of the particles. Retained particulates are held back because they are larger than the pore opening.

Skeletal muscle

Muscle that is generally attached to the skeleton and causes body parts to move; consists of muscle fibers. Voluntary muscle cells that have a striated appearance. These muscles control skeletal movements and are normally under conscious control.

Skeletal system

One of eleven major body organ systems in animals; supports the body, protects internal organs, and, with the muscular system, allows movement and locomotion.
Skeleton
Support structure in animals, against which the force of muscles acts. Vertebrates have a skeleton of bone or cartilage; arthropods have one made of chitin; while many other invertebrates use a hydrostatic skeleton, which is merely an incompressible fluid-filled region of their body.

Skin

One of eleven major body organ systems in animals; the outermost layer protecting multicellular animals from the loss or exchange of internal þuids and from invasion by foreign microorganisms; composed of two layers: the epidermis and dermis.

Sleep movement

In legumes, the movement of the leaves in response to daily rhythms of dark and light. The leaves are horizontal in daylight and folded vertically at night.

Sliding filament model

Model of muscular contraction in which the actin filaments in the sarcomere slide past the myosin filaments, shortening the sarcomere and therefore the muscle.

Slime

Slippery substance consisting of protozoa, algae, bacteria, and polymers. Slimes are often carbohydrate polymers made by bacteria and yeasts from sugars.

Slime molds
Protistans that may represent a transition between protistans and fungi.

Small intestine
A coiled tube in the abdominal cavity that is the major site of chemical digestion and absorption of nutrients; composed of the duodenum, jejunum, and ileum.

Smog
Smog is a type of air pollution; the word "smog" was coined in the mid 20th century as a portmanteau of the words smoke and fog to refer to smoky fog. The word was then intended to refer to what was sometimes known as pea soup fog, a familiar and serious problem in London from the 19th century to the mid 20th century. This kind of smog is caused by the burning of large amounts of coal within a city; this smog contains soot particulates from smoke, sulfur dioxide and other components. Modern smog, as found for example in Los Angeles, is a type of air pollution derived from vehicular emission from internal combustion engines and industrial fumes that react in the atmosphere with sunlight to form secondary pollutants that also combine with the primary emissions to form photochemical smog.

Smooth muscle
Muscle that lacks striations; found around circulatory system vessels and in the walls of such organs as the stomach, intestines, and bladder. Involuntary, not striated cells that control autonomic functions such as digestion and artery contraction.

Snapdragon
Erect plant, woody below of figwort family till 2 metres tall. Spear-shaped or oval leaves till 70 cm. Purple flowers in sticky spikes. Flowers sometimes yellowish. In old walls, rocks and dry places.

Social behavior
Behavior that takes place in a social context and results from the interaction between and among individuals.

Social monogomaysocial Monogamy
The monogamous association between a male and a female that cooperate in producing a clutch of eggs and (often) raising the resulting young.

Societies
The most highly organized type of social organization; consist of individuals that show varying degrees of cooperation and communication with one another; often have a rigid division of labor.

Sodium-potassium pump
The mechanism that uses ATP energy to reset the sodium and potassium ions after transmission of a nerve impulse.

Soil
Weathered rocks and minerals combined with air, water and organic matter that can support plants.

Solute
An ionic or organic compound dissolved in a solvent; for example, the sugar in a cup of coffee is a solute.

Somatic
Relating to the non-gonadal tissues and organs of an organism's body.

Somatic cell
A somatic cell (diploid) is any biological cell forming the body of an organism; that is, in a multicellular

organism, any cell other than a gamete, germ cell, gametocyte or undifferentiated stem cell. By contrast, gametes are cells that fuse during sexual reproduction, for organisms that reproduce sexually; Germ cells are cells that give rise to gametes; Stem cells are cells that can divide through mitosis and differentiate into diverse specialized cell types.

Somatic nervous system

The portion of the peripheral nervous system consisting of the motor neuron pathways that innervate skeletal muscles.

Somatic senses

All senses except vision, hearing, taste, and smell; include pain, temperature, and pressure.

Somatostatin

Pancreatic hormone that controls the rate of nutrient absorption into the bloodstream.

Somites

Mesodermal structures formed during embryonic development that give rise to segmented body parts such as the muscles of the body wall.

Song repertoire

The number of different individual songs produced by a single bird.

Songbird

The common name for members of the order Passeriformes, also called the passerines.

Source population

A breeding group that produces enough offspring to be self-sustaining and that often produces excess young that must disperse to other areas.

Southern ocean

The continuous expanse of ocean between Antarctica and the southern tips of the other continents.

Sparkler

Vessel with porous metal plate to hold crystals.

Special senses

Vision, hearing, taste, and smell.

Specialist

Organism which has adopted a lifestyle specific to a particular set of conditions. Contrast with generalist.

Species

One or more populations of interbreeding or potentially interbreeding organisms that are reproductively isolated in nature from all other organisms. Populations of individuals capable of interbreeding and producing viable, fertile offspring. The least inclusive taxonomic category commonly used.

Species diversity

The number of living species on Earth.

Species packing

The phenomenon in which present-day communities generally contain more species than earlier communities because organisms have evolved more adaptations over time.

Species richness

The number of species present in a community.

Sperm

The term sperm is derived from the word sperma (meaning "seed") and refers to the male reproductive cells. In the types of sexual reproduction known as anisogamy and oogamy, there is a marked difference in the size of the gametes with the smaller one being termed the "male" or sperm cell. A uniflagellar sperm cell that is motile is referred to as a spermatozoon, whereas a non-motile sperm cell is referred to as a spermatium.

Spermatogenesis
The development of sperm cells from spermatocytes to mature sperm, including meiosis.

Spermatophyte
A seed plant.

Spicule
Crystalline or mineral deposits found in sponges, sea cucumbers, or urochordates. They are structural components in many sponges, and may serve a protective function in other organisms.

Spike
(Type of inflorescence) spikes are similar to racemes, but florets are attached directly to the floral peduncle, without stems. The flowers of the mints would be a good example of spikes.

Spinal cord
A cylinder of nerve tissue extending from the brain stem; receives sensory information and sends output motor signals; with the brain, forms the central nervous system. Nerve cell collections extending from the base of the brain to just below the last rib vertebrae.

Spindle apparatus
Microtubule construction that aligns and segregates chromosomes during eukaryotic cell division.

Spiracle
In insects and some other terrestrial arthropods, a small opening through which air is taken into the tracheae. Insects have several spiracles, arranged along the sides of the abdomen.

Spleen
An organ that produces lymphocytes and stores erythrocytes.

Spongin
Proteinacous compound of which the spicules in Demospongiae are composed.

Spongocoel
Central body cavity of sponges.

Spongy bone
The inner layer of bone; found at the ends of long bones and is less dense than compact bone. Some spongy bone contains red marrow.

Spongy mesophyll
Parenchyma cells found in plant leaves that are irregularly shaped and have large intracellular spaces.

Sporangia
The structures in which spores are produced (sing.: sporangium).

Sporangiophore
A stalk to which sporangia are attached.

Sporangium
A chamber inside of which spores are produced through meiosis.

Spore
A single cell that is dispersed as a reproductive unit, or that encapsulates a cell during unfavorable environmental conditions; in organisms with an alternation of generations; the products of meiosis are spores.

Sporocap
A cap of spores as in *Pilobolus* at the end of the clublike sporophore.

Sporophore

Is the stalk of a fungus bearing spores.

Sporophyll

Any leaf which bears sporangia is called a sporophyll.

Sporophyte

The diploid stage in the life cycle of an organism undergoing an alternation of generations. The sporophyte is multicellular and develops from a zygote. The mature sporophyte meiotically produces haploid spores that later generate the gametophyte generation.

Sporozoans

Members of the protists that are referred to as slime molds; may include organisms resembling the ancestors of fungi.

Spy hopping

A form of cetacean behavior that consists of rising vertically out of the water, head first, and scanning the entire surrounding area while rotating.

Stability

One of the phases of a population's life cycle. The population's size remains roughly constant, þuctuating around some average density. Also, the ability of a community to persist unchanged.

Stabilizing selection

A process of natural selection that tends to favor genotypic combinations that produce an intermediate phenotype; selection against the extremes in variation.

Stalk

A leaf's petiole; the slender stem that supports the blade of a leaf and attaches it to a larger stem of the plant.

Stalkless = sessile

Leaves which do not possess a petiole The leaf expands itself directly from the blade.

Stallion

A male horse, more than four years old.

Stamens

The male reproductive structures of a þower; usually consist of slender, thread-like filaments topped by anthers. The male reproductive structures in the flower, composed of a filament and anther.

Stapes

One of the three bones that function in hearing.

Starch

A complex polymer of glucose, used by plants and green algae to store surplus sugar for later use.

Starling flow

A portion of filtrate (permeate) that is driven back through the membrane in the reverse direction near the outlet of the cartridge due to the high permeability of these membranes in the presence of permeate pressure. This phenomenon is most often associated with the operation of micro filtration membranes using permeate flow control.

Start codon

The codon (AUG) on a messenger RNA molecule where protein synthesis begins.

Stasis

A period of little or no discernible change in a lineage.

Steam-in-place, (SIP)

The process of sterilizing a device, such as a hollow fiber cartridge, with steam, without removing the device from the separations system.

Steinkerns

Internal casts of a fossil. Steinkerns may reveal internal anatomy of an organism, such as muscle attachment, and other details of soft tissue structure.

Stem

(Part of the plant) It is a very important part of the plant with the following functions:
1) Maintain the flowers and leaves at a certain distance from the soil.
2) Carry the nutrients and water.

Stem cells

Cells in bone marrow that produce lymphocytes by mitotic division.

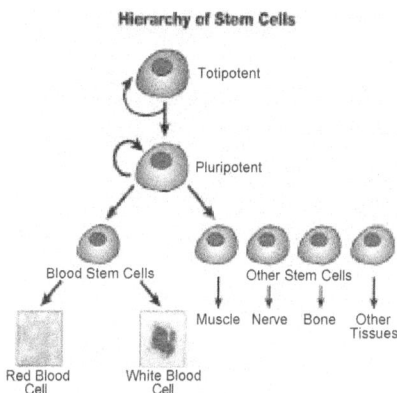

Hierarchy of Stem Cells

Stem group

All the taxa in a clade preceding a major cladogenesis event. They are often difficult to recognize because they may not possess synapomorpies found in the crown group.

Sterile

Devoid of living microbial organisms and/or of toxins generated by living organisms; defined formally by USP or AAMI sterility requirements.

Sterilization

A process that removes/destroys all microorganisms from a solution or a filtration system.

Sternum

The sternum or breastbone, in vertebrate anatomy, is a flat bone. It probably first evolved in early tetrapods as an extension of the pectoral girdle; it is not found in fish. In amphibians and reptiles it is typically a shield-shaped structure, often composed entirely of cartilage. It is absent in both turtles and snakes. In birds it is a relatively large bone and typically bears an enormous projecting keel to which the flight muscles are attached.

Steroids

Compounds with a skeleton of four rings of carbon to which various side groups are attached; one of the three main classes of hormones.

Sticky ends

Term applied to DNA sequences cut with restriction enzymes where the cuts will bond with each other or with another sequence cut with the same enzyme.

Stigma

Part of the female reproductive structure of the carpel of a flower; the sticky surface at the tip of the style to which pollen grains attach. The receptive surface of the pistil (of the flower) on which pollen is placed by a pollinator.

Stimulus

A physical or chemical change in the environment that leads to a response controlled by the nervous system.

Stipe

A scientific term for "stalk".

ipules Strobilus

Stipules
Paired appendages found at the base of the leaves of many flowering plants.

Stolon
(Type of stem) stolons are weak spreading stems, running along the surface of the ground and producing new plants from their nodes.

Stoma
(Part of the leaf) (Plural= stomata) Pore in the surface of a leave or stem, designed for plants to exchange gases.

Stomach
The muscular organ between the esophagus and small intestine that stores, mixes, and digests food and controls the passage of food into the small intestine.

Stomata
Openings in the epidermis of a stem or leaf of a plant which permit gas exchange with the air. In general, all plants except liverworts have stomata in their sporophyte stage.

Stomatal apparatus
The stomata and guard cells that control the size of the stoma.

Stoop
To dive in the air; used especially for falcons in courtship or when attacking prey.

Stop codon
The codon on a messenger RNA molecule where protein synthesis stops.

Stork
(The Stork's bill family - geraniaceae) It comprises about 700 species of plants mainly spread in temperate and subtropical countries. They are herbs and bushes, specially used in gardening, such as geraniums.

Strandings
Whales or dolphins that are found stranded on beaches.

Stratification
The division of water in lakes and ponds into layers with different temperatures and oxygen content. Oxygen content declines with depth, while the uppermost layer is warmest in summer and coolest in winter.

Stratigraphy
The study of rock layers, especially their distribution, environment of deposition, and age.

Stratum
A layer of sedimentary rock; plural is strata.

Stray
An individual bird found in a region outside of its regular range.

Streptophytes
The clade consisting of the plants plus their closest relatives, the charophytes.

Stressed community
A community that is disturbed by human activity, such as road building or pollution, and is inadvertently simpliÞed. Some species become superabundant while others disappear.

Strike
The direction or trend of a bedding plane or fault, as it intersects the horizontal.

Strobilus
A tightly clustered group of sporophylls arranged on a central stalk; commonly termed a "cone" or "flower".

Stroma

The matrix surrounding the grana in the inner membrane of chloroplasts. The area between membranes (thylakoids, grana) inside the chloroplast.

Stromatolite

A sedimentological and biological "fossil" representinmg colonies of bacteria altenating with layers of sediments. Becoming more common during the Proterozoic, stromatolites persist today in marine environments where grazing by herbivorous organisms is limited.

Structural biology

A field of study dedicated to determining the detailed, three-dimensional structures of biological molecules to better understand the function of these molecules.

Structural genomics

A field of study that seeks to determine a large inventory of protein structures based on gene sequences. The eventual goal is to be able to produce approximate structural models of any protein based on its gene sequence. From these structures and models, scientists hope to learn more about the biological function of proteins.

Structure-based drug design

An approach to developing medicines that takes advantage of the detailed, three-dimensional structure of target molecules.

Style

Part of the female reproductive structure in the carpel of a þower; formed from the ovary wall. The tip of the style carries the stigma to which pollen grains attach. Part of the pistil that separates the stigma from the ovary.

Subatomic particles

The three kinds of particles that make up atoms: protons, neutrons, and electrons.

Subcloning

The simple transfer of a cloned fragment of DNA from one vector to another.

Subduction

A geologic process in which one edge of one crustal plate is forced below the edge of another; subduct– v.; subduction zone- n. A long narrow area in which subduction is taking place, e.g. the Peru-Chile trench, where the Pacific Plate is being subducted under the South American Plate.

Subelliptical

Egg shape rounded at both ends but elongated and tapering toward the rounded ends, with the broadest point nearer one end than the other.

Suberin

Waxy, waterproof chemical in some plant cells, notably cork (in stems) and endodermis cells (in roots).

Subfamily

A taxon that is a subset of a family and that contains one or more genera.

Suboscine

"One of two subdivisions of the order Passeriformes."

Subsidence

The sudden sinking or gradual downward settling of the Earth's surface with little or no horizontal motion.

Subspecies

A taxonomic subdivision of a species; a population of a particular region genetically distinguishable from other such populations and capable of interbreeding with them.

Substitution

A type of mutation in which one base is substituted for another.

Substrate

"Supporting surface" on which an organism grows. The substrate may simply provide structural support, or may provide water and nutrients. A substrate may be inorganic, such as rock or soil, or it may be organic, such as wood.

Substrate feeders

Animals such as earthworms or termites that eat the soil or wood through which they burrow.

Subtropical

Habitats and climates that are tropical in nature but found north or south of the tropics.

Succession

In all natural environments a dominant species is replaced by another. Example: weeds, grass, shrubs, trees. Example 2: molds (sugar eating), mushrooms (cellulose eating).

Succulent

(Type of stem) Succulent stems become very fat because of water accumulation. They use it as a reservoir for the long dry periods they have to stand. They are so well adapted to the environment that they have transformed their leaves into prickles, which besides increasing water provision, help the plant to keep herbivores out of range. Cacti are included in this group.

Sudden infant death syndrome

A disorder resulting in the unexpected death during sleep of infants, usually between the ages of two weeks and one year. The causes are not fully understood, but are believed to involve failure of automatic respiratory control.

Sugar

Any of several small carbohydrates, such as glucose, which are "sweet" to the taste.

Superior vena cava

Blood from the head returns to the heart through this main vein.

Supplemental plumage

A generation of feathers, additional to the basic and alternate plumages, found in a few birds that have more than two molts per year.

Suppressor T cells

T cells that slow down and stop the immune response of B cells and other T cells. Immune system cells that shut off the antibody production when an infection is under control.

Suprachiasmic nucleus (SCN)

A region of the hypothalamus that controls internal cycles of endocrine secretion.

Surface filter

A filter in which particles larger than the pores are retained on the surface of the filter.

Surfactant

A surface-active or wetting agent that in solution reduces the surface tension of a liquid, or reduces interfacial tension between a liquid and another liquid or a liquid and a solid. Filters coated with surfactant may be easier to wet out than otherwise, but the surfactant may combine with filtered liquid as an undesirable extractable, thus making the use of surfactants undesirable. Also, molecules with split solubility, with one portion soluble in water, and the other in oil.

Symbiosis

A relationship between two organisms that live in intimate contact with each other; includes mutualism (both organisms benefit, they rely on each other for survival), parasitism (one organism benefits at its host's expense) and commensalism (one partner benefits and the other is neither benefitted nor harmed).

Sympathetic system

The subdivision of the autonomic nervous system that dominates in stressful or emergency situations and prepares the body for strenuous physical activity, e.g., causing the heart to beat faster.

Sympetalous

(Type of flowers) In a flower when the petals are joined , wholly or partly.

Synangium

A cluster of sporangia which have become fused in development.

Synapomorphy

A new trait or structural feature that arises in an evolving lineage that is shared between two or more sister groups that illustrates their close relationship.

Synapse

The junction between an axon and an adjacent neuron.

Synapsid

A vertebrate distinguished by a skull with one pair of openings in the side behind the eyes, e.g., mammals and their close relatives.

Synapsis

The alignment of chromosomes during meiosis I so that each

chromosome is beside its homologue.

Synaptic cleft

The space between the end of a neuron and an adjacent cell.

Synaptic vesicles

Vesicles at the synapse end of an axon that contain the neurotransmitters.

Synchrotron

A large machine that accelerates electrically charged particles to nearly the speed of light and maintains them in circular orbits. Originally designed for use by high-energy physicists, synchrotrons are now heavily used by structural biologists as a source of very intense X-rays.

Syncline

A syncline is a fold, with younger layers closer to the center of the structure. A synclinorium is a large syncline with superimposed smaller folds. Synclines are typically a downward fold, termed a synformal syncline (i.e. a trough); but synclines that point upwards can be found when strata have been overturned and folded (an antiformal syncline).

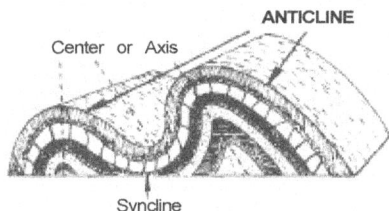

Synergid

Cells in the embryo sac of angiosperms that flank the egg cell. The pollen tube grows through one (usually the smaller) of the synergids.

Syngamy

The process of union of two gametes; sometimes called fertilization. It encompasses both plasmogamy and karyogamy.

Synovial joint

The most movable type of joint. The bones are covered by connective tissue, the interior of which is filled with synovial fluid, and the ends of the bones are covered with cartilage.

Synsepalous or fused

(Type of flowers) if the sepals are partially or wholly joined

Syphilis

A sexually transmitted disease caused by a bacterial infection that produces an ulcer on the genitals and can have potentially serious effects if untreated.

Systematics

The classification of organisms based on information from observations and experiments; includes the reconstruction of evolutionary relatedness among living organisms. Currently, a system that divides organisms into five kingdoms (Monera, Protista, Plantae, Fungi, Animalia) is widely used.

Systemic circuit

The loop of the circulatory system that carries blood through the body and back to the heart.

Systole

The contraction of the ventricles that opens the semilunar valve and forces blood into the arteries.

Systolic pressure

The peak blood pressure when ventricles contract.

T

T cells

The type of lymphocyte responsible for cell-mediated immunity; also protects against infection by parasites, fungi, and protozoans and can kill cancerous cells; circulate in the blood and become associated with lymph nodes and the spleen.

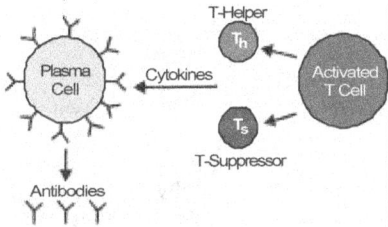

Taiga

Ecological zone south of the tundra and north of the temperate zone, dominated by conifer trees and harsh winters.

Taiga biome

The region of coniferous forest extending across much of northern Europe, Asia, and North America; characterized by long, cold winters and short, cool summers and by acidic, thin soils.

Tail slapping

Dolphins can be seen slapping their tails forcibly on the surface of the water.

Tangential flow filtration

Also called cross flow filtration. In tangential flow filtration, the feed solution flows parallel to the surface of the membrane. Driven by pressure, some of the feed solution passes through the membrane filter. Most of the solution is circulated back to the feed tank. The movement of the feed solution across the face of the membrane surface helps to remove the buildup of materials on the surface. In direct (normal) flow filters, the liquid flows perpendicular to the filter surface, and all the feed passes through the filter. Particles and solutes rejected in direct flow filtration are trapped in or on the pore structure of the filter.

Tap root

A primary root that grows vertically downward and gives off small lateral roots; occurs in dicots. Root system in plants characterized by one root longer than the other roots. Example: carrot.

Taphonomy

The study of the death, decay, burial, and fossilization of an organism. Essentially, taphonomy describes everything that happens to an organism between the time it dies and the moment its remains are discovered. Understanding why organisms are or are not preserved over time helps explain the biases seen in the fossil record. Taphonomy is often broken into two parts, biostratinomy and diagenesis.

Taproot

A taproot is an enlarged, somewhat straight to tapering plant root that grows vertically downward. It forms a center from which other roots sprout laterally. Plants with taproots are difficult to transplant. The presence of a taproot is why dandelions are hard to uproot—the top is pulled, but the long taproot stays in the ground, and resprouts. The taproot system contrasts with the fibrous root system with many branched roots.

Target cell

A cell that a particular hormone effects by its direct action (either passing through the membrane or binding to a surface receptor).

Target molecule (or target protein)

The molecule on which pharmaceutical researchers focus when designing a drug. Often, the target molecule is from a virus or bacterium, or is an abnormal human protein. In these cases, the researchers usually seek to design a small molecule—a drug—to bind to the target molecule and block its action.

Tarsals

The bones that make up the ankle joint.

Tarsus

The lower leg. The major bone in this region of the leg is the tarsometatarsus, which is a fusion of structures called ankle and foot bones in mammals. The avian equivalent of the mammalian lower leg bones (the tibia and fibula) is found in the 'drumstick' or what appears to be the upper leg in most birds.

Tautomer

A molecule which can convert relatively easily from one isomeric form to another.

Taxis

The behavior when an animal turns and moves toward or away from an external stimulus (pl.: taxes).

Taxon

A named group of organisms, not necessarily a clade, but linked by shared physical or genetic characteristics. A taxon may be designated by a Latin name or by a letter, number, or any other symbol.

Taxonomic classification

Hierarchical system for grouping and naming types of living organisms.

Taxonomy

A systematic method of classifying plants and animals. Classification of organisms based on degrees of similarity purportedly representing evolutionary (phylogenetic) relatedness.

Tectonic

Describing the forces that cause the movements and deformation of Earth's crust on a large scale, also describes the resulting structures or features from these forces.

Tectonic plates

Segments of the lithosphere that comprise the surface of the Earth much the way a turtle shell is composed of its plates.

Tegmen

Part of the sead coat. It is the second layer of the seed coat in angiosperms.

Telomere

The ends of chromosomes. These specialized structures are involved in the replication and stability of linear DNA molecules.

Telophase

The final stage of mitosis in which the chromosomes migrate to opposite poles, a new nuclear envelope forms, and the chromosomes uncoil. The last phase of nuclear division in eukaryotes when the segregated chromosomes uncoil and begin to reform nuclei. This is immediately followed (in most cases) by cytokinesis.

Telson

The last segment of the abdomen in many arthropods. May be flat and paddlelike, buttonlike, or long and spiny, as in the horseshoe crabs.

Temperate

Region in which the climate undergoes seasonal change in temperature and moisture. Temperate regions of the earth lie primarily between 30 and 60 degrees latitude in both hemispheres.

Temperate forest biome

Extends across regions of the northern hemisphere with abundant rainfall and long growing seasons. Deciduous, broad-leaved trees are the dominant plants.

Template strand

The strand of DNA that is transcribed to make RNA.

Temporal lobe

The lobe of the cerebral cortex that is responsible for processing auditory signals.

Tendons

A tendon (or sinew) is a tough band of fibrous connective tissue that usually connects muscle to bone and is capable of withstanding tension.

Tendons are similar to ligaments and fasciae as they are all made of collagen except that ligaments join one bone to another bone, and fasciae connect muscles to other muscles. Tendons and muscles work together.

Tendril

Type of stem. They are secondary stems evolved to twist around an object, like the ones developed by the Traveller's joy.

Tentacles

Appendages which are flexible, because they have no rigid skeleton. Cnidarians and molluscs are two kinds of orgnaisms which may have tentacles.

Tepal

Part of the flower. When there is not difference between the calyx and the corolla, because all parts show the same resemblance in texture and colour, we call them tepals.

Terminal buds

Buds located at the end of a plant shoot.

Termination

The end of translation; occurs when the ribosome reaches the stop codon on the messenger RNA molecule and the polypeptide, the messenger RNA, and the transfer RNA molecule are released from the ribosome.

Termination codon

One of three three-base sequences that initiate termination of the protein synthesis process.

Terrane

A general term used to refer to a piece of the crust that is usually smaller than a continent but larger than an island; exotic terrane. terrane that has an unknown origin or a different origin than its surrounding rocks.

Terrestrial
Living on land, as opposed to marine or aquatic.

Territory
A particular area defended by an individual against intrusion by other individuals, particularly of the same species.

Tertiary structure
The folding of a protein's secondary structure into a functional three-dimensional configuration. Shape assumed by protein due to interactions between amino acids far apart on the chain.

Test
A hard shell produced by some unicellular protists; may be made of calcium carbonate, silica, or sand grains.

Test cross
Genetic crossing of an organism with known genotype (one that exhibits the recessive phenotype) with an individual expressing the dominant phenotype but of unknown heritage.

Testa
Part of the seed coat. It is the outer layer of the seed coat in case of angiosperms, above the tegmen. In reference to gymnosperms, it is actually the seed coat. In both cases the testa protects the seed from aggressions included those of the hervivores.

Testes
The male gonad; produce spermatozoa and male sex hormones. Male gonads in mammals. Singular, testis. Paired organs that contain seminiferous tubules in which sperm are produced.

Testosterone
Male sex hormone that stimulates sperm formation, promotes the development of the male duct system in the fetus, and is responsible for secondary sex characteristics such as facial hair growth.

Tethys ocean
A small ocean that existed from the Triassic to the Jurassic; as Pangea was split into Gondwana and Laurasia in the Jurassic, an arm developed westward called the Tethys Seaway or Tethys Sea.

Tetrad
The four chromatids in each cluster during synapsis; formed by the two sister chromatids in each of the two homologous chromosomes.

Tetrapod
An animal with four limbs that evolved from a common fish ancestor during the Devonian Period (~365 million years ago). Tetrapods include amphibians, reptiles, birds, and mammals. Though "tetrapod" literally translates to "four-footed," many animals in this group have limbs adapted for different modes of transportation. Humans walk upright on two legs; the legs of whales, dolphins, and other marine mammals have evolved into fins and flippers; and snakes have lost their legs all together. Tetrapods are generally thought of as terrestrial animals, but some, like dolphins and whales, have returned to marine habitats.

Thalamus
The brain region that serves as a switching center for sensory signals passing from the brain stem to other brain regions; part of the diencephalon.

Thalloid
Plants which have no roots, stems, or leaves are called thalloid, such as liverworts and hornworts.

Theca
General term for any stiff outer covering of a unicellular protist, and usually made up of interlocking plates. dinoflagellates and diatoms are examples of protists with thecae.

Thecodonts
An informal term for a variety of Permian and Triassic reptiles that had teeth set in individual sockets. Small, bipedal thecodontians are the probable ancestors of dinosaurs.

Theory
A hypothesis that has withstood extensive testing by a variety of methods, and in which a higher degree of certainty may be placed. A theory is NEVER a fact, but instead is an attempt to explain one or more facts.

Thermacidophiles
A thermoacidophile (combination of thermophile and acidophile) is an extreme archeon which thrives in acidous, sulfur rich, high temperature environments. Thermoacidophiles prefer temperatures of 70 - 80 °C and pH between 2 and 3. They live mostly in hot springs and/or within deep ocean vent communities. Classified as an Archaebacteria and an extremophile, Thermoacidophiles are found in places where most organisims would not survive.

Thermal stability
The ability of a membrane and filtering device to maintain its performance during and after exposure to excursions of temperature, such as the elevated temperatures experienced during autoclaving or steam sterilization.

Thermiogenesis
The generation of heat by raising the body's metabolic rate; controlled by the hypothalamus.

Thermoregulation
Thermoregulation is the ability of an organism to keep its body temperature within certain boundaries, even when the surrounding temperature is very different. This process is one aspect of homeostasis: a dynamic state of stability between an animal's internal environment and its external environment (the study of such processes in zoology has been called ecophysiology or physiological ecology). If the body is unable to maintain a normal temperature and it increases significantly above normal, a condition known as hyperthermia occurs. For humans, this occurs when the body is exposed to constant temperatures of approximately 55 °C (131 °F), and any prolonged exposure (longer than a few hours) at this temperature and up to around 75 °C (167 °F) death is almost inevitable.

Thigmotropism
Plants' response to contact with a solid object; e.g., tendrils' twining around a pole. Plant response to touch.

Thoracic cavity
The chest cavity in which the heart and lungs are located.

Thorax
In mammals, the part of the trunk anterior to the diaphragm, which partitions it from the abdomen. In insects, the body region between the head and the abdomen, bearing the walking legs and wings.

Thorns
Stems modified to protect the plant.

Thoroughfare channels
Shortcuts within the capillary network that allow blood to bypass a capillary bed.

Threatened species
A threatened species is a native species that is at risk of becoming endangered in the near future.

Throughput
(1) The volume of solution that will pass through a separations device before the filtrate output drops to an unacceptable level.
(2) The rate at which a separations system will generate

Thylakoids
The specialized membrane structures in which photosynthesis takes place. Internal membranes in the chloroplast where the light reaction chemicals are embedded. Collections of thylakoids form the grana.

Thymine
One of the pyrimidine bases in DNA, thymine is replaced by uracil in RNA.

Thyroid-stimulating hormone
A hormone produced by the anterior pituitary that stimulates the production and release of thyroid hormones.

Tight junctions
Junctions between the plasma membranes of adjacent cells in animals that form a barrier, preventing materials from passing between the cells.

Till
Unstratified glacial drift consisting of clay, sand, gravel, and boulders.

Tissue
A group of cells with a specific function in the body of an organism. Lung tissue, vascular tissues, and muscle tissue are all kinds of tissues found in some animals. Tissues are usually composed of nearly identical cells, and are often organized into larger units called organs.

Titer reduction
The measurement of a filter's ability to remove microbes or a virus from a fluid.

Tomentose or downy
Covered with soft hairs.

Topography
The relief features of the Earth's surface, above and below sea level; the set of landforms in a region.

Torsion
A twisting process that gastropods undergo during their development in which the position of their visceral and pallial organs are repositioned by 180°. The resulting arrangement of body parts in the gastropod is therefore asymmetrical.

Toxic
Poisonous, toxicant, toxin poisonous compound produced by a pathogenic bacterium.

Toxins
A toxin is a poisonous substance produced within living cells or organisms; man-made substances created by artificial processes are thus excluded. Toxins can be small molecules, peptides, or proteins that are capable of causing disease on contact with or absorption by body tissues interacting with biological macromolecules such as enzymes or cellular receptors. Toxins vary

greatly in their severity, ranging from usually minor and acute (as in a bee sting) to almost immediately deadly (as in botulinum toxin).

Trace fossil

Evidence left by organisms, such as burrows, imprints, coprolites, or footprints. Trace fossils are not preserved parts of the organism.

Tracheae

Internal tubes through which air is taken for respiration. Vertebrates with lungs have a single trachea carrying air to the lungs, while insects and some other land-living arthropods have a complex network of tracheae carrying air from the spiracles to all parts of the body.

Tracheids

Long, tapered cells with pitted walls that form a system of tubes in the xylem and carry water and solutes from the roots to the rest of the plant. One type of xylem cells. Tracheids are long and relatively narrow, and transport materials from the roots upward. Tracheids are dead at maturity and have lignin in their secondary walls.

Tracheophyte

Any member of the clade of plants possessing vascular tissue; a vascular plant.

Transcription

The first major step in protein synthesis, in which the information coded in DNA is copied (transcribed) into mRNA.

Transduction

Transduction is the process by which DNA is transferred from one bacterium to another by a virus. It also refers to the process whereby foreign DNA is introduced into another cell via a viral vector. Transduction does not require cell-to-cell contact (which occurs in conjugation), and it is DNAase resistant (transformation is susceptible to DNAase). Transduction is a common tool used by molecular biologists to stably introduce a foreign gene into a host cell's genome.

Transfer rnas (TRNAS)

Small, single-stranded RNA molecules that bind to amino acids and deliver them to the proper codon on messenger RNA. The trucks of protein synthesis that carry the specified amino acid to the ribosome. Abbreviated tRNA.

Transformation

In Griffith's experiments with strains of pneumonia bacterium, the process by which hereditary information passed from dead cells of one strain into cells of another strain, causing them to take on the characteristic virulence of the first strain.

Transforming factor

Griffith's name for the unknown material leading to transformation; later found to be DNA.

Transgression

A rise in sea level relative to the land.

Transition reaction

Biochemical process of converting 3-carbon pyruvate into 2-carbon acetyl and attaching it to coenzyme A (CoA) so it can enter Kreb's cycle. Carbon dioxide is also released and NADH is formed (from NAD and H) in this process.

Translation

The synthesis of protein on a template of messenger RNA; consists of three steps: initiation, elongation, and termination. Making of a polypeptide sequence by translating the genetic code of an mRNA molecule associated with a ribosome.

Translocation

1) The movement of a segment from one chromosome to another without altering the number of chromosomes.
2) The movement of þuids through the phloem from one part of a plant to another, with the direction of movement depending on the pressure gradients between source and sink regions.

Transmembrane pressure, (TMP)

The force that drives liquid through a cross flow membrane. During filtration, the feed side of the membrane is under higher pressure than the permeate side. transmembrane pressure = feed pressure + retentate pressure 2 - permeate pressure.

Transpiration

Transpiration is a process similar to evaporation. It is a part of the water cycle, and it is the loss of water vapor from parts of plants (similar to sweating), especially in leaves but also in stems, flowers and roots. Leaf surfaces are dotted with openings which are collectively called stomata, and in most plants they are more numerous on the undersides of the foliage. The stomata are bordered by guard cells that open and close the pore. Leaf transpiration occurs through stomata, and can be thought of as a necessary "cost" associated with the opening of the stomata to allow the diffusion of carbon dioxide gas from the air for photosynthesis. Transpiration also cools plants and enables mass flow of mineral nutrients and water from roots to shoots.

Tree

(Type of plant according to the stem) Plants with ligneous stems, with a superior height of five meters. In this case we call the stems trunks.They do not generally branch up to a considerable distance from the soil.

Triassic period

The first period of the Mesozoic Era between 225 and 185 million years ago. Pangaea began to breakup during this time. The ancestors of dinosaurs were present, as were early mammals and mammal-like reptiles.

Tribe

A taxon that is a subset of a subfamily and that contains one or more genera.

Trichocyst

Organelle in ciliates and dinoflagellates which releases long filamentous proteins when the cell is disturbed. Used as a defense against would-be predators.

Trichomes

Extensions from the epidermis of the plant that provide shade and protection for the plant.

Trilobites

A group of benthonic, detritus-feeding, extinct marine invertebrate animals (phylum Arthropoda), having skeletons of an organic compound called chitin. Trilobites appear in abundance early in the Cambrian period and were dominant animals in the Burgess Shale fauna, before finally becoming extinct at the end of the Permian period.

Triplet

Three-base sequence of mRNA that codes for a specific amino acid or termination codon.

Trisomy
A condition where a cell has an extra chromosome.

Trophoblast
The outer layer of cells of a blastocyst that adhere to the endometrium during implantation.

Tropic hormone
Hormone made by one gland that causes another gland to secrete a hormone.

Tropical
Region in which the climate undergoes little seasonal change in either temperature or rainfall. Tropical regions of the earth lie primarily between 30 degrees north and south of the equator.

Tropical rain forest biome
The most complex and diverse biome; found near the equator in South America and Africa; characterized by thin soils, heavy rainfall, and little þuctuation in temperature.

Tropism
The movement of plant parts toward or away from a stimulus in the plant's environment. Plant movement in response to an environmental stimulus.

True-breeding
Occurs when self-fertilization gives rise to the same traits in all offspring, generation after generation. Now interpreted as equivalent to homozygous.

Trunk
Trunk (or bole) refers to the main wooden axis of a tree that supports the branches and is supported by and directly attached to the roots. The trunk is covered by the bark, which is an important diagnostic feature in tree identification, and which often differs markedly from the bottom of the trunk to the top, depending on the species. The trunk is the most important part of the tree for timber production. Trunks occur both in "true" woody plants as well as non-woody plants such as palms and other monocots though the internal physiology is different in each case. In all plants, trunks thicken over time due to formation of secondary growth (pseudo-secondary growth in monocots).

Trypanosomes
A type of roundworm, responsible for human disease associated with eating raw or undercooked pork.

Tubal ligation
Tubal ligation or tubectomy (also known as having one's "tubes tied" (ligation)) is a surgical procedure for sterilization in which a woman's fallopian tubes are clamped and blocked, or severed and sealed, either method of which prevents eggs from reaching the uterus for fertilization. Tubal ligation is considered a permanent method of sterilization and birth control.

Tubal pregnancy
Occurs when the morula remains in the oviduct and does not descend into the uterus.

Tube feet
Extensions of the water-vascular system of echinoderms, protruding from the body and often ending in suckers. May be used for locomotion and/or for maintaining a tight grip on prey or on the bottom.

Tube nucleus
One of the cells in the male gametophyte in seed plants. The tube

nucleus grows through the stigma, style, and into the ovule, clearing the way for the sperm nuclei to enter the embryo sac.

Tubenoses

Colloquial name for members of the order Procellariiformes, which includes the albatrosses, the shearwaters and petrels, and the storm petrals.

Tuber

Tubers are various types of modified plant structures that are enlarged to store nutrients. They are used by plants to survive the winter or dry months and provide energy and nutrients for regrowth during the next growing season and they are a means of asexual reproduction. There are both stem and root tubers.

Tubercle

Any small rounded protrusion. In pycnogonids and some cheliceramorph arthropods, the central eyes are carried on a tubercle.

Tuberculate

Covered in raised, fleshy protuberances.

Tuberoid

Type of root. Tuberoid roots are fibrous roots that became fat because of the accumulation of nutrients

Tubers

Swollen underground stems in plants that store food, such as the irish potato.

Tubular

Type of flower. Flower longer than wider, in the shape of a tube.

Tubular secretion

The process in which ions and other waste products are transported into the distal tubules of the nephron.

Tubule

Tube-like structure (larger ID fibers than hollow fibers) made from an ultrafiltration or microfiltration membrane and sealed inside a cross flow cartridge. When in use, the feed stream flows into one end of the tubule and the retentate (the material that does not permeate through the walls of the tubule) flows out the other end. The material that does flow through the membrane (walls of the tubule) is called the permeate.

Tubulins

The protein subunits from which microtubules are assembled.

Tuff

A general term for consolidated rocks made of material ejected from volcanic explosions.

Tumor necrosis factor

A type of biological response modifier (a substance that can improve the body's natural response to disease).

Tumor suppressor gene

Genes that normally restrain cell growth but, when missing or inactivated by mutation, allow cells to grow uncontrolled. The P53 gene is an example.

Tundra

A vast, mostly flat, treeless Arctic region of Europe, Asia, and North America in which the subsoil is permanently frozen. The dominant vegetation is low-growing lichens, mosses, and stunted shrubs.

Tundra biome

Extensive treeless plain across northern Europe, Asia, and North American between the taiga to the south and the permanent ice to the north. Much of the soil remains frozen in permafrost, and grasses and other vegetation support herds of large grazing mammals.

Turbidite

Turbidite geological formations have their origins in turbidity current deposits, which are deposits from a form of underwater avalanche that are responsible for distributing vast amounts of clastic sediment into the deep ocean.

Turbidity

A measure of relative liquid clarity. Measurements are based on the amount of light transmitted in straight lines through a sample. The more light that is scattered by fine solids or colloids, the less clear (and more turbid) the solution.

Turbidity current

A bottom fast-flowing current that moves down a slope, depositing suspended sediments over the floor of a body of water

Turbidity flow

A flow of dense, muddy water moving down a slope due to a turbidity current

Turgor pressure

Force exerted outward on a cell wall by the water contained in the cell. This force gives the plant rigidity, and may help to keep it erect.

Turner syndrome

In humans, a genetically determined condition in which an individual has only one sex chromosome (an X). Affected individuals are always female and are typically short and infertile.

Turtle

Turtles are reptiles of the order Testudines (the crown group of the superorder Chelonia), characterised by a special bony or cartilaginous shell developed from their ribs that acts as a shield. "Turtle" may either refer to the Testudines as a whole, or to particular Testudines which make up a form taxon that is not monophyletic.

Tympanic membrane

A membrane of the ear that picks up vibrations from the air and transmits them to other parts of the ear; the eardrum.

Type specimen

A single individual organism that is selected to represent the standard for a particular taxon and which serves as the standard for the original name and description of the species.

U

Ultrafiltration

Ultrafiltration (UF) is a variety of membrane filtration in which hydrostatic pressure forces a liquid against a semipermeable membrane. Suspended solids and solutes of high molecular weight are retained, while water and low molecular weight solutes pass through the membrane. This separation process is used in industry and research for purifying and concentrating macromolecular (10_3 - 10_6 Da) solutions, especially protein solutions. Ultrafiltration is not fundamentally different from microfiltration, nanofiltration or gas separation, except in terms of the size of the molecules it retains. Ultrafiltration is applied in cross-flow or dead-end mode and separation in ultrafiltration undergoes concentration polarization.

Ultrastructure

The detailed structure of a specimen, such as a cell, tissue, or organ, that can be observed only by electron microscopy. Also called fine structure. In eggshell, ultrastructure refers to the three-dimensional arrangement of mineral crystals and organic matter. It is described in terms of calcite or aragonite mineralogy and the transition between different zones of organization within the shell. Distinct zones of organization are called ultrastructure zones.

Umbel

Type of inflorescence. In umbels florets arise from the same point of the peduncle.

Umbilical cord

The umbilical cord (also called the birth cord or funiculus umbilicalis) is the connecting cord from the developing embryo or fetus to the placenta. During prenatal development, the umbilical cord is physiologically and genetically part of the fetus and (in humans) normally contains two arteries (the umbilical arteries) and one vein (the umbilical vein), buried within Wharton's jelly. The umbilical vein supplies the fetus with oxygenated, nutrient-rich blood from the placenta. Conversely, the fetal heart pumps deoxygenated, nutrient-depleted blood through the umbilical arteries back to the placenta.

Unconformity

Any interruption of the continuity of a depositional sequence.

Undifferentiated

Unable to distinguish between. Undifferentiated rocks: rocks for which it is not possible to specify finer age divisions.

Undulipodium

An undulipodium or 9+2 organelle is an intracellular projection of a eukaryotic cell containing a microtubule array. Both eukaryotic flagella and eukaryotic cilia are considered undulipodia. Eukaryotic cilia are structurally identical to eukaryotic flagella, although distinctions are sometimes made according to function and/or length. Flagella use a whip-like action to create movement of the whole cell, such as the movement of sperm in the reproductive tract, and also create water movement as in the choanocytes of sponges.

Unicellular

A unicellular organism, also known as a single-celled organism is an organism that consists of only one cell, in contrast to a multicellular organism that consists of multiple cells. Historically simple single celled organisms have sometimes been referred to as monads

Uniformitarianism

The idea that geological processes have remained uniform over time and that slight changes over long periods can have large-scale consequences; proposed by James Hutton in 1795 and reþned by Charles Lyell during the 1800s. The principle on which modern geology was founded: processes operating today on the earth operated in much the same way in the geologic past. Sometimes expressed as "the present is the key to the past".

Uninucleate

Term applied to cells having only a single nucleus.

Unique sequence dna

The fraction of DNA that comes together again most slowly is unique sequence, essentially composed of single copy genes, or those repeated

a few times. Escherichia coli DNA is mostly all unique sequence.

Uniramious

Among arthropods, uniramous refers to appendages that have only one branch. Insects, centipedes and millipedes, and their relatives are uniramous arthropods; land-living chelicerates such as scorpions, spiders,and mites are also uniramous but probably descended from ancestors with biramous appendages.

Unripe, immature

(It is mainly said of fruits) Fruits which are not completely mature.

Unsaturated fat

An unsaturated fat is a fat or fatty acid in which there is at least one double bond within the fatty acid chain. A fat molecule is monounsaturated if it contains one double bond, and polyunsaturated if it contains more than one double bond. Where double bonds are formed, hydrogen atoms are eliminated. Thus, a saturated fat has no double bonds, has the maximum number of hydrogens bonded to the carbons, and therefore is "saturated" with hydrogen atoms. In cellular metabolism, unsaturated fat molecules contain somewhat less energy (i.e., fewer calories) than an equivalent amount of saturated fat. The greater the degree of unsaturation in a fatty acid (i.e., the more double bonds in the fatty acid) the more vulnerable it is to lipid peroxidation (rancidity). Antioxidants can protect unsaturated fat from lipid peroxidation.

Upland

Pertaining to areas away from coastlines and the floodplains of rivers, streams, and other bodies of water.

Uplift

The process or result of raising a portion of the Earth's crust through different tectonic mechanisms.

Upstream

The feed side of a separations process.

Upstream processing

Cellular separations including: cell lysates, cell harvesting, clarification, and cell culture perfusion.

Upwelling

The raising of benthic nutrients to the surface waters. This occurs in regions where the flow of water brings currents of differing temperatures together, and increases productivity of the ecosystem.

Uracil

The pyrimidine that replaces thymine in RNA molecules and nucleotides.

Ureter

A muscular tube that transports urine by peristaltic contractions from the kidney to the bladder.

Urethra

A narrow tube that transports urine from the bladder to the outside of the body. In males, it also conducts sperm and semen to the outside.

Urine

Urine is a typically sterile (in the absence of a disease condition) liquid by-product of the body that is secreted by the kidneys through a process called urination and excreted through the urethra. Cellular metabolism generates numerous by-products, many rich in nitrogen, that require elimination from the bloodstream. These by-products are eventually expelled from the body in a process known as micturition, the primary method for excreting water-soluble chemicals from the body. These chemicals can be detected and analyzed by urinalysis.

Uterus

The organ that houses and nourishes the developing embryo and fetus. The womb. Female reproductive organ in which the fertilized egg implants.

V

Vaccination

Vaccination is the administration of antigenic material (a vaccine) to stimulate the immune system of an individual to develop adaptive immunity to a disease. Vaccines can prevent or ameliorate the effects of infection by many pathogens. The efficacy of vaccination has been widely studied and verified; for example, the influenza vaccine, the HPV vaccine, and the chicken pox vaccine among others. In general, vaccination is considered to be the most effective method of preventing infectious diseases. The active agent of a vaccine may be intact but inactivated (non-infective) or attenuated (with reduced infectivity) forms of the causative pathogens, or purified components of the pathogen that have been found to be highly immunogenic (e.g., the outer coat proteins of a virus). Toxoids are produced for the immunization against toxin-based diseases, such as the modification of tetanospasmin toxin of tetanus to remove its toxic effect but retain its immunogenic effect.

Vaccine

A preparation containing dead or weakened pathogens that when injected into the body elicit an immune response.

Vacuole

A vacuole is a membrane-bound organelle which is present in all plant and fungal cells and some protist, animal and bacterial cells. Vacuoles are essentially enclosed compartments which are filled with water containing inorganic and organic molecules including enzymes in solution, though in certain cases they may contain solids which have been engulfed. Vacuoles are formed by the fusion of multiple membrane vesicles and are effectively just larger forms of these. The organelle has no basic shape or size; its structure varies according to the needs of the cell.

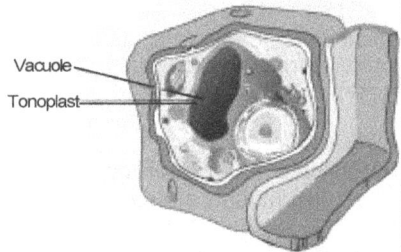

Vagina

The vagina (from Latin va-gi-na, literally "sheath" or "scabbard") is a fibromuscular tubular tract leading from the uterus to the exterior of the body in female placental mammals and marsupials, or to the cloaca in female birds, monotremes, and some reptiles. Female insects and other invertebrates also have a vagina, which is the terminal part of the oviduct. The Latinate plural "vaginae" is rarely used in English. The word vagina is often used colloquially to refer to the vulva or to the female genitals in general; technically, the vagina is the specific internal structure. In humans, this passage leads from the opening of the vulva to the uterus (womb). It lies midway between the anal tract and the urethra.

Valence shell

The valence shell is the outermost shell of an atom. It is usually (and misleadingly) said that the electrons in this shell make up its valence electrons, that is, the electrons that determine how the atom behaves in chemical reactions. Just as atoms with complete valence shells (noble gases) are the most chemically non-reactive, those with only one electron in their valence shells (alkalis) or just missing one electron from having a complete shell (halogens) are the most reactive.

Vas deferens

The duct that carries sperm from the epididymis to the ejaculatory duct and urethra. The tube connecting the testes with the urethra.

Vascular

Refers to a network of tubes which distribute nutrients and remove wates from the tissues of the body. Large multicellular animals must rely on a vascular system to keep their cells nourished and alive.

Vascular bundle

A vascular bundle is a part of the transport system in vascular plants. The transport itself happens in vascular tissue, which exists in two forms: xylem and phloem. Both these tissues are present in a vascular bundle, which in addition will include supporting and protective tissues. Also, it is a vein in the leaf that contains conducting tissues. The xylem typically lies adaxial with phloem positioned abaxial. In a stem or root this means that the xylem is closer to the centre of the stem or root while the phloem is closer to the exterior. In a leaf, the adaxial surface of the leaf will usually be the upper side, with the abaxial surface the lower side. This is why aphids are typically found on the underside of a leaf rather than on the top, since the sugars manufactured by the plant are transported by the phloem, which is closer to the lower surface.

Vascular cambium

The vascular cambium (pl. cambia or cambiums) is a part of the morphology of plants. It consists of cells that are partly specialized, for the tissues that transport water solutions, but have not reached any of the final forms that occur in their branch of the specialization graph. When these cells have divided and specialized further they make up the secondary vascular tissues, secondary xylem and the secondary phloem. The vascular cambium is a lateral meristem in the vascular tissue of plants. The vascular cambium is the source of both the secondary xylem (inwards, towards the pith) and the secondary phloem (outwards), and is located between these tissues in the stem and root. A few leaf types also have a vascular cambium.

Vascular cylinder

A central column formed by the vascular tissue of a plant root; surrounded by parenchymal ground tissue.

Vascular parenchyma

Specialized parenchyma cells in the phloem of plants.

Vascular plants

Vascular plants (also known as tracheophytes or higher plants) are those plants that have lignified tissues for conducting water, minerals, and photosynthetic products through the plant. Vascular plants include the clubmosses, Equisetum, ferns, gymnosperms (including conifers) and angiosperms (flowering plants). Scientific names for the group include Tracheophyta and Tracheobionta.

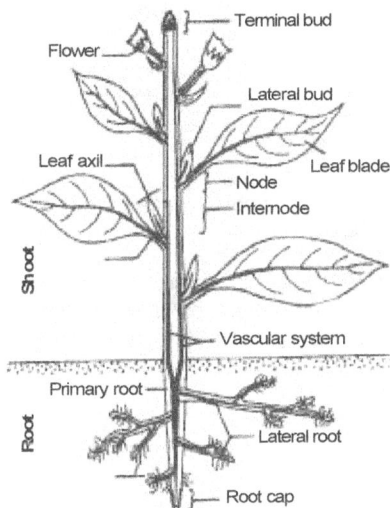

Vascular system

Specialized tissues for transporting puids and nutrients in plants; also plays a role in supporting the plant; one of the four main tissue systems in plants.

Vascular tissue

Vascular tissue is a complex conducting tissue, formed of more than one cell type, found in vascular plants. The primary components of vascular tissue are the xylem and phloem. These two tissues transport fluid and nutrients internally. There are also two meristems associated

with vascular tissue: the vascular cambium and the cork cambium. All the vascular tissues within a particular plant together constitute the vascular tissue system of that plant.

Vascular tissue system

A system formed by xylem and phloem throughout the plant, serving as a transport system for water and nutrients, respectively.

Vasectomy

A contraceptive procedure in men in which the vas deferens is cut and the cut ends are sealed to prevent the transportation of sperm. Surgical separation of the vas deferens so that sperm, while still produced, do not leave the body.

Vectors

Self-replicating DNA molecules that can be joined with DNA fragments to form recombinant DNA molecules.

Vegetative growth

Growth of a plant by division of cells, without sexual reproduction.

Veins

The vessels, like wrinkles or pipes running along the blade. They are really the vascular bundles coming from the stem throughout the petiole into the the surface of the blade.

Vena cava

The superior and inferior vena cava are collectively called the venae cavae. They are the veins that return deoxygenated blood from the body, into the heart. They both empty into the right atrium.
1. The inferior vena cava (or caudal vena cava in animals) travels up alongside the abdominal aorta with blood from the lower part of the body. It is the largest vein in the body.

2. The superior vena cava (or cranial vena cava in animals) is above the heart, and forms from a convergence of the left and right brachiocephalic veins that contain blood from the head and the arms.

Venation

A leaf is an organ of a vascular plant, as defined in botanical terms, and in particular in plant morphology. Foliage is a mass noun that refers to leaves as a feature of plants. Typically a leaf is a thin, flattened organ borne above ground and specialized for photosynthesis, but many types of leaves are adapted in ways almost unrecognisable in those terms: not flat (such as many succulent leaves and conifers), not above ground (such as bulb scales), or without photosynthetic function (consider for example cataphylls, spines, and cotyledons).

Ventilation

The mechanics of breathing in and out through the use of the diaphragm and muscles in the wall of the thoracic cavity.

Ventral

Term applied to the lower side of a fish, or to the chest of a land vertebrate.

Ventral scale

Scale on the underside of a snake's body (usually broader than other scales).

Ventricle

The chamber of the heart that pumps the blood into the blood vessels that carry it away from the heart. The lower chamber of the heart through which blood leaves the heart.

Venules

A venule is a very small blood vessel in the microcirculation that allows deoxygenated blood to return from the capillary beds to the larger blood vessels called veins. Venules range from 8 to 100 m in diameter and are formed when capillaries unite (come together).

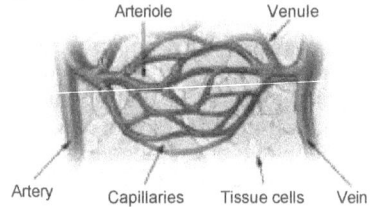

Venules are blood vessels that drain blood directly from the capillary beds. Many venules unite to form a vein.

Vernalization

Artibcial exposure of seeds or seedlings to cold to enable the plant to bower.

Vertebra

A component of the vertebral column, or backbone, found in vertebrates.

Vertebrae

The segments of the spinal column; separated by disks made of connective tissue.

Vertebral

Along the center of the back.

Vertebrata

A subphylum of chordates. Members of this subphylum have cartilaginous or bony vertebrae that surround a nerve cord and a skull that protects the brain.

Vertebrate

Vertebrates are animals that are members of the subphylum Vertebrata (chordates with backbones and spinal columns). Vertebrates are the largest group of chordates, with currently about 58,000 species described. Vertebrates include the jawless fishes, bony fishes, sharks and rays, amphibians, reptiles, mammals, and birds. Extant vertebrates range in size from the carp species Paedocypris, at as little as 7.9 mm (0.3 inch), to the blue whale, at up to 33 m (110 ft). Vertebrates make up about 5% of all described animal species; the rest are invertebrates, which lack backbones.

Vesicles
A vesicle is a bubble of liquid within another liquid, a supramolecular assembly made up of many different molecules. More technically, a vesicle is a small membrane-enclosed sack that can store or transport substances. Vesicles can form naturally because of the properties of lipid membranes (see micelle), or they may be prepared. Artificially prepared vesicles are known as liposomes. Most vesicles have specialized functions depending on what materials they contain.

Vessel elements
Short, wide cells arranged end to end, forming a system of tubes in the xylem that moves water and solutes from the roots to the rest of the plant. Large diameter cells of the xylem that are extremely specialized and efficient at conduction. An evolutionary advance over tracheids. Most angiosperms have vessels.

Vestigal
Pertaining to the part of an animal that is in the process of being lost in the course of evolution and is small, imperfectly formed, and serves little or no function.

Vestigial structures
Nonfunctional remains of organs that were functional in ancestral species and may still be functional in related species; e.g., the dewclaws of dogs.

Vicariance
Speciation which occurs as a result of the separation and subsequent isolation of portions of an original population.

Villi
Finger-like projections of the lining of the small intestine that increase the surface area available for absorption. Also, projections of the chorion that extend into cavities Þlled with maternal blood and allow the exchange of nutrients between the maternal and embryonic circulations. Projections of the inner layer of the small intestine that increase the surface area for absorbtion of food.

Viral clearance
The removal of viral contamination using specialized membranes or chromatography. To ensure that therapeutic drugs derived from certain sources are fully rid of any viral contamination, these protein solutions undergo viral clearance to inactivate or remove viral materials.

Viroids
Viroids are plant pathogens that consist of a short stretch (a few hundred nucleobases) of highly complementary, circular, single-stranded RNA without the protein coat that is typical for viruses. The smallest discovered is a 220 nucleobase scRNA (small cytoplasmic RNA) associated with the rice yellow mottle sobemovirus (RYMV). In comparison, the genome of the smallest known viruses capable of causing an infection by themselves are around 2 kilobases in size. The human pathogen hepatitis D is similar to viroids.

Virus
A non-living particle containing genetic matter (nucleic acid) and covering of

protein. The covering may contain lipid (fatty matter). Viruses can multiply only inside a suitable living cell. Bacterial viruses often contain a hollow tail which injects the genetic matter into a suitable host bacterium. LINK to phage structure page.

Virus particle

A single member of a viral strain, including all requisite proteins and genetic material.

Viscera

The internal organs, especially those of the great central body cavity.

Viscosity

A measurement of a fluid's resistance to shear. A slow flowing liquid such as gear oil, has a higher viscosity than a free-flowing liquid such as water. In a given separations process, higher-viscosity fluids are operated at a lower flow rate through a cartridge than lower viscosity fluids.

Vitalism

The idea that life processes have a component entirely separate from the constraints of the laws of natural science.

Vitamins

A vitamin is an organic compound required as a nutrient in tiny amounts by an organism. In other words, an organic chemical compound (or related set of compounds) is called a vitamin when it cannot be synthesized in sufficient quantities by an organism, and must be obtained from the diet. Thus, the term is conditional both on the circumstances and on the particular organism. Vitamins are classified by their biological and chemical activity, not their structure. Thus, each "vitamin" refers to a number of vitamer compounds that all show the biological activity

associated with a particular vitamin. Such a set of chemicals is grouped under an alphabetized vitamin "generic descriptor" title, such as "vitamin A", which includes the compounds retinal, retinol, and four known carotenoids. Vitamers by definition are convertible to the active form of the vitamin in the body, and are sometimes inter-convertible to one another, as well.

Vivacious

(Type of plant according to the stem) Vivacious plants have aerial stems lasting a single season, but keeping underground structures from which new stems spring again next season.

Void volume

The combined volume of all filter pores, interstices, passages, and the like. Indicates, in general, the solids or contaminant holding capacity of filter cartridges.

Volcanic

Describes the action or process of magma and gases rising to the crust and being extruded onto the surface and into the atmosphere; also applies to the resulting igneous rocks that cool on the surface of the Earth, including beneath water, which typically have small crystals due to the rapidity of cooling.

Volcanic arc

A volcanic arc is a chain of volcanoes positioned in an arc shape as seen from above. Offshore volcanoes form islands, resulting in a volcanic island arc. Generally they result from the subduction of an oceanic tectonic plate under another tectonic plate, and often parallel an oceanic trench. The oceanic plate is saturated with water, and volatiles such as water drastically lower the melting point of the mantle. As the oceanic plate is subducted, it is subjected to greater and greater pressures with increasing depth. This pressure squeezes water out of the plate and introduces it to the mantle. Here the mantle melts and forms magma at depth under the overriding plate. The magma ascends to form an arc of volcanoes parallel to the subduction zone.

Volcanism

The process by which magma and associated gases rise to the Earth's crust and are extruded, or expelled, onto the surface and into the atmosphere.

Voltage-gated ion channel

Voltage-gated ion channels are a class of transmembrane ion channels that are activated by changes in electrical potential difference near the channel; these types of ion channels are especially critical in neurons, but are common in many types of cells. They have a crucial role in excitable neuronal and muscle tissues, allowing a rapid and co-ordinated depolarization in response to triggering voltage change. Found along the axon and at the synapse, voltage-gated ion channels directionally propagate electrical signals.

Volumetric flow rate

The rate of flow of a substance through the determination of the volume it occupies, usually at standard atmosphere in cubic centimeters/cubic inches or cubic meters/cubic feet.

Vulva

A collective term for the external genitals in women.

W

Warning coloration
A combination of contrasting colors that warns that an animal is dangerous. Bands of black and yellow are a typical form of warning coloration, found in stinging insects.

Water flux
Measurement of the amount of water that flows through a cartridge. Clean water flux refers to the flux measurement made under standardized conditions on a new (and cleaned) membrane cartridge.

Water root
(Type of roots) Water roots are those living in the water.

Water vascular system
The water vascular system is a hydraulic system used by echinoderms, such as sea stars and sea urchins, for locomotion, food and waste transportation, and respiration. The system is composed of canals connecting numerous tube feet. Echinoderms move by alternately contracting muscles that force water into the tube feet, causing them to extend and push against the ground, then relaxing to allow the feet to retract. "In echinoderms, a system of fluid-filled tubes and chambers that connects with the tube feet. The fluid in the water vascular system is under pressure, giving the tube feet their shape."

Wattle
A wattle is a fleshy dewlap or caruncle hanging from various parts of the head or neck in several groups of birds, goats and other animals. In some birds the caruncle is erectile tissue. The wattle is frequently an organ of sexual dimorphism. In some cases within the bird world the caruncle has a feather covering, whilst in other cases the feathers are sparse or absent.

Weaning
Weaning is the process of gradually introducing a mammal infant to what will be its adult diet and withdrawing the supply of its mother's milk. The process takes place only in mammals, as only mammals produce milk. The infant is considered to be fully weaned once it no longer receives any breast milk (or bottled substitute).

Weanling
A weanling is an animal that has just been weaned. The term is usually used to refer to a type of young horse, a foal that has been weaned, usually between the ages of 6 months and a year. Once a year old, the horse is referred to as a yearling.

Weathering
Weathering is the breaking down of rocks, soils and minerals as well as artificial materials through contact with

the Earth's atmosphere, biota and waters. Weathering occurs in situ, or "with no movement", and thus should not be confused with erosion, which involves the movement of rocks and minerals by agents such as water, ice, wind, and gravity. Two important classifications of weathering processes exist – physical and chemical weathering. Mechanical or physical weathering involves the breakdown of rocks and soils through direct contact with atmospheric conditions, such as heat, water, ice and pressure. The second classification, chemical weathering, involves the direct effect of atmospheric chemicals or biologically produced chemicals (also known as biological weathering) in the breakdown of rocks, soils and minerals. As with many other geological processes the distinction between weathering and related processes is diffuse.

Weed

A weed in a general sense is a plant that is considered by the user of the term to be a nuisance, and normally applied to unwanted plants in human-controlled settings, especially farm fields and gardens, but also lawns, parks, woods, and other areas. More specifically, the term is often used to describe any plants that grow and reproduce aggressively.[1] Generally, a weed is a plant in an undesired place.

Wetting

Wetting is the ability of a liquid to maintain contact with a solid surface, resulting from intermolecular interactions when the two are brought together. The degree of wetting (wettability) is determined by a force balance between adhesive and cohesive forces. Wetting is important in the bonding or adherence of two materials. Wetting and the surface forces that control wetting are also responsible for other related effects, including so-called capillary effects. Regardless of the amount of wetting, the shape of a liquid drop on a rigid surface is roughly a truncated sphere. Various degrees of wetting are summarized in this article.

White blood cell

White blood cells, or leukocytes (also spelled "leucocytes"; from leuko-Ancient Greek "white"), are cells of the immune system involved in defending the body against both infectious disease and foreign materials. Five different and diverse types of leukocytes exist, but they are all produced and derived from a multipotent cell in the bone marrow known as a hematopoietic stem cell. They live for about 3 to 4 days in the average human body. Leukocytes are found throughout the body, including the blood and lymphatic system.

Whorl

An arrangement of appendages, such as branches or leaves, such that all are equally spaced around the stem at the same point, much like the spokes of a wheel or the ribs of an umbrella.

Willow

Willow family herb family - onagraceae. It comprises about 700 species of annual or perennial plants that live throughout the world. They are mainly herbs, but we also find trees and shrubs. Some genera such as Fuchsia or Oenothera are very valuable in gardening.

Wing-bar

A light-colored bar on a wing, formed by pale tips on the covert feathers or pale bases of the flight feathers.

Winged

It is generally said of the stems. Showing side expansions like wings. Many of thistles, for instance, have winged stems.

Wing-flicking

A rapid movement of the wings of a bird otherwise at rest; seen, for example, in some kinglets and Empidonax flycatchers. Such movements along with pumping of the tail, are sometimes described as 'nervous' habits.

Wood

A secondary tissue found in seed plants which consists largely of xylem tissue.

Woody, ligneous

It is said of the vegetable part bearing the texture of wood.

X

X-chromosome

The X chromosome is one of the two sex-determining chromosomes in many animal species, including mammals (the other is the Y chromosome) and is common in both males and females. It is a part of the XY sex-determination system and X0 sex-determination system. The X chromosome was named for its unique properties by early researchers, which resulted in the naming of its counterpart Y chromosome, for the next letter in the alphabet, after it was discovered later.

Xenophobic alliance

A union or coalition of individual chimpanzees within a group that challenges any conspecific intruders that threaten or encroach upon their territory and its boundaries.

Xeric

A term used to describe a habitat or environment that exhibits extremely dry conditions.

Xerophytic leaves

The leaves of plants that grow under arid conditions with low levels of soil and water. Usually characterized by water-conserving features such as thick cuticle and sunken stomatal pits.

X-ray crystallography

A technique which allows elucidation of the structure of macromolecules. In this technique, an X-ray beam is passed through a crystal of a particular substance. The atoms which make up the crystal cause the X-rays to be deflected. This deflection pattern is directly dependent on the structure of the molecule being analyzed, and can thus be used to help determine the molecular structure.

X-ray diffraction

Technique utilized to study atomic structure of crystalline substances by noting the patterns produced by x-rays shot through the crystal.

Xylem

Tissue in the vascular system of plants that moves water and dissolved nutrients from the roots to the leaves; composed of various cell types including tracheids and vessel elements. Plant tissue type that conducts water and nutrients from the roots to the leaves.

Y

Yeast

Yeasts are eukaryotic micro-organisms classified in the kingdom Fungi, with 1,500 species currently described estimated to be only 1% of all fungal species. Most reproduce asexually by mitosis, and many do so by an asymmetric division process called budding. Yeasts are unicellular, although some species with yeast forms may become multicellular through the formation of a string of connected budding cells known as pseudohyphae, or false hyphae, as seen in most molds. Yeast size can vary greatly depending on the species, typically measuring 3–4 µm in diameter, although some yeasts can reach over 40 µm.

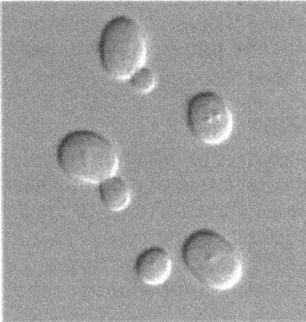

Yield

The amount of particulates or molecules of interest (product) that can be recovered from the cross flow filtration process; also referred to as recovery.

Yolk

An yolk is a part of an egg which feeds the developing embryo. The egg yolk is suspended in the egg white (known alternatively as albumen or glair/glaire) by one or two spiral bands of tissue called the chalazae. Prior to fertilization, the yolk together with the germinal disc is a single cell, one of the few single cells that can be seen by the naked eye.

Yolk sac

The yolk sac is a membranous sac attached to an embryo, providing early nourishment in the form of yolk in bony fishes, sharks, reptiles, birds, and primitive mammals. It functions as the developmental circulatory system of the human embryo, before internal circulation begins.

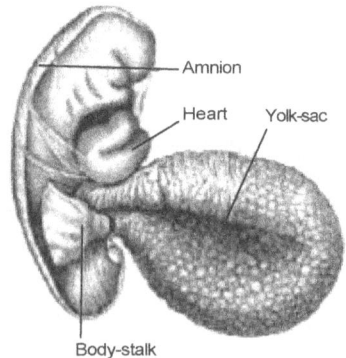

Amnion
Heart
Yolk-sac
Body-stalk

Z

Z lines
Dense areas in myofibrils that mark the beginning of the sarcomeres. The actin filaments of the sarcomeres are anchored in the Z lines.

Zebroid
A zebroid (also zedonk, zebra mule, and zebrule) is the offspring of any cross between a zebra and any other equine: essentially, a zebra hybrid. In most cases, the sire is a zebra stallion. Offspring of a donkey sire and zebra dam, called a zebra hinny, or donkra, do exist but are rare. Zebroids have been bred since the 19th century.

Zone of differentiation
Area in plant roots where recently produced cells develop into different cell types.

Zone of elongation
Area in plant roots where recently produced cells grow and elongate prior to differentiation.

Zone of intolerance
The area outside the geographic range where a population is absent; grades into the zone of physiological stress.

Zone of physiological stress
The area in a population's geographic range where members of population are rare due to physical and biological limiting factors.

Zoned reserve systems
Habitat areas that are protected from human alteration and surrounded by lands that are used and more extensively altered by human activity.

Zoology
The study of animals.

Zooplankton
Zooplankton is a categorisation spanning a range of organism sizes including small protozoans and large metazoans. It includes holoplanktonic organisms whose complete life cycle lies within the plankton, as well as meroplanktonic organisms that spend part of their lives in the plankton before graduating to either the nekton or a sessile, benthic existence. Although zooplankton are primarily transported by ambient water currents, many have locomotion, used to avoid predators (as in diel vertical migration) or to increase prey encounter rate.

Zooxanthellae
Symbiotic dinoflagellates in the genus Symbiodinium that live in the tissues of a number of marine invertebrates and protists, notably in many foraminiferans, cnidarians, and some mollusks.

Zygodactyly
In birds, refers to the arrangement of the toes in which the outer front toe

faces back and as a result, two toes point forward and two backward.

Zygomycetes

One of the division of the fungi, characterized by the production of zygospores; includes the bread molds.

Zygospore

In fungi, a structure that forms from the diploid zygote created by the fusion of haploid hyphae of different mating types. After a period of dormancy, the zygospore forms sporangia, where meiosis occurs and spores form.

Zygote

The product of gamete fusion. In organisms with a haploid life cycle, the zygote immediately undergoes meiosis, but in organisms with a multicellular diploid stage, the zygote is merely the first stage in the diploid portion of the life cycle.

Appendix – I
SI Units

Base and dimensionless SI units

Physical quantity	Name	Symbol
Length	metre	m
mass	kilogram	kg
time	second	s
electric current	ampere	A
thermodynamic temperature	Kelvin	K
luminous intensity	candela	cd
amount of substance	mole	mol
*plane angle	radian	rad
*solid angle	steradian	sr

*dimensionless units

Derived SI units with special names

Physical quantity	Name of SI unit	Symbol of SI unit
frequency	hertz	Hz
energy	joule	J
forcc	newton	N
power	watt	W
pressure	pascal	Pa
electric charge	coulomb	C
electric potential difference	volt	V
electric resistance	ohm	
electric conductance	Siemens	S
electric capacitance	farad	F
magnetic flux	weber	Wb
inductance	henry	H
magnetic flux density (magnetic induction)	tesla	T
luminous flux	lumen	lm
illuminance	lux	lx
absorbed dose	gray	Gy
activity	becquercl	Bq
dose equivalent	sievert	Sv

Decimal multiples and submultiples to be used with SI units

Submultiple	Prefix	Symbol	Multiple	Prefix	Symbol
10^{-1}	deci	d	10	deca	da
10^{-2}	centi	c	10^2	heclo	ii
10^{-3}	milli	m	10^3	kilo	k
10^{-6}	micro		10^6	mega	M
10^{-9}	nano	n	10^9	giga	G
10^{-12}	pico	p	10^{12}	tera	T
10^{-15}	femto	f	10^{15}	peta	P
10^{-18}	atto	a	10^{18}	exa	E
10^{-21}	zepto	z	10^{21}	zetta	Z
10^{-24}	yocto	y	10^{24}	yotta	Y

Conversion of units to SI units

From	To	Multiply by
in	m	2.54×10^{-2}
ft	m	0.3048
sq.in	m^2	6.4516×10^{-4}
sq.ft	m^2	9.2903×10^{-2}
cu.in	m^3	1.63871×10^{-5}
cu.ft	m^3	2.83168×10^{-2}
l(itre)	m^3	10^{-3}
gal(lon)	l(itre)	4.546 09
miles/hr	$m\ s^{-1}$	0.477 04
km/hr	$m\ s^{-1}$	0.277 78
lb	kg	0.453 592
gcm^{-3}	$kg\ m^{-3}$	10^3
lb/in^3	$kg\ m^{-3}$	$2.767\ 99 \times 10^4$
dyne	N	10^5
poundal	N	0.138 255
lbf	N	4.448 22
mmHg	Pa	133.322
atmosphere	Pa	$1.013\ 25 \times 10^5$
hp	W	745.7
erg	J	10^{-7}
eV	J	$1.602\ 10 \times 10^{-19}$
kW h	J	3.6×10^6
cal	J	4.1868

Appendix – II
Simplified Classification of the Animal Kingdom

*Animalia

- Porifera (sponges)
- Cnidaria (i.e. jellyfish, sea anemones, corals)
- Platyhelminthes (flatworms)
  - Tubellaria (planarians)
  - Trematoda (flukes)
  - Cestoda (tapeworms)
- Nematoda (roundworms)
- Mollusca
  - Gastropoda (e.g. snails, slugs)
  - Bivalvia (e.g. oysters, mussels, clams)
  - Cephalopoda (e.g. squids, octopuses)
- Annelida (segmented worms)
  - Oligochaeta (earthworms)
  - Polychaeta (e.g. lugworms)
  - Hirudinea (leeches)
- Crustacea (e.g. shrimps, crabs, lobsters)
- Hexapoda (insects, e.g. bugs, beetles, bees, flies)
- Myriapoda
  - Chilopoda (centipedes)
  - Diplopoda (millipedes)
- Chelicerata
  - Arachnida (e.g. spiders, scorpions, mites)
- Echinodermata (e.g. starfish, sea urchins, brittlestars)

- agnathans (jawless fish; e.g. lampreys, hagfish)
- chondrichthyes (cartilaginous fish; e.g. sharks, rays)
- Osteichthyes (bony fish)
  - Dipnoi (lungfish)
  - Teleostei (e.g. salmon, plaice, eel)
- Amphibia (e.g. frogs, toads)
- Reptilia (e.g. crocodiles, snakes, lizards)
  - Dipnoi (lungfish)
- Aves (birds)
- Mammalia
  - Metatheria (marsupial mammals; e.g. kangaroo, wombat)
  - Eutheria (placental mammals; e.g. carnivores, bats, whales, rodents, ungulates, primates)

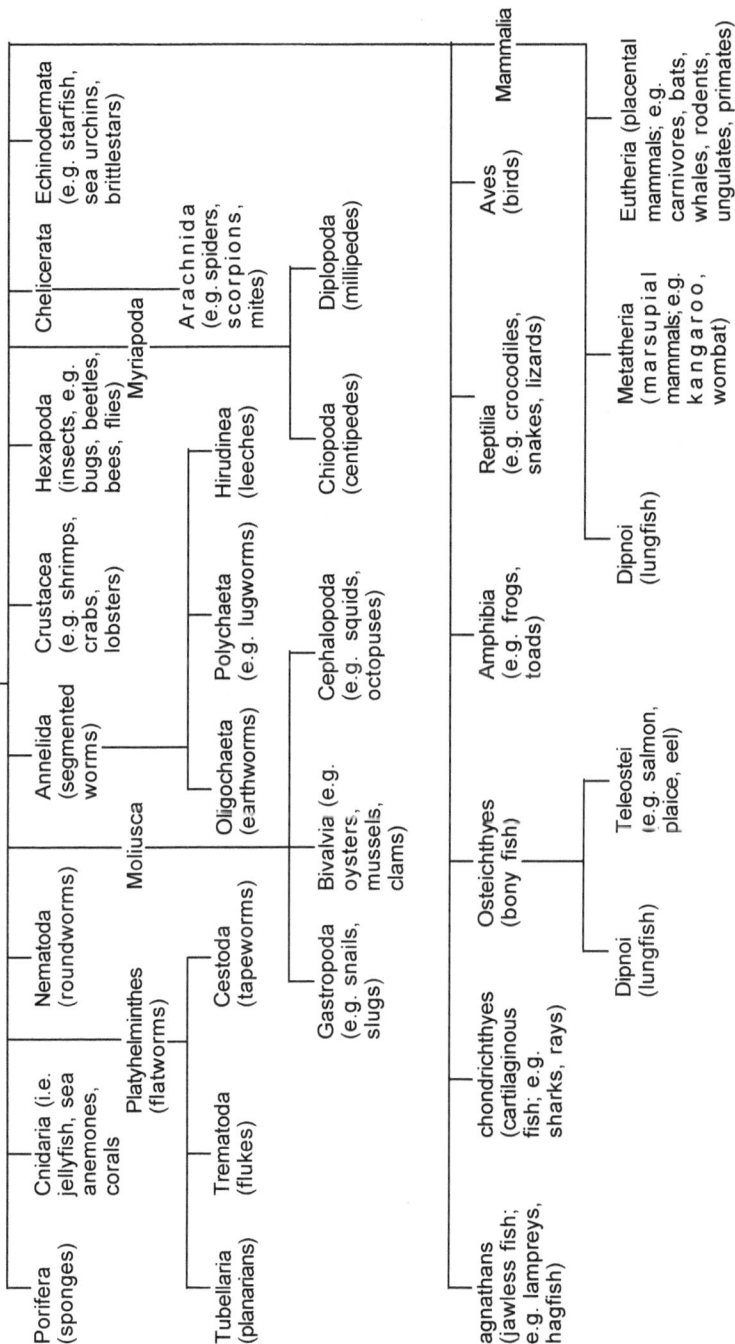

* Only major taxonomic groups are shown

227

Simplified Classification of Land Plants

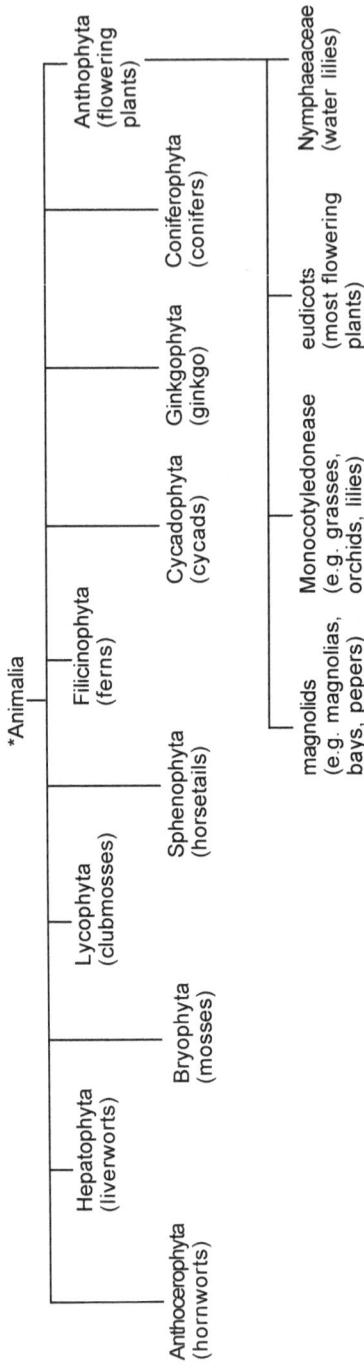

*Animalia

Anthocerophyta (hornworts)

Hepatophyta (liverworts)

Bryophyta (mosses)

Lycophyta (clubmosses)

Sphenophyta (horsetails)

Filicinophyta (ferns)

Cycadophyta (cycads)

Ginkgophyta (ginkgo)

Coniferophyta (conifers)

Anthophyta (flowering plants)

magnolids (e.g. magnolias, bays, pepers)

Monocotyledonease (e.g. grasses, orchids, lilies)

eudicots (most flowering plants)

Nymphaeaceae (water lilies)

* Extinct and mostly extinct groups are excluded

228

Appendix – III
Geological Time Scale

millions of Years ago	Eon	Era	Period	Epoch	Millions of years ago
	Phanerozoic	Cenozoic	Neogene	Holocene	
				Pleistocene	
				Pliocene	
				Miocene	
					23
			Palaeogene	Oligocene	
				Eocene	
				Palaeocene	
					65
		Mesozoic	Cretaceous		
					145
			Jurassic		
					200
			Triassic		
					251
		Phaeozoic	Permian		
					299
			Carboniferous		
					359
			Devonian		
					416
			Silurian		
					444
			Ordovician		
					488
			Cambrian		
542					542
	Proterozoic		Precambrian time		
2500					
	Archaean				
3600					
	Hadean				
4500					4500

Appendix – IV
Model Organisms and their Genomes

Scientific name	Description/ common name	Type of organism	Genome size (Mb)	Haploid no. of chromosomes	No. of genes	Website
Escherichia coli/K-12	nonpathogenic reference strain of E. coli	eubacterium	4.6	1	4576	http://ecocyc.org/
Dictyostelium discoideum		amoebozoan cellular slime mould	34	6	13 600*	http://dictybase.org/
Saccharomyces cerevisiae	budding yeast used in baking and brewing	fungus	12.1	16	6600*	www.yeastgenome.org/
Neurospora crassa	red bread mould	fungus	40*	7	9820*	www.broad.mit.edu/annotation/ genome/neurospora/
Zea mays	maize (corn)	monocotyledonous flowering plant of the grass family	2000-3000*	10 (including supernumerary (B) chromosomes)	7	www.maizegdb.org/
Arabidopsis thaliana	thale cress	dicotyledonous flowering plant of the mustard family	125	5	27 873	www.arabidopsis.org/
Caenorhabditis elegans		nematode	97	6 autosomes + X sex chromosome	19 500*	www.sanger.ac.uk/Projects/ C_elegans/
Drosophila melanogaster	fruit fiy	dipteran insect	16.5	3 autosomes + X and Y sex chromosomes	15 185	http://flybase.bio.indiana.edu/
Danio rerio	zebrafish	teleost fish	1762	25	19 059*	http://zfin.org/cgi-bin/ webdriver?Mival= aa-ZDB_home.apg

Scientific name	Description/ common name	Type of organism	Genome size (Mb)	Haploid no. of chromosomes	No. of genes	Website
Gallus domesticus	chicken	bird	1050	38 autosome + Z and W sex chromosomes	13 000*	http://ensembl.bioinfo. helsink.fi/Gallus_gallus/ index.html
Mus musculus	laboratory mous	mammal	2632	19 autosomes + X and Y sex chromosomes	20 000*	http://www.informatics.jax.org/
Homo sapiens	human	mammal	3000	22 autosomes + X and Y sex chromosomes	20 000-	www.ncbi.nlm.nih.org/genome/ guide/human/

* Approximate or estimated value(s).

Appendix – V
Major Mass Extinctions of Species

Extinction event(s)	Date (millions of year ago)	Organisms most affected	Estimate of percentage of species made extinct	Cause(s)
Late Cambrian (series)	c. 488	trilobites, brachiopods, conodonts (primitive toothed vertebrates), ?soft-bodied arthropods	?	?change in sea level
Late Ordovician	c. 444	echinoderms, brachiopods, triobites, ostracods, nautiloids	70-85	glaciation and fall in sea levels
Late Devonian (series)	c. 360	cephalopods, corals, brachiopods, bryozoans, echinoderms, trilobites, ammonites, agnathans, armoured fishes	70-83	?global cooling and reduced oxygen levels in deeper waters
Late Permian (Permo-Triassic; PTr)	251	corals, crinoids, ammonites, brachiopods, bryozoans, trilobites, land plants, insects, terrestrial vertebrates	<95	?volcanic activity with consequent global warming and changes in marine enviroment
Late Triassic	200	brachiopods, ammonites, bivalve and cephalopod molluscs, marine reptiles, conodonts, labyrinthodonts (primitive amphibians), insects	80	?dimatic changes due to continental drift
Cretaceous-Tertiary (K-T)	65	dinosaurs, flying reptiles, ammonites, fish, brachiopods, planktonic organisms, plants	75-85	?meteorite collision (Alvarez event)

Appendix – VI
Nobel Prizes in Biology

Year	Nobel prize	Name of prizewinners)	Nationality	Nature of work or discovery
1901	Physiology or Medicine	Emrl Adolf von Behring (1854-1917)	German	Developed a diphtheria antitoxin based on serum derived from immune individuals
1902	Physiology or Medicine	Ronald Ross (1857-1932)	British	Established that malaria parasites are transmitted by mosquitoes
1904	Physiology or Medicine	Ivan Petrovich Pavlov (1849-1936)	Russian	Investigated importance of sight and smell of food in stimulating the digestive system
1905	Physiology or Medicine	Robert Koch (1843-1910)	German	Discovered the bacterium responsible for tuberculosis
1906	Physiology or Medicine	Camillo Golgi (1843-1926)	Italian	Identified fundamental aspects of nervous system organization
		Santiago Ramon y Cajal (1852-1934)	Spanish	
1907	Physiology or Medicine	Charles Louis Alphonse Laveran (1845-1922)	French	Identified the protozoan responsible for malaria
1908	Physiology or Medicine	Ilya Ilyich Mechnikov (1845-1916)	Russian	Discovered phagocytosis
		Paul Ehrllch (1954-1915)	German	Studied antisera and immunity
1909	Physiology or Medicine	Emil Theodor Kocher (1841-1917)	Swiss	Studied the physiology, pathology, and surgery of the thyroid gland
1910	Physiology or Medicine	Albrecht Kossel (1853-1927)	German	Identified the chemical nature of cell components, particularly proteins and nucleic acids
1913	Physiology or Medicine	Charles Robert Richet (1850-1935)	French	Discovered anaphylaxis
1914	Physiology or Medicine	Robert Barany (1876-1936)	Austro-Hungarian	Investigated the physiology of the inner ear and devised the Barany test for diagnosing disease of the vestibular apparatus
1915	Chemistry	Richard Martin Willstatter (1872-1942)	German	Determined key aspects of chemical nature of chlorophyll and other plant pigments

Year	Nobel prize	Name of prizewinners)	Nationality	Nature of work or discovery
1919	Physiology or Medicine	Jules Bordet (1870-1961)	Belgian	Discovered the immune component alexin, later called complement
1920	Physiology or Medicine	Schack August Steenberg Krogh (1874-1949)	Danish	Discovered physiological mechanism controlling capillary diameter in the blood vascular system
1922	Physiology or Medicine	Archibald Vivian Hill (1886-1977)	British	Discovered that heat produced following muscle contraction indicated oxygen consumption
		Otto Fritz Meyerhof(1884-1951)	German	Showed that lactic acid produced by contracting muscles was subsequently converted to glycogen by aerobic reactions
1923	Physiology or Medicine	Frederick Grant Banting (1891-1941)	Canadian	Discovered insulin
		John James Richard Macleod (1876-1935)	Canadian	
1927	Chemistry	Heinrich Otto Wieland (1877-1957)	German	Characterized the nature of bile acids
1928	Chemistry	Adolf Otto Reinhold Windhaus (1876-1959	German	Identified key aspects of sterol chemistry and link with vitamin D
1929	Physiology or Medicine	Christiaan Eijkman (1858-1930)	Dutch	Identified cure for beriberi
		Frederick Gowland Hopkins (1861-1947)	British	Discovered vitamins
1930	Physiology or Medicine	Karl Landsteiner (1868-1943)	Austrian	Discovered the ABO system of human blood groups
1930	Chemistry	Hans Fischer (1881-1945)	German	Determined the chemical nature of haem
1931	Physiology or Medicine	Otto Heinrich Warburg (1883-1970)	German	Identified the enzymes involved in cell respiration
1932	Physiology or Medicine	Charles Scott Shernngton (1857-1952)	British	Studied nervous control and integration of muscle reflexes

Year	Nobel prize	Name of prizewinners)	Nationality	Nature of work or discovery
		Edgar Douglas Adrian (1889-1977)	British	Investigated principles of nervous signalling based on impulse frequency
1933	Physiology or Medicine	Thomas Hunt Morgan (1866-1945)	US	Established chromosomes as the physical basis of genetic linkage
1935	Physiology or Medicine	Hans Spemann (1869-1941)	German	Discovered an embryonic organizer
1936	Physiology or Medicine	Henry Hallett Dale (1875-1968)	British	Discovered that acetylcholine is a chemical transmitter of nerve signals
		Otto Loewi (1873-1961)	Austrian	
1937	Physiology or Medicine	Albert von Szent-Gyorgyi (1893-1936)	Hungarian	Discovered fundamental components of cellular respiration
		Walter Norman Haworth (1883-1950)	UK	Discovered ring structures of sugars and synthesized vitamin C (ascorbic acid)
		Paul Karrer (1889-1971)	Swiss	Determined the structure of carotene and synthesized vitamins A and B2 (riboflavin)
1938	Physiology or Medicine	Corneille Jean Francois Heymans (1892-1968)	Belgian	Determined the role of the carotid sinus in regulating heart rate and blood pressure
1938	Chemistry	Richard Kuhn (1900-67)	German	Determined the structures of vitamins A and B2 and synthesized vitamin Bs (pyridoxine)
1943	Physiology or Medicine	Henrik Carl Peter Dam (1895-1976)	Danish	Discovered and characterized vitamin K
		Edward Adelbert Doisy (1893-1986)	US	
1944	Physiology or Medicine	Joseph Erlanger (1874-1965)	US	Identified different classes of nerve fibres according to their conducting velocity
		Herbert Spencer Gasser (1888-1963)	US	
1945	Physiology or Medicine	Alexander Fleming (1881-1955)	British	Discovered, isolated, and purified penicillin
		Ernst Boris Chain (1906-79)	British	
		Howard Walter Florey (1898-1968)	Australian	

Year	Nobel prize	Name of prizewinners)	Nationality	Nature of work or discovery
1946	Physiology or Medicine	Hermann Joseph Muller (1890-1967)	US	Discovered that X-rays cause a high rate of mutations
1947	Physiology or Medicine	Carl Ferdinand Cori (1896-1984)	US	Discovered how glycogen is broken down and resynthesized
		Gerty Theresa Cori (1896-1957)	US	
		Bernardo Alberto Houssay (1887-1971)	Argentina	Studied the effects of pituitary hormones on blood glucose
1948	Chemistry	Arne Wilhelm Kaurin Tiselius (1902-71)	Swedish	Developed electrophoresis as a technique for separating proteins and confirmed the existence of different classes of serum proteins
1950	Physiology or Medicine	Edward Calvin Kendall (1885-1972)	US	Identified the structure and biological effects of the adrenocortical hormones
		Tadeus Reichstein (1897-1996)	Swiss	
		Philip Showalter Hench (1896-1965)	US US	
1953	Physiology or Medicine	Hans Adolf Krebs (1900-81)	British	Discovered the citric acid cycle (Krebs cycle)
		Fritz Albert Lipmann (1899-1986)	US	Discovered coenzyme A and established its importance in intermediary metabolism
1955	Physiology or Medicine	Axel Hugo TheodorTheorell (1903-82)	Swedish	Established mechanism of action of oxidative enzymes
1955	Chemistry	Vincent du Vigneaud (1901-78)	US	Synthesized the hormone oxytocin
1957	Chemistry	Alexander R. Todd (1907-97)	British	Synthesized the purine and pyrimidine bases of nucleic acids and also various coenzymes, including FAD, ADP, and ATP
1958	Physiology or Medicine	George Wells Beadle (1903-89)	US	Formulated the one gene-one enzyme hypothesis (now known as the one gene-one polypeptide hypothesis)
		Edward Lawrie Tatum (1909-75)	us	

Year	Nobel prize	Name of prizewinners)	Nationality	Nature of work or discovery
		Joshua Lederberg (1925-)	US	Discovered genetic recombination and conjugation in bacteria
1958	Chemistry	Frederick Sanger (1918-)	British	Determined the amino acid sequence of bovine insulin
1959	Physiology or Medicine	Severo Ochoa (1905-93)	US	Discovered enzymes that catalyse the formation of RNA and DNA from their respective nucleotides
		Arthur Kornberg (1918-2007)	US	
1960	Physiology or Medicine	Frank Macfarlane Burnet (1899-1985)	Australian	Discovered acquired immunological tolerance
		Peter Brian Medawar (1915-87)	British	
1961	Physiology or Medicine	Georg von Bekesy (1899-1972)	US	Established the physical mechanism of hearing within the cochlea of the inner ear
1961	Chemistry	Melvin Calvin (1911-97)	US	Determined the reactions of carbon assimilation during photosynthesis (the Calvin cycle)
1962	Physiology or Medicine	Francis Harry Compton Crick (1916-2004)	British	Discovered the chemical structure of DNA and its significance for the transfer of genetic information
		James Dewey Watson (1928-)	US	
		Maurice Hugh	New Zealand-	
		Frederick Wilkins (1916-2004)	British	
1962	Chemistry	Max Ferdinand Perutz (1914-2002)	British	Determined the structure of the protein myoglobin using X-ray crystallography
		John Cowdery Kendrew(1917-97)	British	
1963	Physiology or Medicine	John Carew Eccles (1903-97)	Australian	Discovered how ionic movements are intrinsic to nerve cell excitability
		Alan Lloyd Hodgkin (1914-98;	British I	
		Andrew Fielding Huxley (1917-)	British	
1964	Physiology or Medicine	Konrad Bloch (1912-2000)	US	Discovered crucial steps in cholesterol synthesis

Year	Nobel prize	Name of prizewinners)	Nationality	Nature of work or discovery
1965	Physiology or Medicine	Feodor Lynen (1911-79)	German	Identified key role of coenzyme A in fatty acid metabolism
		Francois Jacob (1920-)	French	Formulated the operon model of gene regulation
		Jacques Monod (1910-76)	French	
		Andre Lwoff (1902-94)	French	Determined the mechanism by which bacterial cells infected with bacteriophages undergo lysogeny
1966	Physiology or Medicine	Peyton Rous (1879-1970)	US	Discovered that certain viruses can cause cancer in animals
1967	Physiology or Medicine	Ragnar Granit (1900-91)	Swedish	Discovered fundamental aspects of the neurophysiology of vision
		Haldan Keffer Hartline (1903-83)	US	
		George Wald (1906-97)	US	
1968	Physiology or Medicine	Robert W. Holley (1922-93)	US	Elucidated the genetic code and its role in protein synthesis
		Har Gobind Khorana(1922-)	US	
		Marshall W. Nirenberg (1927-2010)	US	
1969	Physiology or Medicine	Alfred D. Hershey (1908-97)	US	Established that DNA is the genetic material of bacteriophages
		Max Delbruck (1906-81)	US	Demonstrated genetic recombination between viruses
		Salvador E. Luria (1912-91)	US	
1970	Physiology or Medicine	Bernard Katz (1911-2003)	British	Discovered the nature of certain neurotransmitters and the mechanism of their storage, release, and inactivation at synapses
		Ulf von Euler (1905-83)	Swedish	
		Julius Axelrod (1912-2004)	US	
1970	Chemistry	Luis F. Leioir (1906-87)	Argentinian	Discovered the role of sugar nudeotides in glycogen synthesis
1971	Physiology or Medicine	Earl W. Sutherland (1915-74)	US	Discovered cyclic adenosine monophosphate and demonst-

Year	Nobel prize	Name of prizewinners)	Nationality	Nature of work or discovery
				rated its importance as a second messenger in cell signalling
1972	Physiology or Medicine	Gerald M. Edelman (1929-)	US	Determined the chemical structure of antibodies
		Rodney R. Porter (1917-85)	British	
1972	Chemistry	Christian B. Anfinsen (1916-95)	US	Established that amino acid sequence alone determines the biological activity of enzymes
		Stanford Moore (1913-82)	US	Identified the chemical groups contributing to the active site of
		William H. Stein (1911-80)	US	the enzyme ribonuclease
1973	Physiology or Medicine	Karl von Frisch (1886-1982)	German	Demonstrated certain basic aspects of individual and social behaviour in animals under natural conditions
		Konrad Lorenz (1903-89)	Austrian	
		Nikolaas Tinbergen (1907-88)	British	
1974	Physiology or Medicine	Albert Claude (1899-1983)	Belgian	Discovered certain cell components, including lysosomes and ribosomes
		Christian de Duve (1917-)	Belgian	
		George E. Palade (1912-2008)	US	
1975	Physiology or Medicine	David Baltimore (1938-)	US	Discovered the role of the enzyme reverse transcriptase during infection by RNA viruses
		Howard Martin Temin (1934-94)	us	
		Renato Dulbecco (1914-)	us	Established the concept of virus-induced transformation of normal cells into cancer cells
1977	Physiology or Medicine	Roger Guillemin (1924-)	us	Discovered peptide hormones in the brain
		Andrew V. Schally (1926-)	us	
		Rosalyn Yalow (1921-)	us	Developed radioimmunoassay for peptide hormones
1978	Physiology or Medicine	Werner Arber (1929-)	Swiss	Discovered restriction enzymes and their applications in molecular genetics
		Daniel Nathans (1928-99)	US	
		Hamilton O. Smith (1931-)	U5	

Year	Nobel prize	Name of prizewinners)	Nationality	Nature of work or discovery
1978	Chemistry	Peter D. Mitchell (1920-92)	British	Formulated the cherniosrnotic theory of biochemical energy transfer
1979	Physiology or Medicine	Alan M. Cormack (1924-98)	US	Developed computerized tomography
		Godfrey N. Hounsfield (1919-2004)	British	
1980	Chemistry	Paul Berg (1926-)	US	Pioneered recombinant DNA techniques
		Walter Gilbert (1932-)	US	Developed techniques form sequencing nucleic acids
		Frederick Sanger (1918-)	British	
1980	Physiology or Medicine	Baruj Benacerraf (1920-)	US	Determined the genetic basis of histocornpatibility antigens on body cells and their significance in immune mechanisms and tissue transplantation
		Jean Dausset (1916-2009)	French	
		George D. Snell (1903-96)	US	
1981	Physiology or Medicine	Roger W. Sperry (1913-94)	US	Identified the main functional specializations of right and left cerebral hemispheres
		David H. Hubel (1926-)	US	Made key insights into the structural and functional organization of the visual cortex
		Torsten N. Wiesel (1924-)	Swedish	
1982	Physiology or Medicine	Sune K. Bergstrom (1916-2004)	Swedish	Discovered key aspects of the nature, metabolism, and biological actions of prostaglandins and related substances
		Bengt I. Sarnuelsson (1934-)	Swedish	
		John R. Vane (1927-2004)	British	
1982	Chemistry	Aaron Klug (1926-)	British	Developed crystaliographic electron microscopy to determine the structure of protein-nucleic acid complexes
1983	Physiology or Medicine	Barbara McClintock (1902-92)	US	Discovered mobile genetic elements (transposens)
1984	Physiology or Medicine	Niels K. Jerne (1911-94)	Danish	Developed theories explaining antibody specificity and diversity

Year	Nobel prize	Name of prizewinners)	Nationality	Nature of work or discovery
1985	Physiology or Medicine	Georges J. F. Kohler (1946-95) Cesar Milstein (1927-2002) Michael S. Brown (1941-) Joseph L. Goldsteir (1940-)	German Argentine-British US US	Described the hybridoma technique for producing monoclonal antibodies Described the importance in cholesterol metabolism of cell surface receptors for low-density lipoproteins
1986	Physiology or Medicine	Stanley Cohen (1922-) Rita Levi-Montalcini (1909-)	US Itaiian-US	Discovered, respectively, epidermal growth factor and nerve growth factor
1987	Physiology or Medicine	Susumu Tonegawa (1933-)	Japanese	Demonstrated how genetic recombination in immune cells produces the diversity of antigen receptors and antibodies
1988	Chemistry	Johann Deisenhofer (1943-) Robert Huber (1937-) Hartmut Michel (1948-)	German German German	Determined the three-dimensional structure of a photosynthetic reaction centre
1989	Physiology or Medicine	J. Michael Bishop (1936-) Harold E. Varmus (1939-)	US US	Discovered that viral oncogenes are derived from normal cellular genes
1989	Chemistry	Sidney Altman (1939-) Thomas R. Cech (1947-)	Canadian-US US	Discovered the catalytic properties of RNA
1991	Physiology or Medicine	Erwin Neher (1944-) Bert Sakmann (1942-)	German German	Studied the operation of single ion channels in cell membranes
1992	Physiology or Medicine	Edmond H. Fischer (1920-) Edwin G. Krebs H918-)	Swiss-US US	Discovered the importance of protein phosphorylation as a regulatory mechanism for cellular functions
1993	Physiology or Medicine	Richard J- Roberts (1943-) Phillip A. Sharp (1944-)	British US	Discovered 'split genes', consisting of exons and intervening noncoding introns

Year	Nobel prize	Name of prizewinners)	Nationality	Nature of work or discovery
1993	Chemistry	Kary B. Mullis (1944-)	US	Invented the polymerase chain reaction technique
		Michael Smith (1932-2000)	Canadian	Developed the technique of site-directed mutagenesis
1994	Physiology or Medicine	Alfred G. Gilman (1941-)	US	Discovered G proteins and their role in cell signalling
		Martin Rodbell (1925-98)	US	
1995	Physiology or Medicine	Edward B. Lewis (1918-2004)	us	Identified the genes that control the development of Drosophila embryos
		Christiane Nusslein Volhard(1942-)	German	
		Eric F. Wieschaus (1947-)	US	
1995	Chemistry	Paul J. Crutzen (1933-)	Dutch	Made fundamental contributions to understanding of ozone chemistry and the threat posed to the ozone layer by human-derived chemicals
		Mario J. Molina (1943-)	US	
		F. Sherwood Rowland (1927-)	US	
1996	Physiology or Medicine	Peter C. Doherty (1940-)	Australian	Discovered the mechanism by which cytotoxic T cells recognize virus-infected cells
		Rolf M. Zinkernagel (1944-)	Swiss	
1997	Physiology or Medicine	Stanley B. Prusiner (1942-)	US	Discovered prions
	Chemistry	Paul D. Boyer (1918-)	US	Determined the structure and mechanism of ATP synthetase
		John E.Walker (1941-)	British	
		JensC. Skou (1918-)	Danish	Discovered sodium/potassium ATPase (the sodium pump) in cell membranes
1998	Physiology or Medicine	Robert F. Furchgott (1916-2009)	US	Discovered that nitric oxide is a key signalling molecule in the cardiovascular system
		Louis J. Ignarro (1942-)	US	
		Ferid Murad (1936-)	US	
1999	Physiology or Medicine	Gunter Blobel (1936-)	US	Formulated the signal hypothesis whereby proteins are tagged with peptide 'address labels' to specify their destination within the cell

242

Year	Nobel prize	Name of prizewinners)	Nationality	Nature of work or discovery
2000	Physiology or Medicine	Arvid Carlsson (1923-)	Swedish	Demonstrated the mechanism of action of dopamine as a neurotransmitter in the brain
		Paul Greengard (1925-)	US	
		Eric R. Kandel (1929-)	US	Discovered how changes in nerve synapses are the basis of learning and memory
2001	Physiology or Medicine	Leland H. Hartwell (1939-)	US	Identified key genes and proteins involved in regulating the cell cycle
		R. Timothy Hunt (1943-)	British	
		Paul M. Nurse (1949-)	British	
2002	Physiology or Medicine	Sydney Brenner (1927-)	British	Identified crucial genes that regulate organ development and programmed cell death (apoptosis)
		H. Robert Horvitz (1947-)	US	
		John E. Sulston (1942-)	British	
2003	Chemistry	Peter Agre (1949-)	US	Discovered water channels in cell membranes
		Roderick MacKinnon (1956-)	US	Determined the spatial conformation of the potassium ion channel
2004	Physiology or Medicine	Richard Axel (1946-)	us	Discovered the family of genes encoding olfactory recoptors and how olfactory signals are received by the brain
		Linda B. Buck (1947-)	us	
2004	Chemistry	Aaron Ciechanover (1947-)	Israeli	Discovered the process of ubiquitin-mediated protein degradation in living cells
		Avram Hershko (1937-)	Israeli	
		Irwin Rose (1926-)	US	
2006	Physiology or Medicine	Andrew Z. Fire (1959-)	us	Discovered RNA interference
		Craig C. Mello (1960-)	us	
2006	Chemistry	Roger D. Kornberg (1947-)	us	Determined the molecular basis of transcription in eukaryotic cells

Year	Nobel prize	Name of prizewinners)	Nationality	Nature of work or discovery
2007	Physiology or Medicine	Mario R. Capecchi (1937-) Martin J. Evans (1941-) Oliver Smithies (1925-)	us British US	Developed the technique of using embryonic stem cells to create mouse strains carrying targeted gene modifications
2008	Physiology or Medicine	Harald zur Hausen (1936 -) Françoise Barré-Sinoussi (1947 -) Luc Montagnier (1932 -)	Germany France France	Human papilloma viruses causing cervical cancer Human immunodeficiency virus
2009	Physiology or Medicine	Elizabeth H. Blackburn (1948 -) Carol W. Greider (1961 -) Jack W. Szostak (1952 -)	Australia US UK	Protection of chromosomes by telomeres and enzyme telomerase
2010	Physiology or Medicine	Robert G. Edwards (1925 -)	UK	Development of invitro fertilization
2011	Physiology or Medicine	Bruce A. Beutler (1957 -) Jules A. Hoffmann (1941 -) Ralph M. Steinman (1943 - 2011)	US Luxem-bourg Canada	Activation of innate immunity Dendritic cell and its role in adaptive immunity

Note: The physiology or medicine prizewinners listed above have been selected for their contributions to biology; they do not represent an exhaustive list of prizewinners

Popular Science

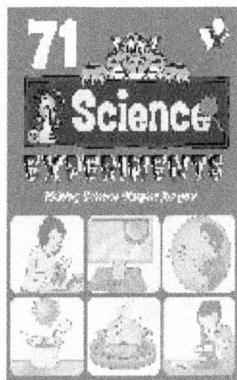

Author: Vikas Khatri
Format: Paperback
Language: English
Pages: 160
Price: ` 110

Experiments are an inseparable part of any scientific study or Research. In this book, the author has tried to simplify science to the readers, particularly the school-going students through easy and interesting experiments. All the experiments given in the book are based on some scientific phenomena, such as atmospheric pressure, high and low temperatures, boiling, freezing and melting points of solids, liquids and gases, gravitational force, magnetism, electricity, solubility of substances, etc. Thus, read and carry out each of these fun-filled experiment in your homes or schools under the supervision and guidance of your teachers, parents or elders.

Author: Dr. C.L. Garg & Dr. Amit Garg
Format: Paperback
Language: English
Pages: 120
Price: ` 140

81 Classroom projects on: Physics, Chemistry, Biology& Electronics for Sec. & Sr. Sec. Students. Science projects and models play a pivotal role in inculcating scientific temper in young minds and in harnessing their skills. Students of classes 10 th, 11th & 12 th have to work on such projects and these carry much weight in the overall performance. All these aspects have been considered during the compilation of the projects and models. This book will also be an ideal choice for parents interested in enhancing scientific temper of their children and for hobbyists.

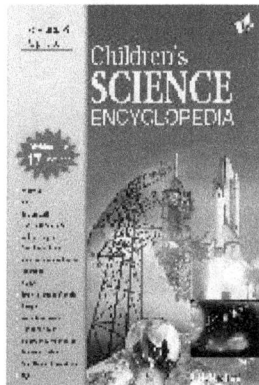

Author: A.H. Hashmi
Format: Paperback
Language: English
Pages: 206
Price: ` 495

Complete science homework compen-dium for children aged 8 to 16. Through Short paragraphs and great pictures the book explains all about, Environment, Transport, Energy, Communi-cation, Electricity & Magnetism, Light & Sound, Chemistry, Universe, Earth, Animal & Plants, Human Body and others in 17 sections! Guaranteed to build scientific temper in children to excel in studies! Equally useful for parents and guardians to understand and explain to the youngsters the different areas of scientific world in which we live. Competitive exam candidates will also be greatly benefitted in getting a short and crisp answer to their inquisitiveness. A must have book for every home!

English Related

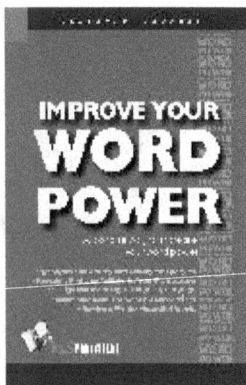

Author: Califord
Sawhney
Format: Paperback
Language: English
Pages: 230
Price: ` 88

We can not ignore the complexities of the English language which sometimes perplex a reader or even a scholar. *Improve your Word Power* by Clifford Sawhney simplifies all these complexities by providing answers to the nagging grammatical queries, syntax, style, choice of words, spellings, etc. This book serves as a complete guide that elaborately explains the usages of nouns, adjectives, adverbs, phrases, proverbs and so on.
Hence, it will undoubtedly serve as a bible for both the lovers and wizards of English language.

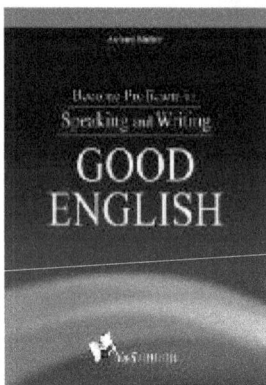

Author: Archana Mathur
Format: Paperback
Language: English
Pages: 148
Price: ` 120

- The book offers practical advice for writing proper and attractive prose.
- It will help improve one's communication ability and skill.
- The topics cover Common Errors, Confusing set of Figures of Speech, Foreign Words and Phrases and various aspects of Grammar and Syntax.
- The entries have adequate and appropriate examples.
- The topics are arranged alphabetically for easy reference.

This work is a contribution to various aspects of writing correct and good English, focusing on the requirements of the Indian writers.

Author: G.C. Beri
Format: Paperback
Language: English
Pages: 132
Price: ` 96

This book contains as many as 460 inspiring quotes classified in well defined 19 groups. This classification itself indicates that all major aspects in human life have been covered.

Even a cursory reading of some quotes will convince the reader that in a small space it presents a mine of wisdom that will always be inspiring.

To one who is passing through some major difficulties and as a result feeling depressed and confused, this book *'Inspirational Quotes and Thoughts'* would bring him out of that disturbed mental state. It will instil in him confidence, inspiration as well as positive outlook that are needed for success and happiness in life.

Quiz Books

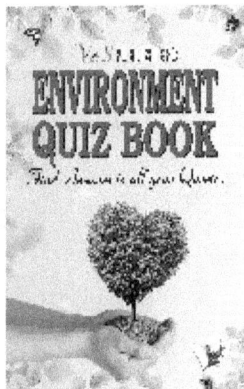

Author: Manasvi Vohra
Format: Paperback
Language: English
Pages: 144
Price: ` 110

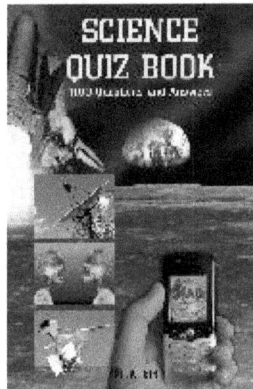

Author: Rajeev Garg &
Amit Garg
Format: Paperback
Language: English
Pages: 192
Price: ` 96

Author: Gladys Ambat
Format: Paperback
Language: English
Pages: 256
Price: ` 120

The study of environment is a must for us as we are an integral part of the environment. It includes composite physical and biological sciences including subjects, such as Ecology, Botany, Zoology, Physics, Chemistry, Soil Science, Geography, etc. Hence, in order to understand and learn more about the environment in which we live in and to find answers to all our queries regarding the mysteries that surround us, *Environment Quiz Book* is an ideal one.

The book includes several interesting and simple:
- Questions & Answers
- MCQs
- Fill in the Blanks
- Crossword
- Word Search
- True & False

That is what your child will find in this A to Z Quiz Series – brilliant books brimming with the latest information and simple explanations of fascinating facts and feats about our constantly evolving world. Designed to boost your child's knowledge base, each page comes alive with new facts in an engrossing form of short Questions and Answers with explanatory illustrations, all of which makes it easy to read, easy to follow and easy to remember.

Each book covers a subject comprehensively. Students, parents and teachers would find these books helpful in boosting the knowledge level of children. These books come in handy for quiz contests, competitive exams, admission tests, career development etc.

Quiz blitzkrieg are brain fitness fundas of a unique kind! The thrill to win or lose gaming session of a quiz programme can give you an optimum level of mental fitness and alertness. You simply bubble over with the sheer joy of challenge. The book is a lively presentation for all youngsters and a pleasant leisure companion for the elders. The veteran author has put together over 4000 exciting quizzes and interesting brain-teasers to get all keyed up. While you race through every page – you could find yourself sitting on the edge of the chair. The book covers:
- Quiz Medley & Quickies
- Palindromes & Proverbs
- Villains in History & Fiction

www.ingramcontent.com/pod-product-compliance
Lightning Source LLC
Chambersburg PA
CBHW070402270326
41926CB00014B/2662